No Babylon

Other publications by the author

Bye-Bye Blackbird: An Anglo-Indian Memoir
Distant Archipelagos: Memories of Malaya
The Singing Tree
The Colour of Asia
Hong Kong Handover
The Long March Back
Hong Kong Style
The Very Nature of Hong Kong
Skylines Hong Kong
Passing Shadows
Lijiang: The Imperiled Utopia
Chinese Symbolism
Another City, Another Age
Hong Kong: What's to See
Building Hong Kong

No Babylon

✦

A Hong Kong Scrapbook

Peter Moss

iUniverse, Inc.
New York Lincoln Shanghai

No Babylon
A Hong Kong Scrapbook

Copyright © 2006 by Peter Moss

All rights reserved. No part of this book may be used or reproduced by any means, graphic, electronic, or mechanical, including photocopying, recording, taping or by any information storage retrieval system without the written permission of the publisher except in the case of brief quotations embodied in critical articles and reviews.

iUniverse books may be ordered through booksellers or by contacting:

iUniverse
2021 Pine Lake Road, Suite 100
Lincoln, NE 68512
www.iuniverse.com
1-800-Authors (1-800-288-4677)

ISBN-13: 978-0-595-38087-9 (pbk)
ISBN-13: 978-0-595-82456-4 (ebk)
ISBN-10: 0-595-38087-5 (pbk)
ISBN-10: 0-595-82456-0 (ebk)

Printed in the United States of America

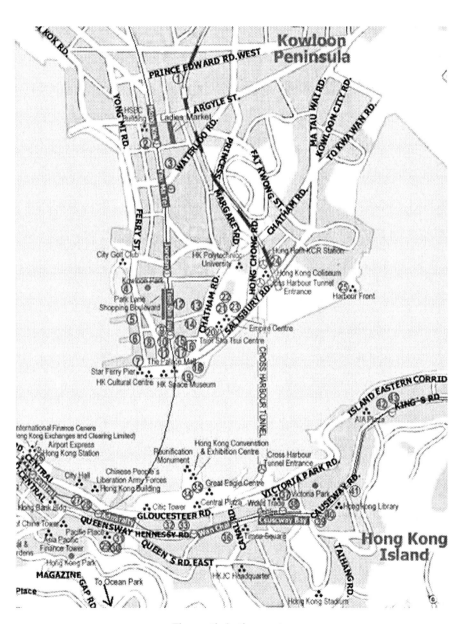

The pestle in the mortar

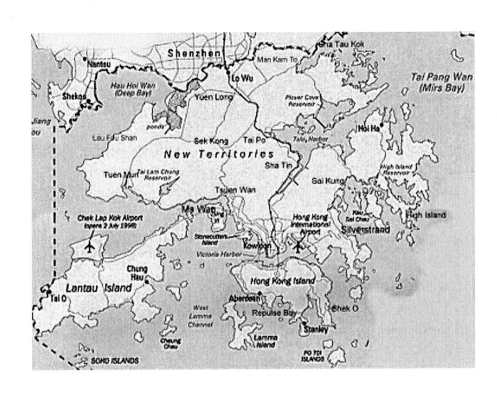

For Brian, Moyreen, Grahame, Lisbet, Gillian,
Mukti, Diosy, Jonathan, Irene, Rino, Daisy and Joyce

No chimera this,
no sailor's tale,
no Babylon of fancy
rearing turrets in the breath
of vagrant clouds,
no vision in the night.

The city is reality,
and all our fickle day
a passing mirage,
lulling us,
momentarily,
with its sweet conceit
of centuries retrieved.

PM: *Return from the Western Approaches* (1970)

Contents

Introduction xi

Edge of the Great Divide. 1

God is Speaking 15

Strictly for the Birds 22

Magic Stone and Replacement Rabbit. 34

Toothbrushes, Cameras and Blue Movies 43

Indivisible Whole 53

Enigmatic Presence 59

The Deluge Now 67

Sailing Below the Wind. 74

The Year of Living Dangerously 90

Escalation 101

Pig on the Thirteenth Green. 116

Detours and Diversions. 124

Beyond the Watershed 138

Before the Killing Fields 148

Moon Dust, Shipwrecks and Landslides 161

Elephant's Ovaries and the Honourable Picnic 175

The New Deal. 193

x   No Babylon

Shamelessly Shirtless in Galle. 206

One of Our Aircraft is Missing 213

A Cork in the Bottleneck. 221

Skittle in a Bowling Alley. 228

The Crochet Club 235

Consorting with the Enemy. 241

Boadecia Redux 245

A Touch of Positive Interventionism 252

Tempting Providence 260

Changing Horses in Midstream. 270

An Imminently Virtual Reality 278

Offerings to the Gods 287

A Gross Miscalculation 296

Farewell the Trumpets. 304

Epilogue 311

Introduction

The last remnants of the once Great British Empire—whose hitherto widespread swathes had straddled the globe in strident shades of red—were fading almost before our very eyes. For me and my brother Paul, born of that Empire and still tied to its apron strings (in Paul's case more loosely than mine) it was becoming a race against time to clamber aboard whatever bits of wreckage were surviving the rapid disintegration.

Guessing which territory would be next to go, and which would linger longest, was like playing the final round in a game of greatly depleted musical chairs. I figured the music for this should be set to the tune of *Old Macdonald's Farm*, transcribed into satirical verse*:*

> "Old Britannia's great empire
> wiped clean off the slate.
> Watch her commonwealth expire
> state by state by state.
> With India gone, Ceylon gone next,
> Burma gone, Malaya gone,
> What the hell is going on?
> The torch that set the world on fire's
> ashes in the grate."

Paul and I were again treading water, waiting for the next life raft to chance by. After eight years in Malaya, which had latterly metabolised into the ungainly archipelago of Malaysia, my employment by the *Straits Times* newspaper group was being steadily undermined by a process termed Malaysianisation. Paul was fed up with commuting to his office in London to promote a revamped but greatly reduced British Rail system he didn't believe in. Thanks to its chairman, Richard Beeching, the network had shrunk from around twenty-one thousand to just twelve thousand miles of track, and even my brother's commuter service wasn't operating on time.

He switched to the public relations office at Odham's Press, but was equally restless there.

All around us was evidence of a flea-bitten Britannic lion limping off to its cave with its tail between its legs. Its retreat from the world stage was applauded rather than deplored by the new breed of Britons taking over the reins of power and punishing yesterday's men for their rank, privilege and class. Nascent public opinion in Britain of the fifties and sixties wanted nothing to do with imperial legacy, and was bent on erasing its last traces with utmost dispatch.

So the question weighing on the minds of both of us was "where next?" Was there any part of that diminished Empire not imminently due for the auction block? We scanned the classifieds for the notices occasionally inserted by the Crown Agents, whose offices were then located at Eland House, Stag Place in London's West End.

The Crown Agents were exactly what their name implied, an agency of Her Majesty the Queen. Founded in 1833, as Crown Agents for the Colonies, they played a vital role in the creation and management of what British historians called the Third Empire. According to Dean Andromidas, writing in *The Executive Intelligence Review* of August 22nd 1997, "While Lord Palmerston, Cecil Rhodes, Prince Edward Albert ('The Prince of the Isles') and Lord Milner were providing the geopolitical theory and ideology to justify Britain's global empire, Crown Agents ran the day-to-day affairs". They printed the stamps and banknotes of the colonies; provided technical, engineering, and financial services; served as private bankers to the colonial monetary authorities, government officials and heads of state; and acted as arms procurers, quartermasters and paymasters for the colonial armies. In effect, Crown Agents *administered* the British Empire, which at one point in the nineteenth century encompassed over three hundred colonies and nominally "independent countries" allied to the British Crown.

I spotted a notice calling for an information officer to serve the "condominium government" of the New Hebrides (now known as Vanuatu). To me this looked like a once-in-a-lifetime dream of an opportunity. The New Hebrides were a scattered archipelago of islands in the South Seas,

Introduction   xiii

that oceanic paradise I had yearned to explore ever since being weaned on the novels of R.M. Ballantyne, H. De Vere Stackpoole and Robert Louis Stevenson. They were the only territory ever simultaneously and jointly administered by both Britain and France, with such comically operatic Gilbert and Sullivan consequences that they promised boundless diversion. I submitted my application, attaching a résumé emphasising my experience as a journalist in what had now become Malaysia.

Weeks went by, winter giving way to spring as I idled in my parents' home at 1, Old Harrow Road, in the wearily démodé and passionless East Sussex resort town of Hastings. I heard nothing. What could have happened? Confiding my disappointment to Paul, I learned that, unbeknownst to each other, we had both replied to the identical advertisement.

I resolved to take matters into my own hands by calling at Eland House in person. I was shown into the office of the particular recruiting agent who had vetted applications for the New Hebrides post. Yes, he recalled receiving my application. He recalled receiving two in fact, both quoting virtually identical early experience with the *Bexhill-on-Sea Observer*. How was he to know that one was from my brother? The system wasn't designed to cater for the anomaly of dual submissions, or at least what *looked* like dual submissions, under the name of P. Moss. And he was very sorry, but the New Hebrides vacancy had been filled.

Were there any others?

He riffled through his files. "There's Hong Kong. They need a senior information officer."

My jaw dropped. Hong Kong was anathema to me; a crowded little belly button of a colony appended to the rotund coastline of communist China. Hardly room to move. Nothing else?

He shook his head. "Not right now. Might be something coming up. But why *not* Hong Kong? You already have eight years Far East experience. You've worked with Chinese. You seem ideally qualified."

I hesitated, remembering that he who hesitates is lost. This was clearly one of those potentially life-changing options, akin to the one that had taken me out to Malaya. My favourite maxim was from Shakespeare's *Julius Caesar*: "On such a full sea are we now afloat. And we must take the current when it serves, or lose our ventures". I had followed this dictum all my life, and my impulse had never led me astray. I could feel the swell surging under my timbers. I said yes.

Six weeks later, just before my thirtieth birthday on June 27th 1965, I landed at Hong Kong's Kai Tak airport. The following year, having rejected an offer of employment in the Solomon Islands (for which I would willingly have traded Hong Kong), Paul landed at Mahe, to take up the post of information officer for the Seychelles archipelago. We had both found our little bits of colonial flotsam to cling to in the wake of that foundering titan of a vessel named *Empire*, he somewhere midway between India and Kenya in the Indian Ocean and I on the shores of the South China Sea.

This personal retrospective of Hong Kong, viewed from my fortieth year of residence, is not intended to offer political insight, for there has been enough of that analysis already. More than two decades have passed since the announcement that this former British colony would be restored to Chinese sovereignty, and in that time Hong Kong has come under the burning glass of international curiosity. Mine is an individual viewpoint, not from the Peak but, figuratively speaking, from somewhere in the Mid Levels.

Peter Moss
Hong Kong
December 2005

Edge of the Great Divide

Few things in life are more saddening than to look back and see how quickly the winds of time have erased our traces; as though we had never trod this path. And few places in the world can more assuredly guarantee that painful discovery than Hong Kong. Here, where nothing survives very long, the past is a dead archive, summarily erased from memory. Which is why my recollections are essentially of a very different place, at a very different time, even if the geographical location remains the same.

When I first landed there in 1965 I found that Hong Kong itself was lucky to have survived. But that was a catch phrase I would hear repeatedly—and learn to employ myself—in the years to come, as this refuge of the forties or the "four T's" (established in 1842 to become a tiny, temporary territory of transients) rebounded, like a resilient ping-pong ball, from one setback after another.

Former Governor Sir Alexander Grantham (1947–58) had watched, back in 1949, as the fragile border between our little enclave and the rest of China was sealed by communist troops, following the demise of Nationalist China and the birth of the People's Republic. Together with many others in Hong Kong at the time, he had half expected those troops to continue marching south, taking over in a matter of days, if not hours, the colony wrested from them by the unequal treaties imposed on the enfeebled and inward-looking Manchu dynasty in the aftermath of two Opium Wars.

As part of the "acclimatisation" course offered all newly-arrived government servants—even those of us admitted via the back door, claiming specialist experience in place of university degrees—I was taken to the border by my barely senior colleague, lanky and languorous Keith Robinson. Keith had reached this tradesman's entrance only a few months before me, clambering aboard from another piece of newly abandoned imperial fallout in the form of Malawi, the central African nation that a year earlier had evolved from the British protectorate of Nyasaland.

The ranks of Hong Kong's still predominantly expatriate civil service were rapidly filling up with discards like ourselves, from those colonies that were about to gain, or had already gained, their independence. Like most of the local population, of whom the great majority were Cantonese, we too were refugees living in—as that great China-hand Richard Hughes would later describe it in his book of that title—"a borrowed place on borrowed time".

We travelled in a government pool car, through open, sparsely populated, thinly agricultural and largely uncluttered countryside, to the "closed area", a cordoned and sanitised frontier zone extending just south of the meandering, twenty-kilometre demarcation line separating Hong Kong from its motherland. Admission to that no-man's-land entailed production and scrutiny of our official pass.

From the entry point the road narrowed into a defile between two hills, where it converged with the railway line inaugurated in 1910 for the Kowloon Canton Railway service to what is now called Guangzhou, and thence to other parts of China. Our arrival at the Lo Wu border crossing coincided with that of one of the regular diesel-engine passenger trains from Kowloon, its dark-green coaches, with their open viewing decks at either end, disgorging passengers and goods for processing through our immigration and customs counters. Most of these cross-border travellers were Cantonese, driven by intense clan loyalties to return to their "roots" in neighbouring Guangdong province, where they would visit relatives who had stayed behind.

"Let's join them," Keith confidently proposed, with half a tongue in his cheek.

"Join them where?" I anxiously countered.

"On the bridge."

"Isn't that in their territory?"

"It's in ours, right up to the highwater mark on their bank of the river."

"Are you sure?"

"This isn't my first time here, remember."

Edge of the Great Divide   3

He had been once before, just a few weeks earlier.

Together we tramped the boards beside the railway track, across which only goods trains were now permitted right of way. Our footsteps echoed under the high-vaulted corrugated iron roof. Those passengers already processed through our immigration controls trotted hurriedly by, some carrying heavy bundles of goods slung at either end of shoulder yokes, others bearing baskets of fruit and clothing as gifts for the kith and kin they would visit in the scattered homeland villages from which they had sprung.

Among these were some of the last of the famous *black-and-white amahs*, whose dress, hairstyle and occupation signified membership of an endangered sorority, rapidly declining in numbers through the depredations of advancing years and their failure to recruit new blood. Prim-faced and pigtailed in their blinding white blouses and black trousers, they were as chaste and unassailable as nuns, married not to the church but to the families to whom they had been bound through loyal and lifelong service. Sold into servitude in childhood, by peasant parents in Guangdong province, they were trained to take charge of everything in the household, from cleaning, cooking and needlework to the care of dogs and children. Their increasing scarcity now rendered them as valuable as much coveted living icons from another age.

Most of these passers-by spared us brief sidelong glances, wondering what we might be up to. We foreigners were a rare sight on this sensitive fault zone between two diametrically opposed political and cultural ideologies.

Every pace we took brought us one step closer to the great divide. My stomach began to constrict in cowardly anticipation as I saw uniformed soldiers of the People's Liberation Army, in their high-collared olive-green jackets and forage caps with five-pointed red star insignia, assemble on their side of the bridge as if ready to resist a large-scale incursion. One of them hurried out of a guardhouse with a camera and began to take photographs at close range.

"Why's he doing that?" I nervously inquired.

Keith smiled obligingly for the photographer. "They take photographs for their records of everyone who approaches the dividing line."

"Where *is* the dividing line?"

Keith indicated a narrow white band painted across the timbered boards almost at the point where the bridge met the embankment on their side of the crossing. He continued walking until he stood a foot or so away from it.

"They can't do anything," he reassured me, "as long as we remain on our side."

"Why provoke them?"

"Custom survives through usage. We have to continue exercising our right to access this bridge unchallenged, even if it means physically toeing the line."

The assembled troops a few yards away from us were looking quite perceptibly and increasingly hostile.

"Well I'm certainly not going to toe that particular line," I insisted.

"Dare you to pass your hand through the Bamboo Curtain."

He meant, of course, the invisible curtain that supposedly separated us from them, the oriental equivalent of the Iron Curtain dividing the two Europes.

"No thanks. I'm not going to be responsible for an international incident. And I don't like the fact that they now have my face on their records."

"They're pretty good at finding out who you are too. They'll have those particulars in their books soon enough."

I cast a final look over the distinctly other world beyond the unsmiling cordon of PLA soldiers. A shabby train waited in an otherwise empty goods siding, and a large blockhouse stood on the right, overlooked by what seemed a barracks on the crest of a hillock. Above the blockhouse flapped the enormous red flag of the People's Republic, with a large gold star, representing the guiding light of the Chinese Communist Party, at its top-left corner, flanked by four smaller stars denoting the four classes united under its wing—workers, peasants, petty bourgeois and capitalists sympathetic to the party.

Edge of the Great Divide 5

I find myself straining to recall just how great was the gulf demarcated by that narrow line of paint on Lowu Bridge. For just as great a gulf now separates that China, on the eve of its Cultural Revolution, from the country that has taken its place. By 1965 China had retreated into almost as great an enigma as ensconced it when Marco Polo probed its mysteries seven centuries earlier.

Thanks to United Nations policy, largely dictated by an America in the sway of paranoid, anti-Red hysteria stirred up by communophobes such as the infamous Senator Joe McCarthy, the world had turned its back on China since Mao Zedong established the People's Republic on October 1st 1949. The only "legitimate China" was the one transposed upon inoffensive Taiwan by the fleeing Nationalist government and their leader Chiang Kai-shek.

Communist China's support for North Korea, during the Korean War which ended with the armistice of 27th July 1953, had further exacerbated the rift and led to an embargo on all trade with the Chinese hinterland. The very rationale for Hong Kong's existence had vanished at the stroke of a pen, forcing the tiny entrepot to "take up arms against a sea of troubles". Not quite the weapons Hamlet had pondered as defence against the slings and arrows of outrageous fortune, these were more the tools of the trade by which Hong Kong must learn to survive as manufacturer and exporter of its own merchandise.

The fifties had ushered in Hong Kong's own revolution, which in a matter of a few crucial years transformed it from a trading to an industrial-based economy. When I arrived in the mid-sixties the "Made in Hong Kong" label had already become widely recognised throughout the world. The principal task assigned me and my fellow senior information officer Keith Robinson was to further promote the image of the colony as source of an increasingly expanding and ever more sophisticated range of Hong Kong-manufactured goods, extending from textiles, shoes and thermos flasks to furniture and wristwatches.

◆　　◆　　◆

I had first come into contact with Chinese on a regular, day-to-day basis during my Malayan years, and had quickly grown to respect them for their resilience, fortitude, adaptability and capacity for sheer hard work. Were I to find myself inexplicably landed on some desert island, I would rather my fellow castaways were Chinese than any other race, because they, best of all, would have the instinct not only to survive but to get things going again in the quickest possible time, no matter what the odds.

In Hong Kong I found a distillation of all those admirable qualities that had turned the Overseas Chinese into the spearhead of economic change, not only in southeast Asia but in so many other areas of the world where they had quietly but unmistakably applied their magic wand. Without their catalytic presence, progress in all of those regions would have been greatly retarded. Like the Jews in Europe, and the Indians in Africa, they were the touchstones around which entire economies crystallised.

But Hong Kong was not just another Chinese refuge. It was their very quintessence, a laboratory effectively on their home turf, in which the bunsen burners of an older, ongoing Chinese experiment were kept ablaze long after those on the adjoining continent were switched to a different flame. Here flagrant capitalism continued to flourish on the doorstep of unbridled communism, because the conditions for its survival and further growth were just right.

Britain's paternalistic colonial administrators employed their predominantly socialist inclinations to create the ideal climate. Many of them young and idealistic, with university backgrounds that had flirted with Marxist-Leninist theories to see how far these could be allied to Keynesian economics, they were left free to pursue their ideas for improving the lot of those they served. Theirs was not the heavy hand of intervention. Instead they paved the course, relaxed the reins and allowed the ponies their heads. It was the perfect symbiosis; humane government and ideal conditions on the one hand and, on the other, the talent and the opportunism best equipped for maximum exploitation. The greater mystery would have lain,

Edge of the Great Divide   7

not in Hong Kong's success but in its failure, for this was a recipe guaranteed to win.

I may not have seen it in those terms then. I may not even have recognised that at least one farseeing visionary, among the top echelons of the communist hierarchy in Beijing, had already resolved to allow the lease of Hong Kong territory to run its full term precisely **because** Hong Kong could serve as forerunner to China's own economic future. But I did see that Hong Kong was nothing less than a phenomenon, which not even Singapore could match, no matter how hard its leader Lee Kuan Yew, and his People's Action Party, might suppress their "nanny" instincts to allow their citizens a modicum of free enterprise.

Looking down on Victoria harbour, from the observation point beside the upper terminus of the Peak Tram station, I was struck less by the sheer spectacle than by the impression that the Kowloon peninsula, on its far side, was a giant pestle descending into the concave mortar of the Hong Kong Island shoreline. It was as if Hong Kong's very topography had fashioned the crucible in which this experiment would find its blazing apogee, and I was happily on the spot, to witness the consequence.

But privileged though I felt to be afforded this opportunity, I saw it as no more than a brief diversion on my way to the outer isles. My head was still filled with dreams of sun-drenched atolls in remote Pacific reaches, and now a funny thing had happened to me on the road there. Where Malaya had proved a delightful sojourn, Hong Kong was looking like a sharp detour leading in entirely the opposite direction. I had envisaged a life of tranquil ease in relaxed and semi-deserted archipelagos, not one of frenzied action amid seething and ambitious masses in a starkly overcrowded one.

◆   ◆   ◆

The feeling of living in a large, makeshift laboratory was reinforced, on closer examination, when I descended into the confines of the canyons and corridors below. Here an improvised, let's-try-and-make-it-up-as-we-go-along conurbation had been grafted onto the few still-visible remains of an earlier, more gracious and less hurried city. The postwar flux of refugees was not the first Hong Kong had experienced. The tidal inflow began even before World War Two, impelled by the onset of the Sino-Japanese war. It had gone only briefly into reverse between Hong Kong's surrender to the Japanese on Christmas Day 1941 and the latter's capitulation of August 14th 1945, the period of occupation that had eviscerated Hong Kong's life and vitality.

Both before and after the war, private developers had stacked up cheap, utilitarian apartment blocks like filing cabinets throughout the city, each accessed by narrow, almost lightless stairwells and fronted by typhoon-prone windows overhung by "eyelashes" of corrugated-iron sheeting. Each shoebox of a room was partitioned, and partitioned again, into bunk-tiered cubicles for sub-rental to families desperate to be as near as possible to work, markets and schooling. The fronts of these depressingly uniform structures bristled with giant signboards, whose brilliantly-illuminated Chinese characters jutted out above the street to advertise the seemingly unlikely presence, within these warrens, of restaurants, bath houses, plastic flower factories and practitioners versed in herbal medicines. The classic anecdote of the "Chinglish" tailor's sign announcing that "ladies can have fits upstairs" suddenly appeared not only accurate but highly probable.

I did not have to look far for evidence of overcrowding. Across a narrow alleyway from my room in the Merlin Hotel, standing where the Kowloon Hotel stands today alongside Nathan Road in Tsim Sha Tsui, were the scruffy windows of a typical flophouse, located in one of those early post-war residential blocks that had sprung up like mushrooms to profit from the incoming floods of refugees. I saw tiered bunk beds stacked so closely together that their occupants had to thread sideways between them in order to reach their allotted berths. And those occupants, I soon came to recognise, arrived at prearranged intervals, so that three different sleepers would successively claim each bed at different points around the clock.

That was how Hong Kong functioned, on a shift basis, a twenty-four-hour factory of a city forever on the go. And most people, men and women, worked at two different jobs, with only a few hours respite in which to snatch some rest before the daily grind commenced again. This was the dark side of capitalism, and it could have fooled the untutored observer into believing there was no redeeming counterbalance. Superficially it looked like a Dickensian nightmare translated from the stygian darkness of nineteenth-century industrial England into this twentieth-century orient. Why had this refugee population chosen to live in such conditions?

Crossing by Star Ferry to my office in central Hong Kong Island, I was surrounded by the slumbering forms of fellow passengers, employing that brief traversal of the harbour to defray some of their sleep deficit as they commuted from one job to another. Looking only slightly less sleep-deprived were the white-collar workers on their way to banks, offices and the lesser cogs of the administrative machine that ground inconspicuously, mysteriously and largely unnoticed somewhere in the background of all that seething commercial consequence.

I was astonished by the profusion of dark-coloured suits, so at odds with the clammy summer humidity and with the open-necked informality I had found in Malaysia. If the men weren't wearing jackets they settled for ties, with almost regulation white shirts and black trousers. The women, if they weren't in *samfoo* pajamas on their way to factories, were invariably in hip-hugging, thigh-revealing *cheongsams*, whose provocatively feminine allure was entirely at odds with their prim, touch-me-not expressions.

Whether factory-bent or office-bound, the brief ride on the Star Ferry—aside from meal breaks—was very likely the only relaxation those thoroughly work-oriented people would see all day. Little wonder most preferred to rent a bed space as close as possible to at least one or other place of work. Little wonder any concept of "home" should be sacrificed to the all-important imperative of proximity to the job. Little wonder, too, that Hong Kong had evolved the way it had, vertically rather than outward, eschewing expansion in favour of concentration to produce the most compact, densely populated city the world had ever seen.

Given the nature of its occupants, this was an inevitable outcome. The Cantonese were a cespitose people, gathering—like plants of that species—in dense clumps and clusters, always seeking out the most crowded places, willing to queue for hours to enjoy the busiest restaurants. And this was the *alfresco* age of living in the streets, when every alleyway and thoroughfare, night and day, was a turbulent river of ceaseless animation. Improvised markets of street barrows and food stalls would mushroom in hours, wherever authority turned a blind eye.

Nobody wanted to abandon the sheer energy and enterprise of that night life until the last possible moment, when they must reluctantly return to their cramped bed spaces to snatch a few hours of sleep. Restaurants were teeming because so few had the means to cook at home. Yet everyone had the right to survival, and the best prospects for doing business were always at the most crowded intersections, where the flow congealed to a crawl in order to negotiate the greatest clusters of hawkers and pedlars.

I once observed a junior official, attached to a patrol squad, attempting to remove a hawker obstructing pedestrian flow in one of the most congested of these corridors. A crowd of bystanders quickly gathered around them, siding not with the municipal minion but with the cause of the obstruction. They berated the officer. Why was he threatening to break this poor hawker's rice bowl? It didn't matter that he was slowing down the traffic and forcing them into the gutter. He had shown admirable initiative in choosing this prime spot, and he deserved all the business that came his way.

The sheer uncomplaining fortitude of these people instilled my deepest admiration. Without making any effort to court such a reaction, without craving understanding or sympathy of any kind, they simply were—just by being so resolutely unwavering—the most remarkable people I had ever encountered. Sheer survival was their incentive. That, and a better tomorrow for their children, for whose education they would scrimp and save every cent. But all of their acts of **individual** survival were pursued in the most competitive of environments, without jealousy, without rancour, without creating the kind of tensions that—in any other community anywhere else—would have defeated such endeavours.

Here was a pot forever on the boil, where yesterday's street hawker might be today's welcomed and unresented millionaire, and yesterday's millionaire today's unashamed and freshly-resolved street hawker. Hence an untended Rolls-Royce could be left in perfect safety, parked beside a back-alley hawker's barrow. It was not seen by the barrow owner as an arrogant symbol of affluence to be scratched, defaced or covered in abusive graffiti for daring to flaunt its ostentatious "have-ness" in a sea of have-nots. He would regard it as proof of what might otherwise seem unattainable, a providential portent of his own dream. He might even buff its bonnet with his cleaning rag for good luck, much as fathers would take their sons to touch the noses of the bronze lions reclining before that sacred cathedral of commerce, the Hongkong Shanghai Bank.

This absence of envy, this lack of any definable class and cast, avoided the stratification that had stultified other societies. Had he discovered Hong Kong first, Karl Marx might never have written *Das Kapital*, for this hubble-bubble of experimental capitalist alchemy contradicted so many of his theories.

In the west, one talked of "returning home" to the pivot of existence. In Hong Kong, where the workplace was the pivot of existence, the equivalent Cantonese phrase was "*faan gung*", or "return to work". "Home" was a bed space or, if one had a family and could not afford a rented cubicle, a squatter shack on a hillside or—if one was lucky enough to qualify—a tiny room in one of the new resettlement blocks that government was building as fast as its finances would allow.

The authorities had at first been reluctant to play landlord to a significant and growing proportion of the population. To do so went against their cardinal tenet of non-intervention in the market forces which hitherto had always shaped their own solutions to problems. But this was a situation whose scale and magnitude lay beyond the capacity of market forces to resolve. And it wasn't going to go away.

A series of disastrous fires, culminating in an inferno which swept unchecked through the congested squatter shacks of Shek Kip Mei on Christmas Day 1953, forced a major review of the woefully inadequate concessions the administration had made in the form of temporary "cottage areas". The decision was taken to embark on a vast construction programme, utilising public funds to establish multi-storey resettlement estates. No limit was set to the size of this endeavour, the policy being to continue building as fast as sites and funds could be made available. Indeed by the time I reached Hong Kong the hope that there *was* a foreseeable end in sight had long evaporated.

By that time the typical resettlement estates—most of them crowded into the northern reaches of the Kowloon peninsula, where they presented the least eyesore to Peak dwellers magisterially surveying the harbour prospect—were variations on the basic, seven-storey H-blocks that had pioneered the programme. They bore all the hallmarks of ingenuity combined with expediency. They shared toilets and bathing facilities in the cross-sections between parallel residential wings, fronted by open balconied common-ways. Within this rudimentary framework whole families piled into bunk beds in their single-room living units and learned the delicate arts of survival in close proximity with a minimum of stress.

A large proportion of an entire generation grew up in this environment, attending classes in rooftop schools while mothers shopped in the outdoor markets cramming the streets below. Hong Kong's longest-running television drama series, entitled *Below Lion Rock*, would later establish its place as Hong Kong's most beloved "soap opera" by depicting the neighbourliness of these crowded estates.

Succeeding the H-blocks would come generations of improved designs, each refining and enlarging until the fundamental concept was altered beyond all recognition. Rising ever higher, like the soaring columns of a graph charting their own progress, these public housing estates would elevate and dramatize the changing Hong Kong skyline. In turn the willing sacrifice by their inhabitants, forfeiting comfort and seclusion to the demands of convenience and accessibility, would dictate the evolution of an ever-changing metropolis and the challenge to which its architects must respond. Hence the refinement of Hong Kong's unique, multi-level complex in which residential apartments were stacked above terraced gardens, which in turn were piled upon sandwich layers of shops, public utilities, transportation systems and, of course, the innumerable and inevitable restaurants.

Edge of the Great Divide   13

If work was the means of life, food was its end. The common Cantonese greeting was not the equivalent of "How are you?" or "Have a nice day" but "Have you eaten yet?" (***nee sek faan mei?***). Whereas in Britain at that time the "pub", or public house, was the pivot of the community, the teahouse and restaurant were its Hong Kong equivalents, their invariably circular dining tables providing rendezvous for business discussions, family gatherings, school reunions, staff parties, gargantuan wedding breakfasts and—more discreetly—lovers' assignations. The larger restaurants were as garrulously gregarious as breeding colonies for sea lions, producing a volume of noise excruciating to the untrained ear.

The Cantonese appetite for food and for life were so intertwined that both found their apogee over the dinner table, where the defences that made it possible to co-exist, as single-celled units in Hong Kong's tumultuous bloodstream, were temporarily discarded. Visitors eager to meet the Cantonese on their thickly tufted home turf could do no better than join them in the restaurant. Here—especially if encountered in the bosom of the family—their guard was lowered, their concentration relaxed and their mood at its most congenial.

Yet, at heart, this mood was still one of "make the most of what we have, while we can". For the dreams of the majority—and indeed my own dreams too—lay beyond this pressure cooker we inhabited. However rapidly Hong Kong was changing through the impact of its all-but-unsustainable immigration, it could not avoid the appearance of being an enormous refugee camp, a tiny, temporary territory of transients. And I sensed, when I looked around at my smiling fellow transients, snatching their brief respite from the daily grind, that wherever they might end up, they would take their China with them; not so much a country, more a state of mind. A state of mind that would outlive and outlast anything to do with politics, or even history itself; the imperishable quality of Chineseness imprinted into their genetic coding.

Wherever they went, and whatever formal nationality they might subsequently obtain, superimposed in invisible but non-erasable ink across the stamp in their passport would be their place of origin, to which they would continue devoting their undying loyalty. To paraphrase the words of a famous advertising slogan, you might take the Chinese out of China but you could never take China out of the Chinese.

God is Speaking

My own workplace was the office I shared with Keith Robinson on the fifth floor of Beaconsfield House, a utilitarian shoebox of a building located in Queens Road Central, directly behind the granite fortress of the Hongkong Shanghai Bank, whose place as Hong Kong's tallest edifice had recently been supplanted by the immediately adjoining pillar of the Bank of China. Through the gap between these two financial bastions our window overlooked a narrow segment of the harbour, affording an occasional glimpse of a passing junk sail or ocean liner. Beyond lay the distant peaks of the Kowloon foothills, separating our metropolis from the agricultural hinterland of the New Territories.

Keith and I sat at desks facing each other beside the window, with another corner of the room occupied by our stenographer Linda Lee, who would prove—over our many years together—the best personal secretary with whom I ever had the privilege of working. As she got to know me better, Linda would learn to safeguard me from my chronic forgetfulness by pinning little scraps of paper to the lapels of my jacket so that, when I donned it, I would know exactly where to go and what time to be there. Sometimes I might forget to remove these reminders, which would contribute to my somewhat curious appearance at meetings.

Next door to our office was that of Bill Fish, a former colleague from the *Straits Times* organisation in Malaya who had joined the Hong Kong Government Information Services some four years ahead of me. Although I knew Bill would vouch for me, I had avoided contacting him when submitting my own application, so as to spare him any suspicion of nepotism. As it turned out, he was accompanying a trade mission to Japan when our director, Nigel Watt, got in touch with him to inquire if he knew me. Bill admitted that he did, and that I would probably prove an acceptable addition to the department's expanding establishment.

16   No Babylon

Buried in the task of writing the government's Annual Report for 1965, Bill was punctilious about checking his facts and ensuring that he maintained the high standards set for this flagship publication, which served as a bible of information on everything there was to know about how government operated, what it had accomplished and what still remained to be done. It was a point of pride in Government Information Services, whose acronym of GIS we construed as "God is Speaking", that ours was the best government annual report ever produced in what remained of the colonial dependencies; the most truthful, the most accurate and the first to achieve publication (within three months of the year it described).

It would be my task to produce the report for 1966, and Keith's to take charge of the year after that.

Bill, meanwhile, was unashamed about admitting his preparations for departure from GIS as soon as his editorial chore was complete. He planned to join the newly created Trade Development Council, heading its promotional wing, for he loved travelling and the TDC (as that embryonic organisation was popularly known) spent most if not all of its time planning and staging overseas trade exhibitions, to boost Hong Kong's reputation as manufacturer and exporter of an increasingly varied and sophisticated range of products.

Other new recruits included Brian Salt, who arrived from the Isle of Man with a generous heart, a goatee beard and a twinkle in his eye to head our film unit. I felt Brian, with his film experience, would have made a much better and more appropriate companion for Madame Bruce, but then Brian never claimed—as I foolishly did—to speak French.

Madame Josette Bruce, Polish, plump, homely and the image of a motherly housewife, was the widow of Jean Bruce, prolific French author of detective novels featuring a secret agent known as OSS 117. Bruce was France's most successful thriller writer, the Gallic parallel (and predecessor) of Ian Fleming with his series on the incredible adventures of James Bond. Born in 1921, Bruce led an extraordinary life. A pilot by the age of seventeen, he worked for the Special Brigade (the equivalent of Interpol), was an active member of the French Resistance during the war, an actor, secretary to a Maharajah, imprésario, agent, safety inspector and jeweller.

He was also a keen horseman and an enthusiastic rally driver, motor racing being his passion. In 1949, he started writing under the assorted pseudonyms of Jean Alexandre, Jean Alexandre Brochet, Joyce Lindsay and Jean-Martin Rouan. His first and most popular creation, Hubert Bonnisseur de la Bath, also known as agent OSS 117, was a household name in France well before James Bond was even a gleam in Ian Fleming's eye, and the OSS 117 novels, together with the movies produced from many of these, transformed Bruce into a millionaire.

Having completed eighty-eight novels—a number the Cantonese would regard as very fortuitous indeed since, in their language, eight also connotes wealth—and having also scripted those that made it to the cinema screen, Bruce died in a hundred-mile-per-hour road accident outside Paris in 1963. The editor of the series then approached his widow, Josette, and asked her to continue the OSS 117 adventures, to satisfy her late husband's avid following of readers and moviegoers. Hong Kong was her first port of call, on a search for locations in which to set the intrepid secret agent's next escapade.

Unhappily, in my application for the job of Senior Information Officer with the Hong Kong Government Information Services, I had very ill-advisedly, inappropriately and quite excessively volunteered the information that I spoke French, based on a vague familiarity with basic "*la plume de ma tante*" sentence-construction acquired in my grammar school years. I had never attempted to speak the language since.

Our director Nigel Watt, who spoke even less French than I did, was at his wits' end to entertain Madame Bruce when she called on him to request the department's assistance. He had his secretary ferret through the staff files and she came up with the information that his establishment included one French speaker; namely myself.

Summoned to Nigel's office, I was introduced to Madame Bruce, informed that she spoke no English and instructed to accompany her, as guide and informant, on a tour of the New Territories. Madame Bruce rose from her chair, her puzzled frown giving way to a smile of relief. Nigel, clearly equally relieved to be rid of her, could not entirely suppress the impatient hand gesture that signalled my dismissal. I tried not to look absolutely terrified.

On our way down the stairs, even before we got to the government pool car waiting for us at the top of Battery Path, just behind our office, Madame Bruce excitedly embarked on a torrent of French which ended with an unmistakable question mark.

"*Naturellement*," I cautiously replied.

The little crease of bewilderment immediately returned to her brow. By now, we had reached the footbridge connecting the office rear entrance to Battery Path, where I could see the designated limousine and its uniformed driver awaiting our appearance.

She must have decided I had either misheard her or had mistaken her question. Undeterred, she pressed on, pausing at the end of an extremely complicated query for my reply.

"*Exactement!*" I ventured, with as much force of conviction as I could muster.

She looked simultaneously both dismayed and defeated. Was this some kind of crude Anglo-Saxon jest? Had she been quite deliberately and insultingly inflicted with a madman?

Taking our places at the back of the car, she turned to me again, determined either to overcome this impasse or establish why it had arisen. Another deluge of deliciously musical but totally elusive French assailed my ears.

I cogitated for a while, rapidly running out of exclamations to offer her. I ventured something more ambitious. "*Malheureusement, je suis inconnu.*"

"*Oh mon Dieu!*" she expressively cried.

Our office driver turned around to look at us. Normally such pool office drivers were required to master just sufficient English to establish where we wished to go, but instead of doing this, he addressed Madame Bruce in perfect French.

I could not have been more surprised had a shaft of light penetrated the roof of our saloon to wreathe his crown in tongues of flame. God is speaking to **me**, I inwardly divined. Quite distinctly, directly and personally.

Madame Bruce was thrilled. What a funny joke! How exquisitely droll and quintessentially English! To saddle her with an incompetent, inarticulate British bureaucrat and then spring the deliverance of a disarmingly literate Chinese chauffeur. *Très divertissant!*

She promptly ignored me and addressed herself to our driver, pouring out her long litany of hitherto unanswered questions.

He listened patiently and then turned to me to render the gist of this in English. Madame Bruce wished to know how many resettlement estates the government had built, how many were housed in them and what proportion of the total populace were thus accommodated.

I trotted out the figures, which were conveyed back to her in French.

Madame Bruce was immensely pleased. Such a charming idea for her hosts to arrange this unusual mode of communication in order to demonstrate the care we took to train even our minor staff in multilingual skills! She was unable to resist patting my knee in a gesture of appreciation. I shrugged, trying to look as if this was indeed what Nigel and I had been planning all along.

And so we progressed, through a very pleasant and memorable afternoon, touring resettlement estates, interviewing residents, moving on to the New Territories to probe some of its agricultural villages and examine their rustic life cycle. Our driver and self-appointed interpreter was at all times the model of courtesy and efficiency, handling the most complicated interrogations with urbane graciousness. I was beginning to suspect that Nigel might have included me as a target for this grand deception, that it was all some elaborate subterfuge for which he had recruited the services of a top linguist to play the role of a mere office driver, from whom one would least expect such virtuosity.

When we reached the traditional lookout point, overlooking the border from the hill at Lok Ma Chau, I waited for our visitor to busy herself with one of the specially provided telescopes, in her search for some hint of a uniformed PLA patrol on the other side of the river, and then confronted our driver, challenging him to reveal his true identity. Wasn't this all some kind of put-up job?

20   No Babylon

He looked pained. Certainly not. His name was Henry Wong, and he was indeed a mere office driver who happened to enjoy learning the French language, which he had acquired through classes at the local branch of Alliance Francais.

"But why, Henry? *Pourquoi, s'il vous plaît?*"

Because he needed something to occupy him while waiting behind the wheel for the various government personnel he was required to convey from meeting to meeting. Such longueurs could destroy idle minds, and he could think of no better use for them than to spend them reading the novels of Baudelaire, Emile Zola and Guy de Maupassant in their original French.

He excitedly discussed these authors with Madame Bruce when we dined on chicken curry (five Hong Kong dollars a dish) at the Better 'Ole restaurant in the yard of the Fanling railway station. This curiosity of an eatery—which was then the only establishment serving western dishes north of the Kowloon hills—had been launched by a retired British sergeant-major as a whimsical tribute to Old Bill, the cartoon creation of Bruce Bairnsfather, who set his grouchy, mustachioed veteran soldier in the trenches of World War One. The name derived from a classic Old Bill retort to a young recruit, huddled alongside the old-timer in a foxhole while shells whistled overhead: "If you know of a better 'ole, go to it".

Slipping unnoticed from the table, in the midst of an animated debate of the late Jean Bruce's OSS 117 novels, I studied the antique collection of naughty postcards pinned to the restaurant walls, most dating from the prewar kiss-me-quick era of typical British watering holes. Many were familiar to me from displays outside promenade kiosks of such spas as Hastings and Southend-on-Sea. "Where's my Little Willy?" I mused, nostalgically.

Although I would never see her again, or learn what she made of the material gathered from that tour, I recall Madame Bruce as a formidable writer. She excelled even the output of her deceased spouse, producing one hundred and forty-eight novels, the last of them completed in 1985, a year before she died. The task of continuing the series then befell her children,

François and Martine Bruce, who went on to keep the OSS 117 tradition alive with a further twenty-four titles.

It is salutary to compare OSS 117 with Ian Fleming's 007. Unlike Bond, Hubert Bonnisseur de la Bath is far less capable of dominating situations. Events sweep him along, seemingly without allowing him time to formulate a plan or develop any clear idea of exactly what is happening. He depends entirely on his fast and instinctive reactions and his ability to exploit opportunities as they arise. We are afforded little insight into his character and not much by way of a physical description, other than the fact that he is tall, slim and handsome and that at times he suffers mild bouts of anxiety. Yet some see him as more human and credible than Bond because of his fallibility and his occasional miscalculations.

Having delivered a thoroughly satisfied Madame Bruce back to her hotel, I shook Henry Wong's hand in grateful appreciation for having saved my career. I admitted that, had he not been miraculously present, I would have so far disgraced myself with my lack of French that Madame Bruce would surely have complained to Nigel, who would then begin to suspect not only my false claim in regard to French but all of my other credentials.

Henry would remain a firm friend for many years to come, frequently visiting me in the government quarter I would eventually be allocated until, much later, he disappeared from my ken, a great deal wealthier but a lot less happy man. A Chinese entrepreneur seeking to promote a stain-resistant carpet conditioner in the French market learned of Henry's linguistic skills and hired him as co-director, on a salary he couldn't refuse. Overnight he became immersed in accounts and office correspondence and lost the free time he had devoted to his French literature.

For him it would no longer be possible to enjoy the delights of "*Chacun à son gout*".

Strictly for the Birds

The Hong Kong civil service turned dangerously uncivil when it came to internecine warfare over government quarters. This contest was adjudicated on a "points" basis, with an allocations committee meeting once a month to determine the fates of scores of anxious public officers nearing the end of their home leave, or stranded in hotels—like myself—because they were newly arrived and at the bottom of the ratings. It was precisely the kind of iniquitous system one might expect of a caste-ridden colonial institution governed by protocols based on rank, privilege and hierarchy.

To further compound my degraded status as a complete nonentity, with barely sufficient "points" to qualify for the equivalent of a cubicle in a resettlement estate, I was a bachelor, the lowest form of life on the evolutionary scale. People like myself were expected to live in "messes" and eat in public cafeterias. Indeed, the lists of available accommodation circulated each month had little else to offer those in my completely worthless category.

The "quartering office" persuaded me to look around just such a newly completed establishment somewhat appropriately named the Hermitage, stuck between Kennedy and Macdonnell Roads in Hong Kong's Mid Levels. The single-room suites, with bathroom and kitchenette, were so small that I felt I would rather be hung and drawn than quartered in such inadequate accommodation.

Every time my applications failed to produce results, I would console myself with another shopping spree to stockpile, in my already crowded hotel room, the household furnishings and appliances for that "better 'ole" that, sooner or later, must surely materialise. When I was finally allocated a quarter, some three months after my arrival in Hong Kong, I required a removals van to shift me out of the Merlin Hotel.

My new home was a ground floor apartment in a recently-built estate overlooking Silverstrand Beach, several miles beyond the Kowloon Hills. The only reason I managed to gain anything that size was because few people wished to live in such a remote corner, tucked away in the southeastern arm of the New Territories. But I had a car, a sky-blue Hillman Imp with a rear-mounted Coventry-Climax engine, good road-holding and its own parking space at a newly-constructed multi-storey car park near the foot of Nathan Road, to which I had unlimited access at a flat rate of thirty Hong Kong dollars a month.

Furthermore I would have chosen Silverstrand Estate even if I had free choice of anything nearer town, if only because it was in idyllic surroundings that reminded me of my beloved Malaya. Behind me were terraced rice fields, still under cultivation, and in front of me a wide vista looking east across the waters of Port Shelter, which harboured Hong Kong's most profligate archipelago of islands and sequestered the rustic port of Sai Kung, with its fleet of junk-sailed fishing vessels. I had not expected Hong Kong to offer anything so serene, peaceful and isolated.

My balcony afforded me a grandstand view of Port Shelter's eastern approaches, and as evening fell the horizon would become an animated frieze of russet-coloured junk sails as scores of fisher families set out for deeper waters. In complete contrast to this seemingly timeless spectacle, our waterway was occasionally commandeered by the artillery, for gunnery practice, or by the navy, for exercises. I described one of the latter in a letter to my parents:

"A couple of sleek R.N. destroyers hid themselves in narrow inlets and lay in wait for a large and imposing cruiser that was presumably attempting to run some kind of gauntlet. Hysterical signals were flashed between bridges when the cruiser hove into sight, and the destroyers opened up with little puffs of smoke from their gun turrets, to which the cruiser retorted with a great belch of industrial-quality smog from its chimney stack, making off with maximum vitesse. It was 'Sink the Bismarck' being played out before my very eyes and it went on for hours, conducted under elaborate rules to which only inscrutable admirals would have the key. Utterly indecipherable though it was, I could hardly tear myself away from my balcony rails."

Together with a spacious living-dining room, my apartment possessed a decent-sized kitchen, two bathrooms and three bedrooms, one of which I slept in, another I used as a guest room while a third I reserved as an aviary, hung with caged birds which I would release by day to fly around in relative freedom. To supplement the standard-issue government furniture, I combed Silverstrand Beach for flotsam and jetsam, returning with glass fishing floats, worn strands of fishnet, timbers from wrecked or abandoned fishing vessels and bric-a-brac of every description, which I arranged at key focal points around the walls.

The latter trend was influenced by a pseudo-Japanese mood and the prevailing style of household effects offered by the local branch of Cost Plus, a chain store that had opened in San Francisco in 1958, when a businessman of that Pacifically-oriented city parlayed his passion for travel into an import business, by selling a shipload of hand-woven wicker down at Fisherman's Wharf. His furniture sold out within a few days, but the idea lived on. A Hong Kong branch had opened at the former Sea Terminal, housed on a converted wharf off the cluttered dockland area along Canton Road in Tsim Sha Tsui. I became a regular client, especially smitten by the hand-painted panels of their Japanese folding screens. Large numbers of these decorated my walls, where they made an unlikely contrast to the acrylics of my own handiwork, salvaged from my tenure in Malaya.

Armed with a simple illustrated guide to cooking, put together by Len Deighton, author of such best-selling spy novels as *The Ipcress File* and *Funeral in Berlin*, I summoned sufficient courage to entertain. With what I subsequently recognised as a painfully obvious sycophantic motive, my first guests comprised my boss, Nigel Watt, his wife Daphne and their three children. The main course, Surprise Rice, was not a success, proving rather more surprising than I had anticipated since the majority of its mysterious ingredients remained distinctly undercooked.

But Nigel, who had come to Hong Kong from a career in photography, put me at ease by requesting second helpings, followed by the loan of one of my sarongs to relax in, claiming my lifestyle reminded him of his last posting in Aden. Meanwhile Daphne, an elocution teacher, cast a critical eye over the décor and was visibly trying to articulate encouraging remarks.

One of the birds, a Chinese Grosbeak, escaped from the aviary, clung to the hanging lamp in the middle of the living room and shrieked at everybody before returning whence it came. This produced a momentary silence in the conversation, following which I was compelled to conduct my guests to view the contents of the third bedroom. The latter was cause for an even more protracted hiatus in communication. Daphne looked at me severely, compelled to admit that she had not expected to find a bachelor living in such surroundings.

I found their young son Graham in puzzled contemplation of one of my nudes, which I had affected to paint in ersatz-Gaugin style, Polynesian, bulky and lying on her stomach, as viewed from above. "Is it a man or a woman?" he asked. Daphne hurried him away before I could reply.

My belief that the evening had not made a favourable impression was soon dispelled when I received an invitation to dinner at the Watts' household on the Peak. They were to prove not only charming but frequent hosts, and in Nigel I discovered a fellow enthusiast, obsessed with collecting. His particular passions were imaginatively carved and ornately decorated walking sticks, arranged in special stands that lined the walls of the dining room, and ivory cases for Victorian prayer cards, together with snuff bottles, displayed in crowded glass cabinets in the living room.

Other early guests at my Silverstrand apartment were Brian and Moyreen Tilbrook, whom I had first encountered when they taught at the Bourne Road military school in Kuala Lumpur. Gazing out of the back windows of Beaconsfield House, across the footbridge that connected us to the top end of Battery Path, I had been amazed to recognise their familiar faces emerging from the former education department headquarters in the cloistered French Mission Building. They too had been posted to Hong Kong within weeks of my advent, and our friendship would survive my culinary ministrations to develop ever-stronger bonds as the years progressed.

But while I enjoyed entertaining, I lacked any real interest in cooking, and it was becoming abundantly clear that one would not prove possible without the other. The only alternative was to hasten the arrival of my adopted Javanese family from Malaya, Mukti bin Mat Sahit, his wife Asarah and their two sons Mazli and Mazlan. I had promised to send for them as soon as I was settled in, and my distinct lack of culinary talents now made it more compelling that I expedite that promise. I wrote to them at their home in Kampong Congo, Kuala Lumpur, and it was agreed that Mukti would come out first, to judge whether the move would be suitable for his family, before we sent for the others to join him.

I picked him up from Kai Tak airport and, to give him the lie of the land, drove him to the crest of Fei Ngo Shan peak, at the eastern end of Tate's ridge along the spine of the Kowloon hills. From there we looked down on Kai Tak runway, jutting out into Kowloon Bay, and watched the jets banking to the right of us, taking that extreme ninety-degree turn below the prominent landmark of Lion Rock before settling into their final approach. To the south stretched the whole of the Kowloon peninsula and, beyond, the distinctive contours of Hong Kong Island. Within that panorama lay the vast majority of our tiny territory's population; the distant hum of traffic and city bustle carrying up to us like the throb of some perpetual-motion dynamo. I tried to gauge Mukti's expression, to see if this was just too much city for him to accept. He grinned in anticipation, impatient to get to grips with it.

Everything worked. He loved the city, the exaggerated Chinese flavour of its pace and style, together with the extreme contrast afforded by our rustic environment at Silverstrand. The thought that he might possibly be the only Javanese—perhaps even the only Malaysian—in all Hong Kong did not deter him in the least, even if this meant he would have to greatly improve his English and gain a fundamental grasp of Cantonese in order to communicate. He took to it like a proverbial *itek dalam ujan* (a duck in the rain) and adapted to his new home much quicker than I did.

Within months he would be joined by his wife and children, but that time couldn't arrive fast enough for him. He set out to make himself so thoroughly indispensable that it would be impossible for me to contemplate sending him home. He took one look at my kitchen cabinets, stocked with virtually nothing but tinned foods, and decided that we were

Strictly for the Birds   27

both going to die of malnutrition unless he taught himself to cook. By the time Asarah arrived with the boys, Mukti had commandeered the kitchen, leaving her to tend to the laundry and the housecleaning. Without ever consulting a recipe book, which he would have been unable to read anyway because of his limited education, he discovered in himself an innate talent for cooking, simply by testing, tasting and trusting his instincts.

The same remained true of his driving skills, so that inevitably he commandeered the car as well, much to my satisfaction as I preferred to be driven than to drive. His driving was not exemplary, for if anything he tended to be even less patient than I was. One morning we ran into totally stagnant traffic in the heavily built-up sector between the resettlement blocks of Wong Tai Sin and the industrial zone of San Po Kong. Private vehicles, including smaller vans, began to circumvent this impasse by taking to the pavement. Without hesitation, Mukti followed suit, but we had hardly progressed a hundred metres before a uniformed expatriate police inspector hurled himself across our bonnet, shouting "What the hell do you think you're doing?"

Raising his head to peer through the windscreen, he recognised me just as I recognised him. He was our neighbour at Silverstrand, a young, fairly newly-arrived overseas recruited officer for whom I had developed a high regard. "Peter!" he protested. "Why are you setting such a bad example?"

I pointed out that others had set it for me. I was only following an established trend.

"Well hang on," he said, "and I'll see what I can do to sort this out."

Within a few minutes of careful orchestration, he managed the seemingly impossible and we were all on our way again.

He never held my misdemeanour against me and I was sorry when, a few months later, he resigned his commission, claiming he was unable to accept the corruption rampant within the force. Unsolicited envelopes, containing money, had started arriving in a drawer of his office desk. He reported these to his senior officer and immediately his career was sideswiped off its tracks and into a holding yard.

Naïvely credulous in my belief that the law was unimpeachable, I could not fully grasp what he told me. Only much later, thanks to the courage of that indomitable campaigner Elsie Elliott (later Elsie Tu), would I comprehend the extent of that blight on the Hong Kong police force and the damage it had wrought to the few conscientious enough to resist.

"You can ride on the wagon," my disenchanted inspector said, "or you can get off and walk. But if you try to stop it, it will run you down."

Mukti settled into a routine in which he would deliver me to the Star Ferry, on my daily commute to work, and then set out to explore the wet markets and open-air stalls crowding the city's teeming back streets and alleyways, picking up provisions, basic bargains and a smattering of the language. To him it quickly became an infinitely more exciting city than Jakarta or Kuala Lumpur or any other place he'd ever seen, and he developed a talent, rivalling that of any taxi driver, for finding his way around it.

While I might be more familiar with the immediate environs of my office in Hong Kong's Central district, then still largely composed of open-fronted shophouses connected by traditional covered five-foot-wide sidewalks lining both sides of the Queen's Road thoroughfare, Mukti became my guide to much of what lay beyond, in the back streets of Wanchai and Kowloon. He knew where to find the cheapest bargains and how to beat down the prices. Often he would keep me out of sight while he conducted the negotiations, knowing that if I were present I would be charged *gwailo* prices, much higher than those applicable to the locals. *Gwailo*, or *"foreign devil"*, was the common Cantonese pejorative for all Europeans. The time would come when we long-term expatriates of Hong Kong would adopt this contemptuous sobriquet as our badge of honour, but that time would have to wait another few decades.

Thanks to Mukti's ability to "shop around", my food bills were greatly reduced. I was eating better and spending less. Furthermore I found my popularity greatly enhanced, as more and more friends proved willing to embark on the long journey out to Silverstrand to enjoy Mukti's popular Malaysian curry. Scrupulous in his accounting for all expenditure, Mukti was appalled to hear, from our friendly caretaker, that I had been observed through the kitchen window, checking the contents of the refrigerator in the middle of the night. I only learned of this when I found him looking

Strictly for the Birds   29

thoroughly abject and I insisted on learning why. It required some effort and perseverance to convince him that it was my habit to explore the fridge in the middle of the night because I was a chronic insomniac, always hunting for a snack at the most awkward hours.

The aviary was a source of special delight to this Javanese bird fancier. His father had owned laceneck turtle doves, the most prized songbirds in the entire Indo-Malaysian archipelago. He took over its management, feeding the birds by hand and adding to their numbers and varieties with visits to the bird market in Mongkok, a crowded alleyway cacophonous with bird calls and bristling with cages—many of them beautifully ornamented. We quickly discovered that, along with fish kept in lavishly equipped and well tended aquariums, cage-birds were Hong Kong's favourite domestic pets. They took up little space, were relatively inexpensive to maintain and rewarded their owners with song, whereas the fish were merely propitious because the Cantonese word for them happened to coincide with the word for wealth.

Hong Kong at the time boasted at least two restaurants catering specifically for bird owners, who would hang their cages on hooks suspended over the tables and order from two separate menus—one listing live or dried insects and a whole range of birdseed and the other offering dim sum and assorted flavours of tea. In parks and gardens all over the city, one would see elderly gentlemen airing their caged companions, hanging them in tree branches to sing their hearts out while the owners sat on benches nearby, reading their newspapers. It was a ritual no more worthy of comment than the traditional exercising of dogs in western capitals.

Yet even in Hong Kong it would be deemed unusual—at that or any other time—to witness what I did one morning at Government House, on my way to deliver a draft press release for consideration by Governor Sir David Trench. I observed an African parrot, one of its legs attached to a delicate lead held by a middle-aged European *mem*, being "walked" across the lawn enclosed by the circular driveway between the main gates and the entrance portico. The parrot had paused to investigate something of interest in a bed of canna lilies, and the gentle nudging of this curiosity with its beak was clearly testing the patience of its companion. "Oh do come *along*, you *silly* bird," the latter was driven to remonstrate. On subsequent inquiry I learned that she was the housekeeper.

My costliest avian acquisition was a Himalayan mynah that reminded me of its loquacious forebear of my childhood in India, a magnificent mimic so versatile in its repertoire that it could sing entire verses of bawdy songs. Unfortunately the one we picked up in Mongkok had been stored in a petshot above a cage filled with puppies, so that its vocabulary was confined to yapping, whimpering, yelping, barking and baying at the moon. Nevertheless it took an inordinate fancy to Mukti, presumably under the impression that it was supposed to be man's best friend. It would perch on his shoulder and accompany him around the house, imparting a decidedly *Long John Silver* effect.

The particular favourite of the two boys, Mazli and Mazlan, then aged five and three respectively, was a younger and more common mynah their father had acquired from the watchman of our estate. This gluttonous bird, weaned on a generous diet of live insects, proved so insatiable that Mukti and his sons would spend hours beating the surrounding shrubbery in search of crickets. At the faintest rattle of fluttering wings, the mynah, like some demanding charioteer that had spotted a deer breaking cover, would whip its steed to greater efforts by digging its talons deeper into Mukti's shoulder and yelling encouragement into his ear.

Sitting on the balcony, with a "sundowner" tankard of beer beside me, I would contentedly watch this odd quartet beating the bushes in the twilight, silhouetted against the chromatic backdrop of Silverstrand Bay, while Asarah quietly padded through the rooms behind me, switching on the lights and returning freshly laundered clothing to my wardrobe. She kept a wary eye on my beachcombing trophies, and would make her own discreet deletions to establish some kind of balance with my latest additions. She thereby endeavoured to preserve a manageable equilibrium that prevented the detritus from becoming too unruly or encroaching too far into our living space. She had a horror of discovering our home infested with marine termites.

Her anxiety on this score grew more pronounced when Mukti and I started returning with large collections of corals gathered from the ebbing

Strictly for the Birds 31

waters of Plover Cove in Tolo Harbour. There an immense freshwater reservoir was in process of creation, through the then novel method of damming a large inlet of the sea, draining its saline water and replacing it with fresh water harvested from rainfalls and the cross-border pipeline supplies that Hong Kong was driven to purchase from China.

In the two years before my arrival in Hong Kong, the colony had suffered prolonged droughts of such severity that domestic supplies had been rationed to four hours every fourth day. Queues of patient citizens had formed in the streets, taking turns to fill buckets and basins at public taps. Hardware stores had done a roaring trade selling plastic and aluminium containers of all shapes and sizes in which water could be hoarded within the restricted confines of rented cubicles and bedspaces. Hong Kong desperately needed another reservoir in which to collect the rapidly depleted run-off from its mountainous terrain, but all land-based resources had already been exploited, so that the only option was to look to the surrounding ocean.

In its day, Plover Cove was a staggering feat of engineering; the largest reservoir ever won from the sea. Once the rudimentary embankment had been completed, applying its tourniquet to the trapped waters within the bay, these were pumped out to expose a huge acreage of raw corals, their vivid hues rapidly fading in the harsh sunlight. Mukti and I were not the only ones to descend upon this unexpected treasure trove. Brian Tilbrook, ever an ingenious gatherer of aesthetically promising natural materials, salvaged even more than we did to embellish the interior of the apartment he shared with Moyreen in Kennedy Road.

Most of our corals ended up on the balcony, and the frequent replacement of my insecticide spray cans drove me to suspect that Asarah was keeping vigorously at bay the infestations of unknown maritime minutiae she suspected them of harbouring.

◆　　　◆　　　◆

As in any place of violent extremes, in Hong Kong it never rains but it pours. After the prolonged droughts of 1964 and 1965, our prayers were too abundantly answered in the summer of 1966, when three heavy and sustained rainstorms killed eighty-six people through drowning and landslide.

In the immediate aftermath of this downpour, most of which was concentrated on Hong Kong Island itself, I could sense, even as far out as where we lived at Silverstrand, that it was going to be tough getting to work. Many of my neighbours decided against making the effort, but I felt obliged to do so because, in anything resembling a crisis, GIS personnel were required to report for emergency duty. Besides, Nigel Watt had tried to discourage me from living in the New Territories on precisely these grounds and I wanted to reassure him that the extra distance posed no great handicap.

In the event, it proved easier for me to reach the office than for the majority of my colleagues, and I could see why, long before I got there. Riding the Star Ferry under leaden grey clouds that morning, not a single passenger was asleep. We were all staring aghast at the spectacle of an island melting like a soggy chocolate blancmange. Down every crease and gully of that granite outcrop ran rivers of mud. Whole slabs of soil cover had slid away, taking with them trees, rocks and substantial boulders. I dreaded to think of the devastation in those flimsy squatter settlements that predominated in areas like North Point and Shau Kei Wan.

Our news room on the sixth floor of Beaconsfield House was already operating as a disaster resource, issuing radio announcements of schools closed, roads rendered inaccessible, bus routes that had ceased functioning and relief centres established for the many hundreds forced to evacuate their homes. The basic message to those citizens not compelled to report for duty was "stay home unless your home has been rendered unsafe".

Landslides had proved a regular occurrence in Hong Kong throughout its history. Steep terrain, intense seasonal rainfall and very dense hill-slope development made it a prime candidate for calamity. In particular, many thousands of substandard man-made slopes had been constructed in the past, chiefly during the years of rapid development following World War Two. A large proportion of these were prone to failure during heavy rainfall. But the rains of 1966 had no precedent in all the years since the Royal Observatory first commenced its records of rainfall statistics.

So many roads had been closed through subsidence that the entire Peak area was rendered inaccessible. Even the Peak Tram, which had merited a description by Kipling as "a tramway that stood on its head and waved its feet in the mist", was knocked out of commission for the longest spell since it commenced operation in 1888. A sizeable section of the track had been swept away, and foundations, rails and cables were severely damaged, along with one of its two cars. The company's chairman, Mr. W A Stewart, noted: "Fortunately no injury was caused to passengers or to any of our crews whose devotion to duty was a marked feature of this emergency."

This meant that anyone living on the Peak, including our director Nigel Watt, had to find some way to walk to work, at the risk of injury through slipping on steep gradients or being swept away in a monsoon drain. It also meant that, for the duration of this impasse, food and other essential supplies could only be delivered by helicopter. Newspapers, when they managed to get through, were dominated by photographs of a sensational nature, including a tangled mess of cars that had been swept to destruction down one of the steeper streets of North Point.

Magic Stone and Replacement Rabbit

The head of our film unit, goatee-bearded Brian Salt, was irrepressibly effervescent in his enthusiasms and ideas. He was a relic from an earlier, more courtly age, always dressed in a suit and tie, no matter what the temperature, and he had been involved in film-making at least as long as I had been alive. Back in 1936 he was credited with the animation of a short film entitled *Equation: X + X = O* and in 1958 he directed and co-wrote, for a production company called World Safari, a children's feature set in Africa and entitled *Toto and the Poachers.*

Brian fell instantly in love with Hong Kong, and established a close working relationship with his subordinates, including talented young cinematographer Charles Wang, who would later leave GIS to head his father's company, *Salon Films.* Between them they were always coming up with intriguing ideas for new ventures.

When Hong Kong was subjected to a brief repeat of the water rationing it had experienced in the early 1960s, Brian employed the bathroom of his government quarter at Chater Hall as the set for a short black and white public service message encouraging economies in consumption. The theme of "Save Water, Share a Bath" was illustrated by a trio of mixed race and sex who set an example by simultaneously doing precisely that, with only a diaphanous shower curtain concealing what the old *Carry On* movies would have described as their "naughty bits".

Nigel Watt was confronted with a dilemma. While the film unit fell under his overall direction, so did the film censor's office, headed by a severely conservative old gentleman called William Hung. Willie was appalled by this unprecedented approach to public education. He felt he could not permit Brian's "Save Water" reminder to be screened in Hong

Kong cinemas without serious cuts, and of course with a message as brief as that the cuts would leave nothing that made any sense. Accordingly "Save Water, Share a Bath" went down the plughole as the only GIS film ever banned by the department that produced it.

Undismayed, Brian pressed on with his next project, a fanciful, twenty-four-minute colour movie entitled *Mong Fu Sek*, or *The Magic Stone*. Subtitled *A Legend from Hong Kong*, this was extremely loosely based on the local fable of Mong Fu Sek, the "husband-watching rock" which the majority of us readily recognised by its more common name of Amah Rock. Situated on the northern slopes of the Kowloon range, overlooking the Sha Tin valley, Amah Rock was a prominent landmark, consisting of a stone pillar which, viewed from certain angles, resembled a woman with a child strapped to her back. The supposed origin of this feature was a faithful fisherman's wife who kept constant watch for the return of a husband lost at sea. I was troubled by the divine intervention that rewarded this fidelity by turning both her and the child to stone. Barring the substitution of salt for granite, wasn't that much the same fate which—for an entirely different reason—had overtaken Lot's wife when she turned to look back at Sodom and Gomorrah?

Brian shared no misgivings on that score. His adaptation married the wife to the inventor of the magnetic compass, thereby killing two fables with one stone. His principal character was Wu Ying, a Chinese fisherman betrothed to a local village woman named Mei Ching. Together, they rejoice that the lodestone they have stumbled across allows Wu Ying to sail far beyond the horizon and return with ever richer harvests from the sea. The lovers marry and produce a son, who is still an infant slung from his mother's back when Wu Ying ventures dangerously far from home. Refusing to accept that his junk has been dashed to pieces on a storm-wracked coast, Mei Ching each day climbs the hill behind their village and watches in sorrow for the husband who will never return, until at last the goddess *Tin Hau* takes pity on her and reunites their spirits.

"But what about their son?" I persisted in asking. "Why should he have to share his mother's fate?"

Brian shrugged that off as a mere detail.

He persuaded Nigel that *Mong Fu Sek* could be produced on a small budget as a tourism promotion for Hong Kong. Cost savings could be achieved by eliminating the need for recorded dialogue and depending largely on a musical score—by Ivor Slaney—to carry the story, which would be "a testament to the power of love and faithfulness to transcend death". Only hearts already turned to stone would resist its appeal.

Researching a feature story I planned to write on the Royal Hong Kong Auxiliary Air Force, I flew out to the Sai Kung peninsula in one of their sprightly new Aerospatiale Alouette III helicopters, which had recently entered service to replace the former Westland Widgeons. Our particular mission was to reconnoitre the wreck of the *Nan An,* a cargo vessel that had gone aground on that rugged coast in a typhoon. Despite appalling conditions, the Alouette's volunteer crew had managed to winch up its sailors from the windswept deck and had received commendations for their bravery.

On the way home I suggested we might drop in at the tiny hamlet of Lung Suen Wan on High Island, at the northern end of Port Shelter, where Brian was shooting *The Magic Stone* on location. This would give us the chance to meet up with the entire film unit team and also with the stars of the production, Ling Yuen, playing the fisherman Wu Ying, and the delectable Nancy Kwan, who had graciously agreed to interrupt a busy Hollywood schedule to play his wife Mei Ching.

Nancy's participation in the project was something of a coup, in part engineered by Charles Wang whose father, T.C. Wang, had introduced her to producer Ray Stark and thereby enshrined her title role in *The World of Suzie Wong*. I had greatly enjoyed that movie, not only because of Nancy's performance, or because she co-starred with William Holden, whom I had encountered in Malaya where he was featured in *The Seventh Dawn*, but because I found *The World of Suzie Wong* the most accurate movie ever to portray Hong Kong's postwar years. It had achieved this with greater fidelity than the earlier *Love is a Many-Splendored Thing*, an over-glamourised rendering of Han Suyin's real-life romance with Ian Morrison, in which Holden also starred, his character's name changed from Morrison to Mark Elliott.

Brian Salt had searched with great diligence for the ideal fishing village in which to set his quasi-historical drama. It had to be remote, unspoilt and still populated by genuine fishermen and their families, pursuing their time-honoured occupations according to zealously-guarded traditions. He found what he wanted in Lung Suen Wan on High Island, when that geographical feature still preserved its insularity, long before it was grafted on to the adjoining Sai Kung peninsula to trap and drain another arm of the sea for yet another reservoir. Certainly the old stone houses, with their swayback roofs, looked authentic enough, but Brian felt they needed an extra touch to reinforce their venerability. He acquired great quantities of straw and arranged for this to be laid over all the village roof tiles, to give the settlement a thatched appearance and add to its charming rusticity.

Unfortunately I didn't know this.

As our Alouette hovered over the picturesque little community, preparatory to touchdown in the forecourt of the Tin Hau temple, we were astonished to see a blizzard of straw whirling into motion under our gyrating blades. My first thought was that we had arrived just in time to witness the onset of some unique catastrophic phenomenon, akin to a Biblical deluge of frogs and toads. But then I spotted Brian, like some enraged Old Testament patriarch, pitting himself against the maelstrom and advancing towards our descending helicopter with upraised fists and a look on his face indicative of his desire to personally pluck our rotors from our fuselage.

I incongruously remembered the words of the popular French song: "*Alouette, gentille Alouette, Alouette, je te plumerai*". Rendered in translation, successive verses describe how "Skylark, sweet skylark, I will pluck you; I will pluck your head, beak, neck, back, wings, knees and feet".

Fortunately Brian was a forgiving man. A halt was called to cinematography while we met with cast and crew to pose for photographs that would preserve this impromptu encounter between two worlds.

The government auditors were less forgiving and a great deal less accommodating. For the climactic sequence culminating in the shipwreck, Brian had purchased, at an auction under the patronage of the fisheries department, a secondhand sailing junk that looked sufficiently vintage and battered to resemble the kind of vessels that had plied the South China coastline for hundreds if not thousands of years. This was not a cheap item in the budget, absorbing a large part of the outlay for the entire film.

The passage in the script, calling for the loss of this vessel and all its crew, read as follows:

> "Far out at sea, while the fishermen work at their nets, a dreadful storm comes up. On their junk, Wu Ying and his crew battle bravely against the elements, but heavy seas sweep over them and they drift helplessly. At last, with its sails torn and its mast gone, the junk is broken against cruel, jagged rocks."

When all of the footage was finally in the can, and *The Magic Stone* had been distributed for commercial release in international cinemas, enjoying moderate success as a supporting feature, the accountants went through the books and were astonished to discover no record of the subsequent disposal of the junk. Dissatisfied with the memoranda and minutes in which Brian endeavoured to explain this absence, they summoned him for an interview. Brian later revealed to his colleagues a condensed version of what transpired.

"You say that the junk was lost at sea. Accidentally?"

"No, deliberately."

"Deliberately?"

"Quite deliberately. It was wrecked in a storm."

"Ah, accidentally then."

"Not accidentally at all. And not in a real storm either."

His interrogators looked dumbfounded. "A manufactured storm?"

"A storm whose appearance we spent many patient days endeavouring to simulate."

"Where did this take place?"

"Off the Sai Kung coast. In heavy but not quite satisfactorily stormy weather."

"During which time the junk…"

"Was slowly battered to pieces on the rocks."

"While you stood by observing this process?"

"Observing and filming, at great length."

"The slow destruction of a large and at that time still serviceable item of government equipment?"

"If you can describe a secondhand sailing junk as an item of government equipment."

"If it was purchased with government funds it was an item of government equipment. Which you, it seems, have quite deliberately, methodically and wilfully set out to destroy. For what purpose?"

"For the sake of the film. Which demanded it. It's in the script if you'd care to read it."

"Could the same effect not have been achieved with a model?"

"Perhaps. But only at greater cost and with far less convincing results. The proof is here, in this can, if you wish me to screen it for you."

The interrogating panel looked at each other and then returned their gaze to Brian, slowly shaking their flabbergasted heads.

A model was employed elsewhere in the film, standing in for the Amah Rock at the close of Nancy Kwan's somewhat extreme metamorphosis. By this time the whole of the Sha Tin valley below had been flooded with the use of bluescreen special effects to represent an inlet of the sea across which her inventive but, in the end, too venturesome husband failed to return. Fade to black.

Like many others before him, Brian fell in love with Hong Kong, and left only with extreme reluctance when age worked against him to deny him a renewal of his contract. Shortly after he joined GIS, Stanley Kubrick contacted him with an offer to work on the movie *2001: A Space Odyssey*, which that genius of a director was putting together with its author Arthur C. Clarke. Kubrick had some animated sequences in mind and remembered Brian's work on *Equation: X + X = O*. But Brian was already too smitten by Hong Kong to cut short his stay, and wrote back quoting a salary he thought would be high enough to frighten Kubrick off. To his dismay, Kubrick came back accepting this figure and leaving Brian no option but to decline, with a fuller explanation as to why he couldn't be spared. He was by then too immersed in his South China Sea saga.

When the time came for him to leave, he chose to do so by taking slow boats home, calling en route at the Seychelles where I had told him my brother Paul was occupying the post of the colony's only information officer. Paul had asked me to establish the cost of a Canon camera, which he would reimburse if I arranged to send this out to him. Brian offered to buy the camera and accept the reimbursement but in the event, after being entertained by Paul and my sister-in-law Mary during his brief sojourn, he refused to accept repayment and—much to Paul's consternation—made him an outright gift of the camera, which in its day was one of the most expensive on the market. It was an act typical of Brian's generosity, and one which Paul never forgot.

Brian made numerous return visits to Hong Kong, invariably as the guest of his former cinematographer Charles Wang, who characteristically remained ever loyal to all his former friends and colleagues. As managing director of Salon Films, Charles would develop close bonds with many of the great stars, producers and directors of Hollywood. Major overseas studios and production houses would seek him out as their first point of contact in Hong Kong, where Salon Films were best equipped to facilitate their ventures.

Ingenuity was Charles' byword. When director Robert Wise was shooting *The Sand Pebbles* in Hong Kong, at the time of my arrival in 1965, Charles was assigned by GIS to provide liaison and assist the production in any way he could. Wise needed a high shot of junks and sampans besieging the *U.S.S. San Pablo*, so Charles volunteered to scale the *San Pablo's* mast to obtain this perspective with a heavy, shoulder-mounted Arriflex camera. On the precarious descent he got into difficulties and split his trousers right across the crotch. Wise immediately sent his measurements to a local tailor, ordering two pairs as replacements.

The Sand Pebbles concerned the exploits of the American gunboat and its crew as they patrolled a tributary of the Yangtze in the revolution-torn China of 1926. Naturally, Sino-American relations having virtually ceased to exist in the aftermath of the Korean War, the film could not be shot on the Chinese mainland. So Wise chose Taiwan to substitute for the bulk of his locations, supplemented with four months of exteriors in Hong Kong

Magic Stone and Replacement Rabbit   41

waters, principally in and around that beautiful Port Shelter area that my balcony overlooked. Ironically our endearing film censor Willie Hung decided the story was too politically sensitive to be shown in Hong Kong cinemas, so that many of the local extras who had contributed to its crowd scenes never got to see the finished product.

Wise had originally wanted Paul Newman for the starring role of engineer Jake Holman, but the part went instead to Steve McQueen, winning him his only Academy Award nomination as best actor.

Once both Brian and Charles had left GIS, our film unit went into steady decline, headed by less talented personnel who brought to their task pedestrian skills that were producing diminished returns. Around us, Hong Kong was becoming more sophisticated in its tastes and less disposed to accept the rudimentary documentary fare we were dishing out.

The last incumbent in the post, who I will remember by his first name of Albert, came to seek my advice in the aftermath of a minor crisis encountered in the course of that day's shooting schedule. This had incurred some unexpected expenditure he now wished to reclaim. He and his team had been preparing a short film to celebrate the Chinese New Year of 1970, inaugurating the Year of the Dog. They had borrowed a terrier to symbolise the appropriate zodiac sign, which would denote loyalty and honesty, mingled with a degree of stubbornness. The latter quality was particularly marked in the canine in question, which was not taking well to instruction on where to sit and how to behave.

Albert had chosen a location just in front of the government quarters at Mount Austin Road, not far from the upper Peak Tram station and overlooking the entire panorama of Hong Kong harbour. Posed against that backdrop, the terrier was briefly coerced into position, gazed fleetingly at the camera, and then caught some stray whiff of an aroma which sent it flying up the staircase of the nearest residential block. Abandoning their camera, lighting and sound equipment, the crew set off in pursuit.

Arriving breathless on the third landing, they encountered a poignant scene. The front door to one of the government quarters, accommodating a senior expatriate civil servant and his family, was wide open, the principal occupant having just returned, bearing a gift for his children. The gift was a tame chinchilla rabbit, of which barely sufficient survived to serve even as a collar for a fur coat. Standing over the savaged carcass of this all-too-recently deceased creature, tossing its remnants impatiently aside and spraying the carpet with blood, was the triumphant harbinger of the new year. Shrieking piteous cries of terror were the recipients of this unexpected presentation. The mother was hysterical, the father furious, Albert tongue-tied in his efforts to explain and the whole production reeking of high drama.

What, I inquired, was the item of expenditure Albert had incurred?

Consumed with guilt, he had called a halt to the day's shoot, returned the offending terrier to its owner and then headed to the nearest pet shop to acquire a replacement rabbit.

Had this proved acceptable to the grieving family?

Albert mournfully shook his head. It was the wrong breed, the wrong colour and the wrong texture.

Why hadn't he been able to get a better match?

Very little of the original remained, so that the sample he supplied the pet shop proprietor wasn't really enough to go on. The family would be getting in touch with Nigel Watt. I took Albert with me to Nigel's office to assist his recounting of events.

"Oh, dear God," murmured Nigel.

Shortly after that, the film unit was finally disbanded and its equipment—with some difficulty—"written off". From there on we commissioned outside contractors to supply our film needs.

Toothbrushes, Cameras and Blue Movies

The Cantonese were nothing if not ingenious and enterprising in their search for novel ways to make a living, even if this meant nudging close to the outer confines of the law. Among the first reports I read in the pages of the *South China Morning Post* was one concerning a court case in which it was argued that the defendant had failed to screen blue movies, a point he unsuccessfully employed—on moral grounds—in his own defence.

Evidence was produced to the effect that the defendant's son touted for business in the street below the tiny Mongkok apartment room the two shared. Surreptitiously promising blue movies, he would assemble perhaps a dozen or more eager voyeurs and conduct them up to the room, where they would be seated on collapsible metal chairs. The defendant would commence carefully threading a spool of 16 mm film into the sprockets of a weather-beaten projector, at which point the son would burst into the room to announce a police raid. Chairs and slippers would go flying as, without waiting to reclaim their admission fees, customers beat a hasty retreat down the back staircase. After a decent interval to allow their dispersal, the whole process would be repeated with another set of patrons, of course leading to another false alarm.

The con went awry only when the son, failing to recognise that one of those he solicited was a previous dissatisfied client, subjected the latter to a repetition of the identical sequence of events. This time the twice-bitten victim went straight to the police. The only footage found on the premises was the spool in the projector, which proved to be a fragment of an innocuous promotion for laundry detergent. Effectively then, the case against the defendant rested on the fact that he had failed to produce the promised blue movies. And his only defence was that, had he done so, the penalty he risked would be even more severe.

Among the earliest reports that I myself filed was a feature story on the metamorphosis of the Haking Wong factory, from toothbrushes to cameras. One of many enterprises that had migrated to Hong Kong from Shanghai, following the fall of the Nationalist government, the Haking Wong company continued producing their staple commodity of toothbrushes until its directors, Doctors Haking Wong and Pauline Chan, decided these were insufficiently challenging to take best advantage of high-tech market trends. Casting around for alternatives, they settled on cameras and optical equipment.

At that time there was no other company in Hong Kong manufacturing anything in this particular range, whose products were almost exclusively emerging from Japan. So Doctors Wong and Chan engaged the services of a highly qualified Japanese technician to train their existing personnel in camera production. Those employees reluctant to make the switch were released with handsome compensation, but the majority elected to acquire the totally new skills necessary for the retooling exercise. Production of toothbrushes ceased while the training programme swung into high gear, at the end of which time Haking Wong re-emerged on the public stage with its entirely new range of products, with which it quickly established a distinguished international reputation.

Shanghai money and know-how provided the final crucial ingredients of the Hong Kong success story. They supplemented colonial paternalism and *laissez-faire*, and the gutsy Cantonese can-do spirit, to furnish the remaining leg of the tripod on which Hong Kong set the theodolite of its future ambitions. Many of the colony's leading industrialists had brought their savings and their expertise with them from that former queen of the South China Seas, lighting the touch papers that sparked new enterprise across the entire range of Hong Kong industry from textile manufacturing to film production.

Charles Wang's father, T.C. Wang, was among the Shanghai immigrants, as was that doyen of Hong Kong film magnates Run Run Shaw. The latter had created the most extensive studio complex in the entire territory. Known as Shaw's Movietown, this spread like some immense theme park, through the valley on the other side of the hill behind my apartment at Silverstrand. I could walk there in minutes through the paddy fields, and find myself lost in labyrinthian coils of ancient China, with its teahouses, market stalls, temples and castles ever undergoing renovation, removal and reassembly in fresh configurations, as dictated by the latest of the many sword-fighting movies currently in production.

Many of the films emerging from Shaw Studio is those years of the mid to late sixties were destined to become classics of a genre that would greatly influence future film makers like Quentin Tarantino (*Pulp Fiction* and *Kill Bill*) and Ang Lee (*Crouching Tiger, Hidden Dragon*). In fact Pei-pei Cheng, who played Jade Fox in the latter film, launched her career with such Shaw classics as *Come Drink with Me*, *Hong Kong Nocturne* and *Dragon Creek*.

Gimlet-eyed, lean and aquiline, Run Run looked like a sort of oriental Don Vito Corleone, from a Chinese translation of Mario Puzo's *The Godfather*. He had the same courtly manners, perceptive gaze, shrewd judgment and all-pervading air of absolute authority. You felt that nothing would be allowed to stand, for very long, in his way. But you also felt that the removal of whatever may temporarily impede his progress would be accomplished with the utmost tact and discretion.

Although a martinet to work for, keeping his famed stable of starlets confined in a dormitory from which they would be released only under the closest supervision, he was also a consummate host who enjoyed entertaining and revelled in a wide circle of influential friends. Because I was a neighbour, and would come, in later years, to work closely with him when he chaired the Hong Kong Arts Festival, I was a frequent guest at his dinner parties. These were held in a sort of miniature Hearst Castle on a hill overlooking Movietown, approached by a narrow and tortuous ramp and commanding fine views northward across Port Shelter. Dinner would be preceded by the preview of some forthcoming Hollywood release in a cosy, almost subterranean theatre, after which we adjourned upstairs for a sumptuous buffet at which one might encounter, picking gingerly at the asparagus and abalone, such unexpected celebrities as Elizabeth Taylor.

It was at one of these dinners that the topic arose of filming James Clavell's *Taipan*. At that time the book was practically the only historical fiction Hong Kong had ever inspired, short of thrillers dealing with triads, white slavers, opium cartels and the espionage activities which outdated perceptions so readily attributed to this allegedly less than fragrant harbour. I had personally found *Taipan* a disappointment, not least because of its contrived finale, in which another gust of typhoon came and took away another piece of house. I had much preferred the authentic history offered by Maurice Collis in his *Foreign Mud*, in which I luxuriantly wallowed not just because of its superior prose but because it related a more eventful saga that had the added merit of truth.

Run Run at that time held the screen rights to *Taipan* and didn't know quite what to do about it. Clearly it would be impossible to recreate the early colonial origins of Hong Kong as they would have appeared in the first half of the nineteenth century. No trace of those foundations remained, and there was no room left in the crowded metropolis to permit their simulation through artifice and special effects. Suggestions were put forward regarding the feasibility of leasing some unpopulated island in the Adriatic Sea, constructing the embryo Hong Kong settlement there and populating it with thousands of extras drawn from the Chinese laundries and restaurants scattered throughout Europe.

Nothing came of those proposals and many years passed before the rights were transferred to the De Laurentis Entertainment Group. By then China had opened its doors to foreign investment, so that producer Raffaella De Laurentis could negotiate, with the authorities in Guangzhou, the rights to recreate both Hong Kong, and its antecedents in that city's former "foreign factories", along the banks of the Pearl River. Charles Wang lent technical equipment and support to the undertaking, which on its release in 1986 proved a costly and terrible fiasco.

Critic Roger Ebert was particularly scathing in his review for the *Chicago Sun-Times*. "*Tai-Pan*" he said, "is the embodiment of those old movie posters where the title is hewn from solid rock and tiny figures scale it with cannons strapped to their backs, while the bosoms of their women heave in the foreground. It tells the saga of men who were larger than life, except for their brains, and of the women who loved them, lost them, left them, returned to them, double-crossed them, bore their children, oppressed their servants, and still found time to rend their hearts and their underwear."

During our sojourn at Silverstrand, Shaw Studios experimented in cross-cultural links with their affiliated studios in Singapore, importing Malay movie stars to feature in frothy romantic comedies with Hong Kong settings for the Malaysian market and dispatching Hong Kong stars in the opposite direction to spice up locations for productions targeted at Hong Kong audiences. This brought into our orbit such Malay heartthrobs as Jins Shamsuddin and Aziz Jaafar, and their female leads Saadiah and Sharifah Hanim, all of whom came to join us for our "at homes", with Mukti's curry and satay on the menu.

Jins Shamsuddin would later become a director, bringing to the screen, among other movies, a fairly accurate historical reconstruction of the communist siege of the Bukit Kepong police post during the darkest days of the Malayan Emergency. There twelve Regular Malay Police, two Special Constables, four Auxiliary Police and four of their dependants, numbering a total of twenty-two in all, fought to the death at the Battle of Bukit Kepong, which would go down in local history as Malaya's "Alamo".

◆　　　◆　　　◆

My feature assignments, which I was free to choose myself, took me all over Hong Kong and the New Territories, repeating the freedom of exploration I had enjoyed in my journeys through peninsula Malaya. The territory I covered may have been less extensive but, surprisingly, the variety it offered was as great, or greater. Like the equally variegated but much larger British Isles, Hong Kong seemed to have mastered the art of compacting an astonishing richness and diversity into the smallest of spaces. A circuit of the New Territories could easily be accomplished in a day, but in that span I would traverse civic splendours, industrial slums, docksides, shipyards, ancient villages slumbering in groves of bamboo, bays filled with sailing junks, acres of marshes and fishponds, mountainous prospects of

48   No Babylon

hidden valleys, oceanic outlooks, remote beaches, mangrove swamps, vegetable gardens, rice fields ploughed by yoked oxen and serene vistas of bird-haunted forests.

There was clearly a great deal more to Hong Kong than had immediately met my eye, and I was granted the luxury of thrusting my chopsticks at will into this gargantuan repast spread before me. Yet again, as had been my experience in Malaya, I was hindered by my lack of the *lingua franca*. In Malaya I had overcome this problem through the total immersion method of virtually adopting a local family who spoke no English. And Malay, anyway, was a language one quickly learned to speak badly. Now that this family had joined me in Hong Kong, we were all encumbered with the same handicap, some of us coping with it better than others. Mukti picked up Cantonese very quickly, and his sons in due course would do the same. Asarah's own grasp of it would improve rapidly once she found herself a job in a factory assembling plastic parts. I was slowest of all and, in the end, proved a complete failure.

Cantonese is a very precise monosyllabic language, though some would argue that it ranks as no more than a dialect. Its words embrace a miscellaneous variety of meanings, pinned down to particulars only by the tones and contexts in which they are uttered. I could never get the intonation right, so that the recipients of my carefully rehearsed inquiries would stare at me in blank bewilderment. Also I never met with any kind of encouragement. My Cantonese friends and colleagues, too impatient to bother with sorting out my intentions, were invariably much more concerned to practice their English than to help me with my Cantonese. At times it seemed they preferred to keep their language largely inaccessible to us foreign devils, preserving it as a secret means of communication, rather like those messages hidden in mooncakes that, during the August Moon Festival of 1368, had brought about the downfall of China's pastry-shunning Mongolian rulers.

Nevertheless I persevered in my efforts to master at least enough of the language to venture beyond the confines for our comfortably English-speaking urban environment. So I attended the government language school, in those days housed in a three-storey concrete block beside the

Toothbrushes, Cameras and Blue Movies 49

parade ground of Fire Services headquarters in Admiralty, roughly where the Admiralty office tower block stands today. There, amid fellow students who were largely strapping young police inspectors newly recruited from Britain, I grimly grappled with the six distinct tones I was expected to master: the high-level (or high-falling) tone, mid-rising tone, mid-level tone, low-falling tone, low-rising tone and low-level tone. I seldom remembered which to use in which particular context. Not only did the tonality completely lack any recognisable musical form, but it all seemed hideously and unintelligibly mathematical, and whereas music had been among my favourite subjects at school, mathematics had been my anathema.

Since it seemed that shopping expeditions would provide my only opportunity to practice what I learned, I ventured my first attempt at bargaining in one of the mainland China products stores scattered through different areas of Hong Kong. These offered amazingly cheap merchandise ranging from clothing, footwear, toys, furniture and electric appliances to superbly crafted ornaments in cloisonné, jade and ivory. Naturally no loyal American dare be seen shopping in those Aladdin's caves of treasures for fear of betraying leftist tendencies, but for the rest of us shamelessly apolitical expatriates they were a godsend. I especially coveted their tiny, beautifully clay-wrought teapots, available in many exotic shapes for no more than three Hong Kong dollars apiece.

However I always mixed up the Cantonese for three and four, so that when I was quoted "*saam mun*" (three dollars) I ponderously responded that this was far too expensive and I wasn't prepared to go higher than "*sei mun*" (four dollars). This produced, at first, an incredulous silence all around me for a distance of some ten metres, following which the store was filled with expanding ripples of laughter as word carried through it of a mad *gwailo* who insisted on paying more than the specified sum. I quietly resolved that, while the Cantonese might rank high among my favourite fellow beings, their language—poetic and expressive though it undoubtedly was—must forever remain a mystery to me.

Even without the language, it was still possible for me to do then what it is no longer possible to do now—namely make myself understood virtually everywhere I went. The use of English in those days was far more widespread, and the quality of graduates from Hong Kong University so high that they were as polished and articulate in the international idiom as they were in their own. Furthermore most signs, and nearly all advertising, were in both languages, so that one never felt lost for directions, completely mystified by the import of some large, apparently significant but totally incomprehensible hoarding or struggling to make sense of a leaflet thrust into one's hands by a street tout. Hong Kong was then still a truly global village, whereas it has now reverted to a thoroughly parochial one, desperately striving to be just another Chinese city and negating the very reason why China wanted it back.

◆　　　◆　　　◆

Among my earliest assignments was a feature on the floating clinic operated by the medical and health department. This provided precisely the service its name implied, cruising the remoter villages along the territory's extensively indented seaboard on a regular weekly schedule to bring to their occupants the same quality of health care afforded to urban dwellers, while sparing them the equivalent waiting time at much frequented hospital outlets.

Our particular route that day lay along the corrugated eastern littoral of the New Territories, stopping mainly at insular settlements deprived of any road communications. I had flown over much of this coast by helicopter, but had failed to take in its sheer scale. Skirting precipitous cliffs, whose chiselled columns of basalt vied with any equivalent geological formation elsewhere, I was staggered by the unspoilt beauty of its grandeur, and curiously reminded—but for the substitution of windswept pines for dripping rain forests—of the Langkawi archipelago I had grown to love in Malaya.

Out last ports of call that day were the islands of Tap Mun (Grass Island), at the mouth of Tolo Harbour, and Kat O Chau (Crooked Island) in Starling Inlet. Not far from the latter, in April 1898, Commodore George Dewey, spurred by the aggressive Assistant Secretary of the US Navy, Theodore Roosevelt, had assembled his Asiatic Squadron to prepare an assault on the Spanish fleet in Manila. Despite America's belated imperial ambitions, spurred by the expansionist trends of its *Manifest Destiny* and already vaulting the Pacific to the Philippines, Dewey may not have entertained any notion of annexing Chinese territory. But his reasons for being there at all were not quite so manifestly obvious to startled British merchants barely twenty miles away on Hong Kong Island.

They had argued for years that Hong Kong's mere existence continued to be threatened by the aspirations of rival colonial powers. While it may have sprung from inauspicious beginnings, the embryo colony had prospered beyond expectation, and had attracted the covetous eyes of rival empire-builders.

Governor Sir William Robinson had persistently pressed the Colonial Office to seek an extension of Hong Kong's boundaries in the interests of "securing the defence" of the colony. "Sir William Robinson," commented the Foreign Office, "seems a somewhat impulsive gentleman." To which remark the Colonial Office added its own: "Can he so far have lost his head that he wants to annex Guangzhou?"

Nevertheless London had been made increasingly aware of the extent to which competitors—principally France, Russia and Japan—were spearheading their own infiltrations into the Celestial Empire. Renewed representations by the Hong Kong Chamber of Commerce and, at home, by the China Association and the Navy League, were eliciting a more sympathetic response. Dewey's cheeky naval incursion—without so much as a "by your leave"—seems to have settled the issue once and for all.

The *Sino-British Kowloon Extension Agreement* was signed in Beijing on June 9th 1898 and set to take effect on July 1st 1898. Submitting the convention to Emperor Guangxu for approval, the Tsungli Yamen, China's foreign affairs ministry, stressed that it was only a ***lease*** the British were seeking:

> "Extending boundaries is not the same as ceding a city port. As the lease is temporary in nature, we are still in control."

Which of course would prove exactly the case ninety-nine years later, when the communist government in Beijing would reassert its claim to sovereignty and put an end to long-nourished expectations, in Hong Kong, that they would somehow suffer a lapse of memory and forget all about it.

That cricket-humming, late October day in 1966, when I climbed the hill above the gray slate roofs of Kat O Chau to gaze across Starling Inlet at the startling proximity of mainland China, it seemed I contemplated the green coiled loops of an immense but languorous dragon, asleep in the afternoon sun. Hardly anything stirred. I could imagine George Chinnery seated with his sketchpad on the rocks below. Had that famed illustrator of life on the early China coast ventured this far, he would have found in this familiar prospect much to his taste and satisfaction.

So peaceful was it that our floating clinic called in at Sha Tau Kok, the town bisected down its high street by the boundary line. Its whitewashed markers, hardly more conspicuous than traffic cones, extended down the length of the jetty where we disembarked, careful to keep to our side of its narrow concrete deck. Nobody troubled us as we walked down the high street. Local residents, free to cross at will, exercised their right to do so without sparing us more than a passing glance of curiosity.

There seemed nothing to differentiate "us" from "them". The open-fronted shops on their side seemed to offer goods identical to those on ours. Without the markers, this could have been any little market town anywhere in the New Territories, totally devoid of any suggestion of the "frontier" feeling I had anticipated, and vastly different in atmosphere from the tension that Keith Robinson and I had inspired on the Lo Wu bridge. Little could I suspect how dramatically that scene would alter over the next few months.

Indivisible Whole

The supposed boundary afforded by the street of that name bisecting the Kowloon peninsula had long ceased to serve any such purpose. Here one was made immediately aware how absurd it was to believe that, should China reclaim the New Territories once the lease was up, Hong Kong and Kowloon could continue to survive as a viable entity. The extent of the spillover from those ceded territories, into the technically ancillary area north of this anachronistic demarcation, made it abundantly clear there was no going back. Like an inoperable case of Siamese twins, the conjunction had bonded all into an indivisible whole.

The airport lay north of Boundary Street, as did the great majority of the factories powering the colony's economic engines. The first satellite township of Kwun Tong was already well established by the time I arrived, and a second, even larger, was taking shape at Tsuen Wan, northeast of the Kowloon hills. There inlets with names quaintly suggestive of early Victorian boating parties and picnic expeditions, such as Gin Drinker's Bay, were being filled in with refuse to lay the foundations for still further development.

The official report of proceedings in the Legislative Council, just a year before my arrival, carried a statement by the Colonial Secretary, the Honourable Edmund Brinsley Teesdale, in response to a familiar complaint regarding "more filth in the harbour, in the surrounding waters, and at our beaches than ever before":

> "…there seems little doubt that the recent deterioration to which my Honourable Friend refers is due principally to damage at Gin Drinker's Bay refuse dump during the past few months. Part of the dump collapsed in April and floating refuse escaped through the gap in the log boom through which refuse barges have access to the dump."

It is tempting to hope that among the escaped detritus was a bottle or two of very ancient and not entirely consumed gin.

I went to Tsuen Wan to write a feature story on that township's greatly accelerated growth. Lying in a bay overlooking the granite massif of Tsing Yi Island, and backed by Hong Kong's highest mountain, Tai Mo Shan, Tsuen Wan was a patchwork quilt of old and new. Surviving enclaves of largely unchanged and untouched ancestral village were surrounded by barricades of high-rise factory and apartment blocks. From the tiny windows of those embattled relics, wizened faces stared out in consternation as, on all sides, there arose a ceaseless Anvil Chorus of piledrivers.

The din of construction and reconstruction had never left Hong Kong throughout its history. When George Chinnery paid a brief visit from his beloved Macau in 1846, four year's after the colony's official inception, he found not so much an established community as a grandiose building site. As Patrick Conner remarks in his excellent biography of the artist:

> "The streets seen in Chinnery's drawings are evidently still under construction, with boulders by the roadside and—in some cases—Chinese stonebreakers at work with hammers and pickaxes. 'Go where you would,' a visitor observed, 'your ears were met with the clink of hammers and chisels, and your eyes were in danger of sparks of stone at every corner'."

Even before the Korean War, and the UN embargo on Chinese goods, forced Hong Kong into its industrial revolution, Tsuen Wan had led the way by launching the colony's first textile mills. By the mid-1960s these, and the larger enterprises that had followed them, formed the hub of the township's expedited satellite development. Touring one of the largest undertakings, where mechanised looms never ceased around the clock, and operatives were employed on a three-shift cycle of eight hours apiece, I could see why the union-ridden Labour Government in Britain was looking askance at its prodigiously productive colonial offspring.

It was a Labour Government that washed its hands of India in 1947, and I could readily see it looking for the least excuse to play Pontius Pilate to the fate of Hong Kong. Prime Minister Harold Wilson's administration was steadily disengaging from the Commonwealth, offsetting Britain's greatly diminished global stature by increasing its role in Europe. Wilson was weary of the aftermath of Empire, and embarrassed by his failure to reach a settlement with the white supremacist regime in Rhodesia (now Zimbabwe), which unilaterally declared itself independent of Britain in 1965. In the end I would be proved right, but not in the way I had envisaged and only because a future Labour Government would inherit the legacy of failed Conservative manoeuvering to prolong the New Territories lease.

If a week is a long time in politics, thirty years was to prove vastly more so. And in those three decades the corporate entity of colonial Hong Kong would prove even less divisible than it seemed to me in 1966.

Wang Yincheng comments on the dilemma posed by the New Territories in *The Return of Hong Kong*:

> "...because of Hong Kong's development, the New Territories, which accounts for 92 per cent of the area of Hong Kong, has become an inseparable component of Hong Kong. Losing the New Territories would mean the loss of a big part of Hong Kong's industrial zone, all its farmland, the majority of its water supply system, the Kai Tak Airport, the railways and highways linking it with the Chinese mainland and its many other important properties. Without the New Territories, the Island of Hong Kong and southern Kowloon could not exist. The issue of the New Territories was not an isolated one. It was closely linked with the entire Hong Kong."

Yet conjecture as to what might have been, had Hong Kong not acquired its Achilles' heel, remains futile. Without the New Territories, it would have been denied any possibility of further expansion, and would quickly have stultified. Unlike the flag-flying Rock of Gibraltar, it could not have resisted, fortress-like, the tides of time and change. Change was fundamental to Hong Kong's existence. Like a fish that must keep restlessly swimming in order to oxygenate its lungs through the flow of water past its gills, Hong Kong could sustain itself only through ceaseless momentum. Quite simply, the New Territories prolonged the life of the colony by a further exciting and eventful ninety-nine years.

♦   ♦   ♦

Speaking of fish, marine engineers and fisheries experts of the agriculture and fisheries department had come up with a design for a new deep-sea trawler to replace the long-serving but now somewhat old-fashioned junks that ventured ever further into international waters for their diminishing catches. They invited me aboard their prototype vessel for its maiden voyage.

I boarded its freshly painted and varnished decks at the fish market in Aberdeen. Named after Viscount Palmerston's successor, Lord Aberdeen, this bustling anchorage, occupying a narrow channel between Hong Kong Island and the diminutive islet of Ap Lei Chau, was already a thriving fishing port when the British arrived in 1841. Most of its occupants were Hoklo and Tanka boat people, ethnically distinct from Han Chinese and historically regarded as itinerant "sea gypsies". A long-defunct imperial decree had forbidden them to reside ashore, and indeed they had become averse to doing so, restricting their shore excursions to shopping, trading and occasional sightseeing. The landing party sent by Captain Charles Elliot, to raise the flag at Possession Point on January 25th 1841, had therefore prompted little more than a shrug of their forebears' shoulders.

Aberdeen's was a floating population in every sense of the word. Giant junks—like aquatic versions of the nursery rhyme shoe in which the old woman lived with so many children that she didn't know what to do—housed entire families and sub-families of ocean-foragers, briefly home from the seas to offload catches and replenish supplies before their next prolonged absence in faraway waters. Meandering through the gaps between their closely-packed hulls, like minnows sporting with whales, *wallah-wallahs* conveyed tourists to palatial waterborne restaurants while humbler sampans plied their wares of steamed dumplings and beancurd or dispensed hot and cold beverages.

Alongside those mammoth trawlers, built on elegantly scooped traditional lines, the prototype of their putative replacement looked lean, functional and totally devoid of romance; something to be regarded askance by overweening neighbours until its powerful engines started up and stirred their decks to a welter of curiosity.

We headed out through the harbour arms into the East Lamma Channel, where we lowered the trawling net and started a practice sweep. All went well until the entire vessel came to a sudden, shuddering halt which threw us off our feet. We looked at each other in amazement. What the hell had gone wrong? An uncharted shoal in mid-channel? A rock? A whale? A submarine?

From the evident stress on the trawling gear it was clear that whatever its nature, the obstruction had been encountered by the net rather than the hull. And there was no way to release the net without cutting it entirely free; a costly loss for this experimental undertaking. It was decided we should try hauling it in, no matter what this might dredge up. With winches straining, and the booms in danger of buckling under the sheer weight, the "catch" was slowly elevated until we caught our first metallic glimpse of it just below the surface.

I thought *Oh my God, it **is** a submarine! The Americans will be furious!*

But on second thoughts, no. Why should they be sneaking into the harbour in this submerged mode when their only possible reason for being here would be one of the frequent rest and recreation visits for their crew?

As it rose higher still, we made out the huge, inflated outline of a rubber tyre, attached to what was clearly a large section of aircraft undercarriage. When finally hauled aboard, this mass of rubber and metal took up most of the rear deck. I knew where I had seen that shape before. It clearly belonged to a Dakota DC3, the aeronautical veteran that had made its first flight on December 17th 1935, some six months after I was born. I felt a distinct sense of kinship with the "Dak", then still in service with minor airlines virtually all over the world. I had travelled aboard those twin-engined "Gooney Birds" many times, when they comprised the bulk of the Malayan Airways fleet.

But whence had this one come? And what had happened to it?

We scraped off some of the barnacles encasing the main supporting rod of the undercarriage structure and were amazed to find the metal underneath so little touched by corrosion that it was virtually unblemished. We also discovered a serial number, of which my friends in the fisheries department took due note in the hopes of tracking down the identity of the aircraft to which it had belonged. The only record of a DC3 crash in Hong Kong dated from April 9th 1951, when weather conditions had deteriorated on the final approach of a Siamese Airways Dakota into Kai Tak airport.

The crew had decided to divert to Taiwan, but had learned that Taiwan had closed due to bad weather, forcing their return to Hong Kong. They attempted a night-time visual approach beneath a four hundred foot cloud base, but ended up in the sea, with the loss of all five crew and eleven passengers. Given as probable cause of the crash was the finding that "The captain allowed the aircraft to lose flying speed while attempting to turn quickly in order to avoid flying into higher ground during the approach to the airport in darkness and rain."

But the Kai Tak approach lay well to the north of Hong Kong Island. Could even just a part of the debris have carried so far south as the East Lamma Channel? My companions shrugged. Given the fifteen years that had elapsed since the crash, the strength of tidal drift etc., it was just conceivable…

Enigmatic Presence

In a city restlessly bent on recreating itself, the very concept of rest and recreation, as understood by visiting American servicemen, might seem anathema. But Hong Kong thrived on catering to U.S. military personnel operating in eastern waters, who were growing significantly in numbers every year as the morass of the Vietnam War sucked in more and more money and manpower.

It was a common sight, when crossing the harbour, to see the latest arrivals from the U.S. Seventh Fleet anchored off the Wanchai waterfront. The overpowering juggernaut mass of some aircraft carrier like the *Valley Forge, Saipan, Kitty Hawk* or *Coral Sea* would be flanked by an accompanying battleship or cruiser, under whose huge, overshadowing hulls a diminutive fleet of sampans would be nestled like eggshells seeking protection from an anvil.

In the second half of the twentieth century, the aircraft carrier had become emblematic of the United States' status as a superpower. Essential to Allied victory in the Pacific during World War Two, such leviathans subsequently acquired an even more prominent role as the "forward military presence" of the United States, arriving like giant boots ready to stamp out the first hint of trouble. Since 1946, when the USS Franklin D. Roosevelt was sent to Greece to symbolize support for the pro-western side during Greece's civil war against the communists, carriers had shown up everywhere on the globe where an alarm light began to glow ominously red. Their unmistakable purpose was to warn potential enemies—invariably communist—that America was watching.

The rest of us, assuming we weren't communist ourselves, were supposed to derive comfort from these formidable displays of unassailable might, but—knowing America's trigger-happy mentality, paranoid sensitivities and naïve grasp of geopolitics—I invariably experienced the oppo-

59

site sensation. American determination to stop communism in its tracks in Southeast Asia smacked of the crusading mentality of Middle Aged knights in armour, so blinded by the visors of their helmets that they couldn't see the boiling oil descending from Saracen battlements.

The contrast between all that floating metallic mass, and its boyish, slightly insecure and infinitely more vulnerable occupants, created an impression of utmost poignancy. Decanted into *wallah-wallahs* for their brief spells of shore leave, what could those sailors and soldiers, marines and airmen, know of the nature of the Asiatic country they had been sent to defend? I saw theirs as a fragile insouciance, compounded in equal parts of innocence and ignorance and endangered by their nation's massive prejudice and self-righteousness, against which they could do nothing to prevail.

Whatever fears they might secretly entertain for their own survival were temporarily set aside in the welter of Wanchai. And in their absence the fishing fleet would get to work. Sampan Jenny's "side party" of plate scrapers and hull painters, wielding long-handled implements and brushes while maintaining their balance from the rocking decks of those eggshell-tiny sampans, would set about the towering flanks of the vessels alongside them like barberfish cleaning the hides of slumbering whales.

Sampan Jenny was as beloved a character to Hong Kong's visiting sailors as Tonkinese Bloody Mary was to the Marines on Esperito Santo in James Michener's *Tales of the South Pacific*. Her girls, all dressed in traditional *samfoo* jackets and black trousers, were trained to perform minor miracles of dexterity, unfailingly cheerful and obliging in all weathers. When it was finally time for the navy to set sail again, the flag-bedecked fishing fleet would stand by on their bobbing cockleshells, with farewell banners unfurled, waving handkerchiefs and blowing kisses.

Meanwhile, on shore in what was widely known as "The Wanch", girls of other talents and persuasions would have catered to servicemen frantically pursuing their own forms of restless recreation, plying them with expensive drinks and offering them, through slits in their *cheongsams*, glimpses of the largely unattainable. For getting those girls to part with more than their smiles and brittle chatter was a feat beyond the persuasive powers and wallets of most patrons. Wanchai's Lockhart Road was one long bar-crawl of low dives and sleazy clip joints, interspersed with some of the better-known watering holes like the Pussycat, the Hollywood and the New Ocean. The shore patrols would have their hands full as neon-lit nights advanced towards rosy-fingered dawns.

This was the classic domain of Suzie Wong, the "hooker with the heart of gold" as portrayed by author Richard Mason in his novel of that title, and as played by Nancy Kwan in the movie based on his book. Unhappily the former's depiction of Wanchai, and the latter's rendering of its principal character, had proved too painfully accurate for some.

In *Suzie Wong Revisited*, Asian journalist H. Y. Nahm records that the very name Suzie Wong "offends a generation of Asian Americans who grew up in its shadow. It doesn't matter that most have never actually seen *The World of Suzie Wong*…or that almost no one alive seems to have read the original Richard Mason novel. What matters is that after the film's release the most superficial (and offensive) aspects of the Suzie Wong character single-handedly usurped the image of Asian womanhood in the western imagination. Its spectacular success may be *Suzie Wong*'s greatest sin, the reason that the name still carries a strongly negative emotional charge."

Suzie's fictitious character was far removed from the real-life actress who portrayed her. Nancy Kwan today remains as charming and unspoilt by success as she was when I first met her in 1966. Following in the footsteps of that equally intelligent, sophisticated and beautiful pioneer of Asian women on Hollywood screens, Anna May Wong, Nancy moved on to other, sometimes better but always less famous roles. She even employed her ballet training to good effect in *Flower Drum Song*, the screen version of the Rogers and Hammerstein musical in which virtually all the cast were Asian.

But the world that her initial screen persona had inhabited lingered on unchanged. Wanchai remained a neon-lit, polychrome overlay, superimposed on the drabness of otherwise largely residential back streets. Its flashy-signed, high-decibel bars and night clubs were grafted onto the frontages of tenement blocks that had seen better days and less raucous nights. In adjoining alleyways, the febrile flux of this glittering mainstream quickly petered out into dark and narrow labyrinths of boarded-up street stalls and refuse bins, interspersed with alfresco tables and benches of all-night *dai pai dong* noodle vendors, whose elderly patrons crouched over bowls, chopsticks and glasses of steaming tea. One felt that the bar girls, at the end of their nightly stint, would quickly shed their workaday *cheong-sams*, make-up and singsong accents to don *samfoo* pajamas and melt back into the drab obscurity of this other, parallel and palpably less Suzified world.

By then their hell-bent, pleasure-seeking clients would have been rounded up for the return trip to their respective vessels, the more sober among them having spent quieter, less lustful evenings in the venerable China Fleet Club, just a few minutes' walk from their disembarkation point at Fenwick Pier. With its bowling alley, silver service dining room and duty-free shopping complex, the club was a stress-free home from home for those seeking relaxation rather than exposure to the risk of vicarious misadventure.

My own world lay elsewhere. I spent my lunch breaks and other off-duty hours searching for what little remained of an older Hong Kong. I went in quest of a city that had seized the imagination of myriads who never visited it, and had lingered in the memories of the relatively few who had, earning a reputation out of all proportion to its size.

Hong Kong was a name to be conjured with, an enigmatic presence in a still mysterious sea, its location dictating its inevitable inclusion on the itinerary of virtually every serious "globetrotter". It had come into its own in the age before air travel when, unless bound for Australasia—and very often even if one was—it was impossible to circumnavigate the world without calling here. Visitors had lauded it, writers had extolled it, while its resident business community, though not quite the nabobs of the Indian Raj, had turned its trading offices and banks into temples of homage to the gods of commerce.

That was the Hong Kong I sought, and largely failed to find. Even forty years ago this phantasma compounded of other people's dreams and memories was busy obliterating its traces. The panoramic magnificence of its harbour, and principal ingredient of its fame, remained of course, and was then—in the age before container ships—still performing its time-honoured service. Ships of all sizes and flags were tethered to buoys dotted all over that immense anchorage, surrounded by lighters and barges off-loading cargoes that required manhandling because they didn't come in neat, standardised modules.

But elsewhere much of the character of the port was changing. The Sea Terminal, itself of relatively recent invention, was scheduled to be pulled down and replaced by an Ocean Terminal jutting out at a tangent from the tip of Kowloon peninsula, alongside the Star Ferry piers. Older wharves and warehouses along the western flank of the peninsula were already in process of demolition. You could still see the occasional junk tacking slowly and majestically through the shipping lines, its rust-coloured, heavily-patched sails as emblematic and unexpected as an old and extremely valuable postage stamp on an otherwise thoroughly modern postcard. But even this beloved symbol was fast becoming a rarity and—one felt—could not long survive with any credibility on the logo of the Tourist Association.

Surveyed from the waterfront of Tsim Sha Tsui, on the opposite side of the harbour, the profile of Hong Kong Island remained, even then, a paradigm so instantly familiar as to seem a visual cliché. With the exception of the adjoining headquarters of the Bank of China and the Hongkong Shanghai Bank, the relatively newly-built City Hall and Mandarin and Hilton Hotels, and the freshly inaugurated replacement for Prince's Building, the architecture had not risen to the point where it got in the way of the view.

In the mind's eye one could yet superimpose on that scene a filigreed frame of junks and sampans against a backcloth of solid worthiness, mounting the lower slopes of a massive bulwark of highly distinctive hills with the Peak as their pivotal point. You unfailingly recognised it as the setting for one of the world's great visual dramas, containing all the ingredients for a myriad hand-tinted photographs and travel posters. You could almost smell the fragrance of the harbour which had reputedly given Hong Kong its name—even though you might have your suspicions as to whence the aroma derived.

Most appealing of all was Hong Kong's summation of everything one had come to expect of the East. It was the Orient in microcosm, condensed, instantly accessible and rendered safe for even the most nervous of explorers. Without actually needing to venture any deeper into a continental land mass barred to outsiders, one could claim to have visited China—if only briefly knocking on its doorpost. Those were still the days when, as did Madame Bruce, visitors would flock to the gently elevated border hillock of Lok Ma Chau, to peer through binoculars across the river separating two virtually identical pastorales. Anxiously they would scan the narrow roadway on the far side in hopes of spotting an olive-green uniform of the People's Liberation Army.

Blue-rinsed American matrons would excitedly babble to each other:

> "Yes he *is*, Gladys. He's in that green bit over there. He's carrying a rifle and looking in this direction. What's he doing now? Oh my God he's undoing his flies and he's...he's *pissing*. In this direction! I'm sure it's quite deliberate."

> "Let *me* see! It's *my* turn!"

My own journeys back in time were pursued closer to home, on Hong Kong Island. The farther I forged west, along meandering Hollywood Road, with its rabbit-warren antique shops spilling their open-fronted largesse onto narrow pavements, the more distinctively oriental my surroundings became. Following a serpentine course that roughly paralleled Queen's Road West on a lover level, with which it was connected by steeply-inclined alleyways or "ladder streets", Hollywood Road had been named by an early colonial administrator—not after the Mecca of the movies but in memory of his estate back in the British Isles.

Here was a Mecca of another kind, whose pilgrims were collectors of the last genuine treasures still seeping out of China before the destructive frenzy of the Cultural Revolution gathered sufficient momentum to erase what remained. Not everything in Hollywood Road was genuine, but certainly some of it was, and the rest was so well replicated that it could sometimes fool even the most discerning eye. Nowhere else in the world could you find such a cornucopia of riches harvested from the disappearing traces of the world's longest-surviving civilisation.

Here too was historic Man Mo Temple, curiously dedicated to an uneasy union between the gods of literature (Man) and war (Mo), as if bent on preserving the perpetual balance between our civilised aspirations and our chaotic nature. I saw in this juxtaposition the Taoist equivalent of the ambivalent and many-sided Hindu god Siva. Opposite this walled enclosure, whose darkened inner courts were hung with coiled spirals of eternally-burning incense, the island's contours fell away into yet further tiers of crowded old tenement dwellings. These were traversed by even more authentic looking "ladder streets", whose steps had once rung to the laboured footfall of straining sedan-chair coolies. The whole area somehow reminded me of a disorderly accumulation of weather-beaten slabs of long-congealed lava, cluttering the lower slopes of an extinct volcano, in whose fertile crevasses teemed all manner of exotic species of life.

Almost directly opposite the Man Mo Temple was the area known as "Cat Street", a combination of Upper and Lower Lascar Roads, whose visitors had the greatest difficulty tracing it because of its official non-existence as an identifiable location on the map. Cat Street survived, in collective memory, from a mispronunciation of the word "catch", in the days when Upper and Lower Lascar Roads were the places one went to "catch bargains". They were still crowded with junk stalls and trays of curios, cheaper and less pretentious than the produce of Hollywood Road and reassuringly full of little old men squatting on their haunches to examine jadestones through pebbled glasses, as if they knew what they were doing.

Beyond the western extremity of Hollywood Road lay the beginnings of the area known as Kennedy Town, where meandering arteries tortuously navigated by trams, buses, cars and taxis, along the ever-narrowing configuration of habitable hillside, converged into almost impossibly confined proximities. If unmistakably Chinese Hong Kong could be said to possess a quintessential core, this was its "China Town". It was fronted by the wharves of an ancient, authentic-looking *praya*, where scores of battered old coastal vessel from a variety of Chinese ports arrived to unburden themselves of all manner of cargoes, from livestock to sacks of rice, from crates of flattened squid, sharks fin and pressed duck to jars of hundred-year-old eggs.

None of this would ever be seeing American markets, even if consumers there were adventurous enough to sample them. The Americans had instituted an expensive monitoring and vetting system for Hong Kong imports, querying every detail of their provenance. One of their inspectors had even proposed barring eggs from Hong Kong duck farms because the duck mothers that laid them may have originated in mainland China farms.

It struck me that few sights in the world, at that time, could be more incongruous than the spectacle of a giant US "flat top", putting out to sea at the end of its rest and recreational sojourn, glimpsed through a thicket of blood-red communist flags proudly hoisted at the sterns of mainland Chinese coastal vessels. But the chains of coolies, toiling backwards and forwards up and down the narrow wooden planks between the decks and the wharves, remained oblivious of that departure, as if it simply didn't register. As indeed it probably didn't, anywhere in Hong Kong except in the bars of Wanchai, where the owners were taking invoice of their tills and laying off some of their part-time bar girls until the next R&R flotilla was due to hit town.

The Deluge Now

Like the two-headed Pushme/Pullyou llama in Hugh Lofting's *The Story of Doctor Doolittle*, the Star Ferries didn't have sterns. They only had prows at both ends, designed to ensure what would have been a fast "turn-around" but for the fact that the vessels didn't actually need to turn around. They could run equally well in both directions; a fact tourists were slow to cotton on to because they made no attempt to reposition the angles of seat backs inherited from disembarking passengers. This left them staring at hosts of correctly-oriented "regulars" who had instinctively swung the seats the other way and were now stonily refraining from noticing the only row oriented in the wrong direction.

There was little to distinguish the upper, "first class" deck from the "second class" deck below, except that the latter was unprotected by awnings from high winds and rain, and was generally more crowded because it was cheaper. When living at the very edge of one's income, and having to use this conveyance for one's daily commute, a difference of a few cents could pose an enormous strain on one's budget—a fact that the government failed to properly appreciate when, in 1966, they approved the Star Ferry management's application for a five cent raise in fare.

It is not in the nature of the Cantonese to readily make a fuss, so that when they do one can quickly gauge that they have been provoked beyond endurance. The Star Ferry fare increase proved to be that proverbial last straw. Elsie Elliott, stalwart campaigner on behalf of the underdog, beloved by the masses and belittled by her many critics among the expatriate community, led a protest march that gathered considerable support but also, in due course, attracted malcontents unused to public demonstration and bent on exploiting this opportunity to raise a little ruckus.

The demonstration quickly got out of hand, a sizeable area of Kowloon came under curfew and the police fired tear gas to disperse a looting, rampaging mob. The rioters were largely youngsters, in an age where Hong Kong's population of just over three million was a great deal more youthful than is the profile of today's total of more than double that figure. In *Shouting at the Mountain,* the joint autobiography she later wrote with Andrew Tu, whom she had subsequently married, Elsie describes how, on the night of the riots, "a Chinese lady had visited our school, which was also my home, to warn me that the police in Mong Kok were preparing to frame me by forcing young boys to sign statements that I had paid them to throw stones".

When the boys subsequently confirmed this charge, Elsie volunteered her services as witness on their behalf. Testifying at a public inquiry into the causes of the riots, she found herself mercilessly grilled as though she were on trial for fermenting unrest. Steadfastly refusing to disclose the identities of the sources who had warned her she would be framed, she was effectively informed that only her age and standing in the community spared her a more severe penalty than that which the Commission of Inquiry decided to inflict—which was to send her "before the bar of public opinion for censure".

The public were quick to make their opinion known. In the elections for the Urban Council that followed a few months later, Elsie was returned with the highest number of votes on record.

Busily compiling the government's annual report for 1966, with my own opinions somewhat biased in line with the prevailing official view of Elsie as the gadfly buzzing around our well-protected flanks, I saw the Star Ferry riots as a passing aberration, a momentary glitch in the otherwise reassuringly regular heartbeat of a city state purposefully striding onward and upward. In writing so positively and fervently about Hong Kong's progress, I had come close to brainwashing myself into a Doctor Pangloss view of my temporarily adopted home as—if not the best of all possible worlds—at least the best of all available worlds.

My immediate predecessor as annual report editor, Bill Fish, had devised a scheme which ensured widespread global distribution of our public relations materials. Realising that no conscientious editor would stoop to use a blatant piece of self-advertisement bearing the imprimatur of its issuing authority, he had taken pains to expunge, from our press releases and features, any reference to the Hong Kong Government Information Services. Instead of God speaking, the good word was broadcast by a tame disciple, masquerading as a commercial news syndication service. The beauty of this system was that our articles not only appeared in a fairly respectable range of newspapers, magazines and periodicals, but we actually got paid for them, our tame agency returning us monthly accounts setting out our collective share of the revenues earned.

If Keith and I wanted to pose as impartial commentators on Hong Kong affairs, we had merely to select from our wardrobes an appropriate pseudonym from the many we had perfected for this purpose. In addition to writing under my own name I was also, variously, Ishmael Iskander, Frank Watson, Muskus Major (derived from my Latin name at grammar school, to distinguish me from my brother Paul, who was Muskus Minor) and Alphonse Avoirdupois. The latter was a little risqué because of its blatantly satirical leanings, but I thought it just might conjure a thoroughly reliable Agatha Christie image of a slightly overweight Hercule Poirot.

It went without saying that, since our essays were constantly being submitted to the same outlets, we had to evolve distinctive styles for each of our alter egos, and we also had to inject an occasional note of mild criticism, or even reproof, to blend a streak of discolouration into the whitewash. But overall, of course, despite the odd shortcoming here and there, the cumulative import of our prose was that Hong Kong was doing a masterful job against almost insurmountable odds. Each piece that went out added a few more puffs to the brave little engine that could.

So immersed were we in our promotional crusade that we could barely see the trees for the leaves. The result was that we awoke one morning with a rude shock to discover that peaceful little Macau, barely a couple of hours' ferry ride west across the mouth of the Pearl River, was effectively paralysed by an unseasonable wind from the north.

70   No Babylon

◆   ◆   ◆

For the Chinese, a wind blowing from the north connotes winter, hard times and a need for patient endurance until it passes. In the China of 1966, winter came early. That wind, if only metaphorically, was already blowing in the aftermath of Mao Zedong's amazing decision, announced in August at the Eleventh Plenum of the Eighth Central Committee, to launch the Cultural Revolution. China's schools were closed and, during subsequent months, Mao encouraged Red Guards to attack all traditional values and "bourgeois" things. He also called on them to test party officials by publicly subjecting them to criticism. Mao believed that this measure would be beneficial both for the young people and for the party cadres they attacked.

His urge to renew the spirit of the Chinese revolution may have been impelled by a foreboding that this would be his last decade in power. He feared China would develop along the lines of the Soviet model. Tensions with the Soviet Union convinced him that the Russian revolution had gone astray. Remedial measures undertaken by his colleagues and subordinates, to bring China out of the economic depression caused by the Great Leap Forward, made him doubt their revolutionary commitment. They had turned him into a totem, a figurehead, a plaster bust on countless shelves and mantels, a face on a billion badges. He was still alive, still in charge, and he resented the deification that diminished his continuing role in the nation he had founded.

He especially feared urban social stratification in a society as traditionally elitist as China. But most of all, he was increasingly concerned for his place in history. The phrase "Après moi, le deluge" had been wrongly attributed to French monarch Louis XV, and Charles de Gaulle had made the prediction very much his own. But Mao wasn't prepared to wait. He wanted the deluge now, while he was still alive to command the flood.

He adopted four goals for the Cultural Revolution: to replace his designated successors with leaders more faithful to his current thinking; to rectify the Chinese Communist Party; to provide the new generation in

China with its own revolutionary experience; and to achieve specific policy changes that would make the education, health care and cultural systems less elitist. The country's urban youth were mobilised into groups called Red Guards, and Mao ordered the party and the army not to get in their way.

He put together a coalition of associates to help carry out this revolution. His wife, Jiang Qing, brought in a group of radical intellectuals to rule the cultural realm. Defense Minister Lin Biao was tasked to ensure that the military remained Maoist. Mao's longtime assistant, Chen Boda, worked with security men Kang Sheng and Wang Dongxing to carry out Mao's directives concerning ideology and security. The strains and conflicts that developed within this coalition contributed as much to the stormy history of the new revolution as the dictates of Mao himself.

His monumental effort to reverse the course he saw China taking threw the country into turmoil. From the scant, frequently inaccurate information seeping out of that sealed cauldron it was clear that a period of extraordinary chaos had descended on the land. The Red Guards were running amok, quick to tear down and destroy but not so quick to replace with viable alternatives. Officials were attacked, publicly humiliated, hauled around in carts with dunce's caps on their heads, sometimes driven to suicide or even murdered in the collective frenzy that ran unabated and out of control. This was not reformation but anarchy. They even wanted to change all the traffic lights because they claimed red should denote "go" rather than "stop".

It seemed the only sane voice was the one not publicly heard, the voice of Premier Zhou Enlai, who played an essential role throughout all the mayhem, simply by staying in the background and keeping the country running. Like a benign *éminence grise*, one sensed his quiet presence in the background, and was grateful for it.

Macau paid a terrible price for not knowing what it was dealing with. When revolutionary fervour swept the streets of that quiet little Portuguese colony the authorities over-reacted, in a high-handed fashion, and were taken severely to task. We saw news photographs of Governor Nobre de Carvalho forced to stand bare-headed in the sun to accept a number of demands, among which was the expulsion of KMT militants allegedly using Macau as a base for anti-communist subversion.

Without Macau, there would never have been a Hong Kong. The Portuguese had long stolen a lead over all other western powers by securing this tiny footing—or perhaps more realistically a toenail-hold—on the South China seaboard back in 1557. The Chinese had agreed to a Portuguese settlement there without recognising Portuguese sovereignty. Although a Portuguese municipal government was established, the sovereignty question remained unresolved, and in fact the events of 1966 proved so unsettling that the Portuguese endeavoured to hand the enclave back to China.

China effectively said "No, we're not ready for that yet. You continue running it so long as you do as you're told." It was an ignominious fate for a once proud colony to which Hong Kong owed so much.

It was from Macau, in the late eighteenth century, that the British East India Company launched its forays into the China trade, inserting the thin end of an ever more troublesome wedge into the flanks of a celestial empire frustratingly resistant to its overtures. It was from Macau that Lord Macartney had embarked on his failed embassy to Beijing in 1793, to persuade Emperor Ch'ien-Lung to adopt a more liberal commercial policy. Bearing credentials bestowed on him by King George III, Macartney was denied further concessions for those British merchants who had secured the right to live, part of the year, in a ghetto-like compound of trading factories set up on the outskirts of Guangzhou, where their activities were channeled through a monopoly guild of Chinese merchants.

It was from Macau too that, when China confiscated the opium through which these traders had sought to undermine its resistance, the latter engineered the pretext for the first of two devastating Opium Wars that would prise open the hitherto invulnerable clam and leave China at the mercy of all greedy opportunists from the west. Not that the Portuguese ever got much out of it. Their greatest historical mistake was to be too hospitable, too accommodating, in permitting Macau to become a Trojan horse at China's gates. And not checking too closely into the intentions of those smuggled within.

♦　　♦　　♦

Macau's bitter taste of it in 1966 brought the Cultural Revolution uncomfortably close. It also served as a lesson in what **not** to do should it spill over the border into Hong Kong. The obvious conclusion was that one should avoid over-reaction, moving with the utmost caution and a licked finger raised in the breeze to test both the direction and temperature of prevailing political currents.

We were spared any immediate repercussions. Genuine winter, with its chill and blustery north winds bringing welcome respite from the heat and humidity of summer, came and went. I gave Mukti and his Muslim family their first collective experience of a typical Christian Christmas, with deco-rated tree, presents, turkey and Christmas pudding, which would serve as the role model for all their Christmases to come, and then wrapped up the last chapters of the government's annual report. As a bookmark for this publication I chose a design and brief account of the prevailing year of the Fire Horse in the Chinese zodiac.

Returning in a sixty-year cycle, the Fire Horse is viewed askance by the Chinese as a year in which almost anything can happen—either spectacu-larly good or disastrously bad. Nothing about the Fire Horse occurs in moderation. The last time the Fire Horse prevailed was 1906, the year of the Great San Francisco Earthquake. Women born in this year are deemed so headstrong as to be unmanageable—and therefore unmarriageable. In less enlightened times they would have been left exposed on hillsides at birth.

With the Chinese New Year of February 9th 1967, we left the domain of the Fire Horse and entered that of the Fire Goat, whose temperament is aggressive, dramatic, lively, motivated by deed and can be malicious. We might be out of the frying pan but we were still very much on the stove.

Sailing Below the Wind

To celebrate the wrap-up for *Hong Kong 1966* I took my first long break since arriving in Hong Kong almost two years earlier. I had wanted to visit Borneo ever since reading, long before returning east, Agnes Keith's memoir *Land Below the Wind*.

An American journalist married to a very English conservator of forests, and based in Sandakan, the prewar capital of British North Borneo, Keith had won praise and prizes, together with a large readership, for her whimsical portrayal of an outpost so close to the equator that it lay beyond the reach of tropical cyclones. But not beyond reach of the Japanese. She and her baby son George were imprisoned by the invaders during World War Two, and their experience provided another book, *Three Came Home,* which was subsequently filmed with Claudette Colbert playing Agnes.

I tracked down information on sailings from the copious bulletins appearing in a special section of the *South China Morning Post*, and found that the Norwegian Asia Line could offer me my own cabin for a month-long voyage around the northern coast of Borneo, for an all-in fare of one thousand and fifty Hong Kong dollars, equivalent to well under a hundred and fifty US. It was my chance to see, for the first time, the other half of that incongruous assemblage of former colonial dependencies contrived by Britain through its promulgation of Malaysia in 1963, whereby Sabah and Sarawak were tagged on to the Malay peninsula.

Our first port of call was Jesselton, now known as Kota Kinabalu, which in 1947 had replaced Sandakan as capital of British North Borneo. There I stayed overnight with Peter Harris, an old friend from Malayan days who was teaching art at a local college. On our first evening together we explored what little there was of Jesselton's night life, most of it revolving around an indifferent eatery called the Hong Kong Restaurant, whose menu offered nothing to justify that name.

But I took a liking to Jesselton. It put me in mind of an embryonic Malaya as it might have appeared before World War Two. Illegal Filipino migrant workers added to the multi-racial blend and the thoroughly laid-back demeanour of a population totalling less than a hundred thousand in all. Why had fate not brought me here, I briefly but disloyally mused, before remembering why I had been forced to leave the other half of Malaysia in the first place—namely because I had arrived too late for fate to contrive such happy consequences.

Peter, who had moved here from Kuala Lumpur with the benefit of his academic connections, assured me that Hong Kong would prove the better and wiser choice. As if to underline this point, he walked over to the Hong Kong Restaurant's jukebox and fed in a coin for a replay of the Beatles singing "Yesterday, all my troubles seemed so far away". He himself was merely biding his time to move on to his desired destination in Queensland.

He was clearly still abed when I awoke the next morning, so I padded down to the kitchen in my sarong. Busy looking for something to eat, I felt my right ankle gripped by fierce talons that left me both in a state of acute apprehension and in a position where I was unable to ascertain its cause, because my head was buried in the refrigerator. Guilty for being caught red-handed, I slowly withdrew from the icebox while the talons worked their way up my calf, thigh, hip and right flank until they came to rest on my right shoulder. I felt a beak inserted into my right ear.

"Hello, hello, **hello...**" crooned the beak, with an upward lilt to the last duo-syllable that left me half expecting a constabulary supplement of "What have we here then?"

I slowly turned to face a mirror over the kitchen sink and discovered that my apprehender was a large African parrot of gorgeous colouration and, on the whole, rather disappointingly profane vocabulary. I had interrupted its dawn patrol and enhanced its air of self-righteousness by allowing it to get to grips with an unidentified marauder, of whom it remained in firm possession until my namesake eventually materialised to effect introductions and relieve me of its custody.

My last memory of Jesselton, before re-embarking for the next leg of our voyage, was of the *Rajah Brooke* preparing to sail from the dock which occupied the key prominence on the Jesselton seaboard. Built in 1948, the second vessel of the Sarawak Steamship Company to bear the name of the founder of the White Rajah dynasty that had ruled North Borneo as a feudal patriarchy well into the twentieth century, the *Rajah Brooke* carried her regal lineage like a breath of history from the pages of Joseph Conrad. The sides of her hull were hinged open for fresh air, revealing a hold resembling the interior of a floating Dayak longhouse.

In the pale electric glow, long-haired Ibans with more tattoos than clothing on their superbly sculpted torsos were slinging their hammocks, storing their spears, blowpipes and baskets of worldly goods and bedding down for the voyage to Kuching. Beyond the silhouetted outline of the ship's superstructure and funnel, the western sky was a blazing red flamboyance of a dying age.

Sailing Below the Wind   77

♦   ♦   ♦

From Jesselton we journeyed west ourselves, across the southern reaches of the China Sea and safely below the equatorial typhoon belt, to the island of Labuan which, in 1963, had joined Sabah and Sarawak as an appendix of Malaysia. Sir James Brooke, the original White Rajah, had been deprived of the governorship of this coal-rich possession in 1851, following unproven charges of financial impropriety in regard to payment of "head money" for the elimination of pirates haunting these waters in the early half of the nineteenth century.

Labuan was small but rich in historical eccentricities. The ransacking of graves by head-hunters looking for an easy and convenient source of skulls was a great problem for early settlers. Sir Hugh Low, at first colonial secretary and then governor over some thirty years, emulated the Egyptian pharaohs in their fear of tomb-raiders by making remarkable arrangements for disposing of his wife's remains. On the night she died he directed that fifteen graves be dug, in only one of which did he secretly inter her himself. He then filled in all the others to mystify and thwart potential pillagers. People even wrote out their wills to specify they be buried at sea, to prevent this ignominious end to their mortal remains. You never knew in whose longhouse your skull might come to rest.

After his long sojourn on Labuan, Low went on to become governor of the Malay state of Perak, where he set up a model for enlightened civil administration that was widely emulated by other British residents. He was one of that protean breed, in the footsteps of Sir Stamford Raffles, who could simultaneously lead many diverse lives, blending administrative skills with exploratory curiosity, varied fields of interest and a consuming thirst for the esoteric. In particular, Low was a prime example of that adventurous group of nineteenth century European botanical collectors whose commercially-driven expeditions to lesser-known corners of the planet made enormous contributions to botanical knowledge.

Though his long stint on Labuan curtailed the kind of collecting expeditions that had briefly occupied him during his previous two years in

Sarawak, Low managed to fit in occasional excursions to mainland Borneo that contributed further glories to his promising botanical career. There he discovered a number of spectacular new orchids and other flowers, specimens and paintings of which were duly sent to Kew Gardens. Labuan may have diverted his interests to economic horticulture, but his expeditions to Mount Kinabalu and other parts of the Borneo coast resulted in the discovery of the giant Nepenthes and numerous other plants.

Succeeding Low as governor of Labuan was his son-in-law John Pope Hennessy, who had married Low's beautiful half-Malay daughter. This did not prevent Hennessy from attempting to have his father-in-law arrested on a charge of running a gambling establishment. The evidence? A single worn playing card found in the home of Low's Malay mistress. She had used it as a spool for her darning thread.

My urge to visit Labuan, in particular, had developed though meeting with Pope Hennessy's grandson James, whose immensely entertaining biography of his irascible forebear I had greatly enjoyed. While researching this book, entitled *Verandah: Some Episodes in the Crown Colonies 1867–1889*, James had spent a weekend with me at Fraser's Hill in Malaya, regaling me with extraordinary tales of a truly remarkable colonial life, whose excesses could only have been tolerated when Britain was at the apex of a vastly more extraordinary empire.

James had led a life out of the ordinary himself. He told me he experienced his first love pangs in his perambulator, in the charge of his nurse aboard a London omnibus. It was not the nurse but the bus conductor who caused this premature arousal by chucking the infant James under the chin and crooning, rather in the manner of Peter Harris's parrot, "What have we here then?"

I was greatly saddened, many years later, to learn of James' murder at the hands of a virtual stranger he unwisely took him with him to his flat in London's Ladbroke Grove, when he was literary editor of *The Spectator*. His biography of *Queen Mary, 1867–1953*, had been something of a best-seller in its day and would be followed by a biography of Anthony Trollope, who modelled his *Phineas Finn* on James' infamous *grand-pere*. Trollope may also have had Sir John in mind when he wrote, in *Doctor Thorne*:

"To any honourable gentleman who really felt his brow suffused with a patriotic blush, as he thought of his country dishonoured by Mr. Romer's presence at Hong Kong—to any such gentleman, if any such there were, let all honour be given, even though the intensity of his purity may create amazement to our less finely organized souls."

There were many who had felt that Sir John's presence in Hong Kong brought less than honour to the British crown. As governor of the place his grandson James would describe as a *Half Crown Colony*, in the book of that title, Sir John had been cordially hated by the small but all-powerful expatriate community and joyously regarded by its suppressed Chinese majority.

One of Hong Kong's earliest "tourists", Isabella Bird, arrived in the thick of things to find Sir John playing his gubernatorial role under highly unusual circumstances. Her ship happened to dock against a background, straight from a Hollywood epic, of a city in flames. In her much read travel memoir *The Golden Chersonese*, Isabella paints a dramatic fresco of "dense volumes of smoke rolling and eddying, and covering with their black folds the lower slopes and the town itself". These elements, she admits, constituted "a surprising spectacle":

"...and even as we anchored came off the rapid tolling of bells, the roll of drums, and the murmur of a 'city at unrest.' No one met me. A few Chinese boats came off, and then a steam launch with the M. M. agent in an obvious flurry. I asked him how to get ashore, and he replied, 'It's no use going ashore, the town's half burned, and burning still; there's not a bed at any hotel for love or money, and we are going to make up beds here.' However, through the politeness of the mail agent, I did go ashore in the launch, but we had to climb through and over at least eight tiers of boats, crammed with refugees, mainly women and children, and piled up with all sorts of household goods, whole and broken, which had been thrown into them promiscuously to save them. 'The palace of the English bishop,' they said, was still untouched; so, escaping from an indescribable hubbub, I got into a bamboo chair, with two long poles which rested on the shoulders of two lean coolies, who carried me to my destination at a swinging pace through streets as steep as those of Varenna. Streets choked up with household goods and the costly contents of shops, treasured books and nick-nacks lying on the dusty pavements, with beds, pictures, clothing, mirrors, goods of all sorts; Chinamen dragging their possessions to the hills; China-women, some of them with hoofs rather than feet, carrying their children on their backs and under their arms; officers, black with smoke, working at the hose like firemen; parties of troops marching as steadily as on parade, or keeping guard in perilous places; Mr. Pope Hennessey, the Governor, ubiquitous in a chair with four scarlet bearers..."

It was one of Sir John's shining hours, but it didn't last. We need not wait long to detect, in Isabella's prose, a ring of criticism against Pope Hennessy's policies. We need only follow her up the gradient to Victoria Prison:

"In the prison, which was threatened by the flames, were over eight hundred ruffians of all nations, and it was held by one hundred soldiers with ten rounds of ammunition each, prepared to convey the criminals to a place of safety and to shoot any who attempted to escape. The dread of these miscreants, which was everywhere expressed, is not unreasonable, for the position of Victoria, and the freedom and protection afforded by our laws, together with the present Governor's known sympathies with coloured people, have attracted here thousands of the scum of Canton and other Chinese cities, to say nothing of a mass of European and Asiatic ruffianism, much of which is at all times percolating through the magnificent Victoria prison."

By "coloured people", Isabella meant, of course, primarily the Chinese. And she echoed the sentiments of most of the supposedly imperilled expatriate minority when she lays the blame for the influx at least partly at Pope Hennessy's door.

Whatever political expedience may have prompted Britain to send a succession of Irishmen to govern Hong Kong certainly found its apogee in Sir John. He followed in the footsteps of Sir Hercules Robinson, Sir Richard Graves MacDonnell and Sir Arthur Kennedy, all fellow-countrymen who, through variations on the extremes of severity and moderation, had either bullied or cajoled Hong Kong's troublesome colonials into a state of relative harmony that would be entirely disrupted by their replacement.

Sailing Below the Wind   81

Sir John went to places no previous governor had deigned to visit, and espoused the wholly unwelcome proposition that the Chinese population of Hong Kong might actually be doing rather better business than the European community for whom the colony had been created. Tabling a paper on the *Census Returns and the Progress of the Colony, 1881*, he said:

> "I may mention that a short time before the late Mr. Kwok Acheong died, I went with him and two or three other Chinese gentlemen interested in the factory at Yau-ma-ti, to examine the factory, which was in a more or less rude state, the buildings not being then completed. I was glad to see what they were doing. In addition to making soy, they made ketchup for the European market, and they had also a manufactory for preserving fruits. Now, the ketchup is sent in hundreds of barrels every year direct from Hong Kong to a well-known house in London—that well-known provision merchant whose good things most of us have, from time to time, enjoyed. He sends out thousands of little bottles of his ketchup to Chinese as well as to European storekeepers here, so that, in short the ketchup we consume as English ketchup is manufactured by Chinese in Hong Kong, sent to England, and this famous provision merchant in England returns it to us for retail."

This was thoroughly unwelcome news indeed to the honourable members of the Hong Kong Legislative Council, whose feathers had already been ruffled by Sir John's insistence on appointing, to their distinguished midst, the first and only Chinese in the form of barrister Ng Choi. They had at least thought their ketchup was stainlessly and unassailably British in its provenance.

In answer to critics of the increased sale of land to what were thought to be "speculative" Chinese buyers, Sir John added:

> "On the whole, it is manifest we have in this Colony an increased Chinese community of great importance to the commercial interests of England, and, therefore, we may at once answer the question as to this large dealing in land, and may admit it was a just and natural process, and that this transfer of property from European to Chinese was not of a merely speculative kind."

Good God, man, what tendentious, almost treasonable rhetoric! And from a governor of Hong Kong! One of whose predecessors, Sir George Bonham, had discouraged the study of Chinese on the grounds that it "warped the intellect and undermined the judgment"?

While the Chinese majority might quietly have rejoiced at this testimonial to the vitality of their economic contribution to Hong Kong, the expatriate community closed ranks against their governor, demanding his recall. Unrepentant Sir John quarrelled with everybody, including virtually all his own staff, most of whom asked to be transferred out of his reach. He was repeatedly accused of giving too much encouragement to the Chinese who flocked to the colony during his term. He certainly reorganised all the administrative arrangements for dealing with them, and made it clear that by doing so he intended to put himself more directly in touch with Chinese affairs.

Such flagrant fraternization with the natives was considered dangerously revolutionary. He had been so bold as to state, in his speech to the Legislative Council of June 3rd 1881:

> "Now I believe that the duty of a governor, in dealing with a community such as I find here, is to avoid the encouragement of any body or of any class, but to simply hold the balance evenly between all men."

Could any declaration have more clearly stated his refusal to toe the party line? Where Sir Arthur Kennedy, before him, was content to adopt the suggestion of a Chinese police force for a predominantly Chinese population, saying "We shall learn to rely on them more than at present", Pope Hennessy went so far as to suggest opening up an area close to the military barracks for residential use by the Chinese. General E.W. Donovan strongly opposed this proposition on both military and health grounds, provoking the unseemly spectacle of the colony's two most prominent Irishmen squabbling in public. And leading to a feud with all the trappings of a vendetta.

Sir John was distrusted even by the Colonial Office, with some of whose directives he simply refused to comply, thereby impelling them, in exasperation, to advertise those instructions in the Hong Kong press so that citizens would know they had at least tried. Isabella Bird didn't much trust him either. He had, she said, "a mouth that perpetually smiled and eyes that never did." Clearly too enlightened for the Hong Kong of his time, Hennessy was transferred to the governorship of Mauritius, where it was felt he might do less harm but in fact managed to ferment even more trouble by advocating home rule.

◆   ◆   ◆

Alas our stay in Labuan was too short, even for so small an island. And for me it was made shorter by the fact that I was jumping ship for a longer sojourn in Brunei, where our vessel would not be calling. Brunei was not one but two neighbouring, though separated, slivers of territory left behind by the slow and steady erosion of a once powerful sultanate that ruled much of the north Bornean littoral.

The history of this enormous tract of a still more vast island is essentially one of *Perfidious Albion Redux.* In the early nineteenth century, virtually all of it, including the state of Sarawak, formed part of the hereditary domains of the sultan of Brunei, though his control over it was more apparent than real. The Dayak tribes and pirates inhabiting Sarawak were fiercely independent, frequently rejecting the sultan's authority. James Brooke, a young English adventurer of the *Boy's Own Paper* mould, straight out from India where he had served as an army officer in Bengal, arrived on the scene in the late 1830's and detected a rare opportunity.

Entering the sultan of Brunei's service, he set about pacifying the wild regions of Sarawak with his yacht, the aptly names *Royalist*, in return for which he secured appointment as the sultan's governor. This wasn't good enough for James, who obtained assistance from the Royal British Navy to further entrench his position. When a now angry and aggrieved sultan tried to put a stop to this, Brooke attacked his stronghold at Brunei and forced him to sign a treaty that relinquished Sarawak entirely to Brooke's personal fiefdom. Thus began the long rule of the self-appointed White Rajahs who would progressively wrest further tracts of the former sultanate away from Brunei's once all-encompassing sway.

Given these historical circumstances, it seemed to me a monumental irony for contemporary Britain to have won such loyalty, and blatantly Anglophile affection, from the old sultan's heir, albeit several generations removed. The result was that independent Brunei, having rejected the offer to join the fabricated patchwork quilt made up of its former dependencies, continued to employ British officers and Gurkha troops long after neighbouring, and all-but-engulfing Malaysia had dispensed with their services.

My first sight of Brunei's capital, Bandar Seri Begawan, remains imperishably fixed upon my mind. As we sped in our open-decked express ferry, past stilted riverine homes bordering their maze of canals in Kampung Ayer, the floodlit golden dome of the Omar Ali Saifuddin mosque reared up against a twilight sky like an apparition from the *Arabian Nights*. Named after the twenty-eighth sultan of Brunei, this grandiloquent structure was built in 1958 and stands next to the Sungai Kedayan in its own artificial lagoon. It remains one of the most impressive edifices in southeast Asia.

But there was no time to linger. I had to get to the other end of the country by nightfall, my destination being Seria, more than a hundred kilometres southwest of the capital. While I might have been able to inquire about bus routes and cheaper modes of transportation, I decided I'd be safest making the journey by taxi. It proved an uneventful ride at high speed down arrow-straight and—once released from Bandar's suburbs—all but deserted roads.

◆　　　◆　　　◆

Arrived at the relatively tiny and inauspicious township of Seria, I soon tracked down and inflicted myself upon former *Malay Mail* colleague Kevin Voltz and his lovely Chinese wife Evelyn, both of whom deftly concealed any regret they might entertain for having proved immensely friendly and hospitable when I first descended on then in Kuala Lumpur nearly nine years earlier. They were once again overwhelmingly kind, plunging me into Seria's small but highly sociable community life, which revolved around the hub of an important oil-producing area that included several offshore wells. A pipeline carried Seria's oil to Lutong, thirty-seven kilometres further southwest across the border with Sarawak, where some of it was refined.

Kevin and Johnny Calver, that fellow survivor of our former "When-aye" days in Kuala Lumpur, were among the only residents of Seria not actually involved either in the oil business or in securing the safety of Brunei with the help of the Gurkha contingents stationed in the area. They were jointly editing the *Borneo Bulletin*, a weekly newspaper headquartered in Kuala Belait, another of Brunei's scattered coastal settlements situated some thirty kilometres to the west.

The *Borneo Bulletin* was first published in 1953 as a community newspaper for expatriates working in the Belait District. In 1959, the founders sold the press and newspaper to the *Straits Times Press* of Singapore, who eventually persuaded both Kevin and Johnny to return from long absences in Australia and New Zealand and assume control. The two had but recently taken over from an editor who, at one stage, had been taken prisoner by insurgent Indonesian troops. The latter had crossed the border from Kalimantan at the height of the *Konfrontasi* launched by President Soekarno against the Malaysia he regarded as a British inspired conspiracy to undermine his grip on one of the world's largest archipelagos.

Poor old Soekarno had been looking under the wrong mattress. He paid the price for his extremities in allegedly supporting a failed communist coup that plunged his country into a bloodbath. Following Indonesia's "night of the long knives", during the early hours of October 1st 1965, he was toppled from power to make way for a victorious General Suharto, who emerged very firmly in control. Kevin and Johnny could have kept me awake all night with their tales of "When-aye was in Tutong" or "When-aye was on patrol with the Gurkhas along the border".

From Seria I sped on next day across the Sarawak border to Miri, where a lighter returned me to my ship at anchor in the stream. Casting off, we headed down the coast to nose our way up the Batang Rajang, Malaysia's longest and busiest river. Sibu, second largest town of Sarawak after Kuching, is located some hundred kilometres upstream, at the confluence of the

Rajang and Igan rivers, and effectively serves as main portal to the Rajang's mighty waterway. From here local speedboats provided the chief means of communication to all neighbouring settlements.

Sibu was a product of the timber industry, already depleting the hinterland of its resources faster than natural regeneration could make amends. Its wealth was largely founded on its enterprising, hard-working and exploitive Foochow community, who arrived in Sarawak from Southern China during the reign of Rajah Charles Brooke (1900–1917), as a result of which the town was frequently referred to as "New Foochow". Along our serpentine course to reach it, we occasionally glimpsed the longhouses of Ibans, half hidden in jungle undergrowth, like elderly spinsters drawing the blinds to conceal the extent to which the neighbourhood was changing.

As they had at Jesselton, the seemingly tireless Norwegian officers in charge of our crew, immaculate in their white linens, seemed more preoccupied by the speedy offloading and taking on of cargo than by any thought of snatching some brief spell ashore. We were only there for a few hours, barely enough time for me to hotfoot it to the nearest bank and grab a few spare rolls of film for my camera. Sibu looked small but inviting, with that seductive look outstation townships of Malaya used to have. I was sorry not to see more of it, but Kuching, considerably older and more crucial to Sarawak's history, was already close at hand and proving by far the louder and more tempting siren.

I was not disappointed when we worked our way up the convoluted lower intestine of the Sarawak river the following day to draw alongside Kuching's moss-covered roofs of crumbling tile. I hastened to disembark, and found the local bazaar much the same as it must have looked when it inspired in Somerset Maugham some curiously undetached thoughts, coming from a writer better known for his immersion in expatriate follies than for his susceptibility to local colour. Maugham, in *A Writer's Notebook*, records that:

> "The bazaar consists of narrow streets with arcades like those of Bologna and each house is a shop in which you see the thronging Chinese pursuing the busy life of the Chinese town, working, eating, talking.

On the banks of the river are the native huts, and here, living their immemorial lives, are the Malays. As you wander in the crowd, as you linger watching, you get a curious, thrilling sense of urgent life. You divine a happy, normal activity. Birth and death, love and hunger; these are the affairs of man. And through that press of people passes the white man who rules them. He is never part of the life about him. So long as the Chinese keep the peace and pay their taxes he does not interfere with them. He is a pale stranger who moves through all this reality like a being from another planet. He is no more than a policeman. He is the eternal exile. He has no interest in the place. He is only waiting for his pension, and he knows that when he gets it he will be unfit to live anywhere but here. In the club they often discuss where they shall live when they retire. They are bored with themselves, bored with one another. They look forward to their freedom from bondage and yet the future fills them with dismay."

I could never read that passage without hearing how it would sound from the inimitable lips of the late Sir John Gielgud. I could imagine Gielgud, playing perhaps a more elderly Maugham, immaculate in white, open-necked shirt and a cream blazer, standing under a crumpled linen hat to shield him from the sun, in the midst of that throng, surveying all with a magisterial eye. What a pity no one ever thought to put him there.

Finding a table at an outdoor market, whence I watched young Malay officers strolling by as identical in their "civvies" as they would be in their military uniforms—each with a sealed cylindrical tin of *State Express 555* cigarettes bulging in his shirt pocket—I indulged in my own reverie. I too was surely unfit to live anywhere but here. And yet circumstance had eased me out of this age of innocence and cast me into the hurly burly of Hong Kong. How would I ever survive there?

The rest of the month-long voyage went by in something of a blur, reading novels from the ship's small but sensibly stocked library and keeping a journal (which has not survived). Occasionally I raised my head from my deckchair to stare out at the unravelling scroll of mangrove swamp and palm tree, interrupted by an occasional strand or rocky promontory and backed by eternal mountains, as we retraced our course east along the coast until, with the towering triangle of Mount Kinabalu in the distance, we rounded the northeast extremity of Borneo and forged south down the island's eastern seaboard.

We paused at Sandakan, just long enough for me to go ashore and get a taste of that former capital of Sabah, reassuring myself it could not have changed much since Agnes Keith's days, and then pushed on to infinitely less interesting Tawau, our last port of call. Tawau had the businesslike look of an entirely functional town that had never heard of tourism and had no wish to inquire further. Its purpose was to expedite fast turn-arounds and discourage lingering. We took the point and were soon on our way, heading north through the pirate-infested waters of the Sulu Sea, passing Zamboanga to port and keeping the low, treacherous and seem-ingly interminable outline of Palawan to starboard. Our captain required a careful watch at all times for the approach of the low, fast, outboard-pow-ered catamarans that plied these waters like the darting black shapes of long-legged pond beetles. "Don't let them get too close," we were advised.

Surprisingly, after all that overdose of nostalgia, when we entered Hong Kong harbour at dusk through Lei Mun passage, I felt an unexpected sense of homecoming, a consoling familiarity in all those towering slabs of multi-faceted light, jostling each other for shoulder room on all sides. It was so very different, so very unlike the "terribly jungly place" Maugham had found Sarawak to be. Even distracted governors of an earlier century had been moved to poetry by that spectacle. Sir William Des Voeux (1887–1891) recorded in his memoirs a nocturnal prospect of the harbour from Government House:

> "The sky, though clear of clouds, was somewhat hazy, so that the small-magnitude stars were not visible, though some of the larger ones were plain enough. Beneath, however, the air was quite clear, and con-sequently, though the vessels in the harbour were invisible in the dark-ness, their innumerable lights seemed like another hemisphere of stars even more numerous than the others, and differing only as being red-der."

Mukti was at the dockside to drive me back to Silverstrand, impatient to gauge my reaction when I discovered what he had done in my absence.

He had improved the rock garden on my balcony through a minor miracle of landscape gardening. But he had also cemented it all firmly and indissolubly into place in our temporarily occupied government quarter. I didn't have to try hard to look enormously pleased because—despite whatever official recriminations might ensue—I was.

This time I wasn't going to react hysterically, in the way I had when he constructed for his sons an enormous traditional Malayan kite, with a wingspan some two metres across. He had allowed this to soar until it was a mere speck in the sky, anchored it to the railings in our back yard, and had then gone about his business while the whole apartment, and doubtless those of our neighbours too, was filled with a low and unsettling dynamo hum. Finally tracing the source of this disturbing sound, I noted a helicopter that seemed on the point of cutting the kite cord—along with its rotors—and released a scream that brought the family running and set our family hen nervously clucking.

The hen too was the product of an earlier Mukti inspiration, dating back before the arrival of Asarah and the boys. He had brought it home live from the market to slay it in our kitchen, *halal* style, by gently slitting its throat. Most definitely not, I insisted. I wasn't going to have livestock slaughtered under my roof. If he wanted *halal* food there were Muslim shops that could provide it, and if necessary I would pay whatever additional cost that entailed.

So the solitary chicken lived on in our back yard to a ripe old age, gratefully producing, like clockwork, an egg for my breakfast each morning and becoming, in due course, a much loved family pet because it brought a touch of the *kampong* to our spartan concrete surroundings. Mukti was relieved, because he confessed he had never actually killed a chicken before.

The Year of Living Dangerously

It didn't take me long to sense that something about Hong Kong wasn't quite the same. The mood was different, the atmosphere more tense. A labour dispute at an artificial flower factory in San Po Kong was looking uncharacteristically aggressive. There were agitators present to provoke and sustain a chorus of chanting that had not accompanied previous demonstrations of that nature. Little red books of Chairman Mao's thoughts were making an appearance, clenched in serried ranks of upraised fists.

Mukti had taken to dropping me at the Star Ferry's Hung Hom terminal, because this cross-harbour departure point considerably shortened the travelling time to downtown Tsim Sha Tsui, more than compensating for the longer voyage to Central. One morning I joined the crowd waiting to board at Hung Hom and could not understand why I was receiving sidelong glances. Granted I was the only *gwailo* present, but this was an extremely unusual reaction from a people not normally disposed to notice one's existence. The looks I received were not hostile; merely curious, with now and then a polite little nod and a hint of a smile. Wonder of wonders—in Hong Kong, of all places!

Even if I was wearing something remarkably silly, like a Mohican haircut, or had forgotten to put on trousers, the response would have been a stony indifference, a positive, iron-willed refusal not to look my way. Because it would not have been good Cantonese form to do so. What could now have changed all that? What could possibly be wrong with me?

Then I noticed the crude, hand-painted, big-character posters. All over the place. I didn't need to read the calligraphy to get the message. Each was accompanied by caricatures of terrified little white-skinned pigs and yellow running dogs being crucified, garroted, bayoneted or—at the very least—kicked soundly in their diminutive butts by indignant Chinese patriots holding little red books and scowling righteous scowls.

90

There were more of these when we boarded the ferry. And yet nothing remotely like them in the expressions I saw around me. In the faces of my fellow passengers I read discomfort, disquiet and, when they looked my way, a hint of compassion mingled with apology. In the extreme silence which enveloped us, it was as if they were saying, without needing to put it into words "Look, please realise we have nothing to do with all this and we certainly don't wish you any harm. We're as upset about it as you must be. This isn't us. This *isn't* Hong Kong."

I felt a flood of elation I had not experienced since first setting foot in the colony. It almost brought tears of joy to my eyes. I sensed a real kinship with these people. I was a Hong Konger too, and they accepted me for that. All thoughts of my *gwailo* nature were set aside. We were literally in the same boat, and we would see this through together, whatever might transpire.

I was grateful for those hopelessly misconceived posters, which had produced the very opposite of their intended effect. They had put me in touch with the real character of a city in which I had spent all these months feeling my way, trying to plumb its underlying drift and gauge how I might swim with its currents. Now, suddenly, without a word of Cantonese to connect us, invisible doors had been opened and I had been embraced into the stream. I had joined the club.

It was the start of our Year of Living Dangerously, borrowed from the phrase coined by Soekarno to describe his last year in power. But for us it was not a prelude to an end but the dawn of a beginning. It would turn out to be that necessary rite of passage that would forge our first real sense of belonging; the year when we abandoned our ephemeral existence as a tiny, temporary territory of transients and started being a community of fellow citizens.

◆　　◆　　◆

Left-wing agitators succeeded in inflaming the labour dispute at the artificial flower factory and carrying its embers through the rest of the heavily industrial area of San Po Kong and on to the remainder of

Kowloon. Along with colleagues from the GIS newsroom, I was assigned to report on these developments, in my case from the police headquarters at Mong Kok, which looked as if it had been built, many years earlier, for precisely such a contingency. In common with other district police headquarters, it was surrounded by high walls, topped with barbed wire, whose corners were surmounted by defensive pillboxes commanding wide fields of fire for machine-gun emplacements. Resembling a refined version of an early US cavalry outpost in the Apache badlands, it seemed designed to serve less as a police base than as a prison. But given the exceptional circumstances that had descended on us during those eventful May nights, I was grateful for its redoubtable appearance.

The man in command of this fortress was equally redoubtable Charles Sutcliffe, who had responsibility for the entire Mong Kok district, where some of the worst rioting was taking place. I watched him at work in the operations room, backed by a wall of maps on which red pins indicated the trouble hotspots. He was a tall, elegant individual with an upraised chin and eyes that probed great distances; the kind of face you associated with some key supporting role in a cinematic epic of empire. A man not easily ruffled, he was in radio communication with a Chinese inspector in charge of a platoon confronting a stone-throwing mob in Nathan Road, outside the Astor cinema.

The rest of us in the ops room listened spellbound as Sutcliffe proceeded to calm his unseen and clearly highly agitated subordinate at the other end of this conversation. It was the sort of "don't shoot until you see the whites of their eyes" kind of exchange, except that in this case the only shooting—if it ever came to that—would be of tear gas canisters, since the police were under strict orders to apply minimum force and, wherever possible, keep their distance. Sutcliffe's performance that night provided a lesson in why the trouble-makers were failing to provoke the Hong Kong authorities into the harsh retaliation that had proved the downfall of Macau a year earlier.

When it was clear the Astor incident was under control, Sutcliffe approved the delivery of key documents to a police launch berthed beside the Star Ferry piers at Tsim Sha Tsui. I was given permission to accompany this supply run through the gauntlet of the curfew that had descended over the entire Kowloon peninsula. The Mong Kok police canteen had failed to appease my appetite and I had a hankering for the salmon sandwiches available at the Hilton Hotel coffee shop, right alongside our GIS offices at Beaconsfield House. Over the phone I had arranged for one of my colleagues on the Hong Kong side to take delivery of this snack on my behalf, and was relieved to find it safely aboard the police launch.

On the trip back up Nathan Road our Land Rover dutifully paused at a traffic light, still functioning despite the lack of any except police and military vehicles, and in the silence I could distinctly hear, from all around us, the clatter of mahjong tiles. Craning my neck to look upwards through the protective wire mesh screening our windows, I saw tiers of lighted tenements, whose occupants were clearly using the brief and unaccustomed holiday provided by the curfew to pursue their favourite occupation. Our Chinese driver turned to me and grinned, as if he sensed what was on my mind and was proud of the spirit that would carry us through this uneasy interlude.

◆　　　◆　　　◆

The following morning I crossed the harbour to report to Beaconsfield House and encountered a scene straight out of George Orwell's nightmare vision of *1984*. Rebounding off the walls of buildings on all sides of Statue Square, the open plaza fronting the Hongkong Shanghai Bank, strident broadcasts were disseminated from batteries of loudspeakers affixed to the Bank of China. In keeping with the red, big-character banners draped all over this building, their inflammatory messages denounced the "white-skinned pigs" of the Hong Kong government and the "yellow running dogs" who supported them.

If these condemnations were devised to incite the masses to rebel against colonial authority, they were falling on literally deafened ears. Instead of being drawn to the scene in rivers of fist-shaking righteousness, the public were keeping well clear. Statue Square's deserted appearance only served to reinforce the unreality of the bizarre spectacle. But if it wasn't drawing the crowds, the harsh scream of the female announcer's accusatory voice was at least in danger of paralysing Hong Kong's financial hub. Her raucous tones grated on the eardrums like nail files. How the hell was anyone going to work under these conditions?

In the absence of Nigel Watt, who was away from Hong Kong on home leave, Deputy Director Michael Stevenson was running GIS, and we could not have asked for a better "man of the hour". Tall and gangling, Mike was an Edinburgh Scot with an elongated face and engaging grin, so sure of himself that he might have spent his entire life preparing for the challenge of this moment. Through his links with the military, he borrowed the largest loudspeakers the Army could spare and arranged for these to be installed on our roof, directly facing the Bank of China on the opposite side of Queen's Road Central.

Using tapes of music from the Chinese Opera archives of Radio Hong Kong, this formidable public address system blared back at the bank, countering its incendiary blasts with melodies that were intended to soothe and entertain but—at this volume—were drowning out the vitriol and invective. It was the equivalent of disguising an unendurable earache by pulling out one's teeth, but it had the desired effect. Before long the bank's tirade subsided and a state of relative peace and calm descended on central Hong Kong. We had won the battle of the louder speakers.

Mike took me aside and instructed me that I was to cease my normal duties and serve as second-in-command of his newly organised counter-propaganda unit, housed at the western end of Beaconsfield House's fifth floor. Alongside us was a room allotted to police Special Branch, where officers with binoculars, telephoto cameras and sensitive sound-detection equipment were monitoring activities in the bank across the way. For by now there was no doubt that the Bank of China was playing host to whichever faction was directing the disturbances.

On our side too, things were hotting up. Jack Cater left his position as Secretary for Security to form a special group handling the situation. The group was chaired by Cater and its members included Michael, Denis Bray and Robert Locking. Also represented were Special Branch and Radio

Hong Kong, together with an Assistant Secretary for Chinese Affairs. During the long hot summer of 1967 the group met every morning to inform Governor David Trench what had happened the night before and to discuss the best response to the latest turn of events. Although the decisions of the special group were never publicized during the period, and no reports were ever produced for public consumption, it played a crucial role in informing and influencing public opinion against the leftist campaign of anti-government propaganda.

Government Information Services issued daily information bulletins to explain the government's purposes and policies, the transport department reported on arrangements made to alleviate the impact of the disturbances on vital transport operations and Radio Hong Kong increased its special interest broadcasts to reassure listeners with news of the government response to the "struggle campaign". Young, newly recruited Irene Yau, who would much later become our department's longest serving Director of Information Services, had the daily task of scanning the headlines of the Chinese press and providing Cater's committee with a transcript of the most salient topics.

◆   ◆   ◆

Desperate to create the impression that this was a campaign of resistance that enjoyed full public backing, the local communists commanded everyone with mainland connections, whether employed in banks, shipping offices, department stores, trade organisations or schools, to participate in mass protests against "police atrocities". Here at last was some visible facsimile of the opposition they had hoped to generate. Yet its very appearance served to distinguish it from the broad mass of the populace, who continued to keep their distance, apprehensive and distrustful of where all this was leading.

From our windows in Beaconsfield House we looked down on regimented columns of identically-dressed men and women, marching with robot-like synchronisation and chanting in unison with their little red books waving like poppies in the wind. Past the Hilton Hotel and up Garden Road this procession coiled, to assemble before the closed gates of Government House in Upper Albert Road.

Time magazine of May 26th 1967 reported the British reacting with "extraordinary cool":

> "When 2,500 or so more orderly demonstrators headed on foot and by car to Government House, the residence of Governor Sir David Trench, 51, Hong Kong police politely waved the Red autos to a lot marked 'Official Petitioners' Car Park.' Sir David reported that he was not a bit disturbed by the constant cacophony, but allowed that his poodle Peter had become so unnerved that he had to be packed off to an animal shelter."

With the exception of the leftist press, it was by now clear that most Hong Kong media were opposed to this unwelcome spillover of the Cultural Revolution and calling for more decisive action to put an end to it. Of the four English-language newspapers in circulation at that time—the *South China Morning Post, China Mail, Hong Kong Standard* and the *Star*—the last was particularly strident in its demands for a firmer hand.

The *Star's* editor, Grahame Jenkins, was a man I had first encountered in Malaya, when I was reporting for the *Malay Mail* and he was briefly engaged by the *Straits Times Press* to manage our Kuala Lumpur office. He was a stern task-driver and a boss you wouldn't want to meddle with. Making his mark as Reuter's correspondent in Shanghai, he joined the ranks of Hong Kong's respected old China hands, training first-class journalists who remained loyal to him to the end. From its debut appearance in 1965, around the time I first arrived in Hong Kong, the *Star* quickly became the newspaper you couldn't afford not to read because it toppled so many sacred cows and supplied, among its titillating scandal columns, some of the best-informed accounts of what was happening behind the bamboo curtain.

There were reasonable grounds for complaint in Jenkins' editorial calls for a more decisive government answer to the 1967 troubles. While it was understandable that the authorities should wish to avoid following Macau's example by stumbling into the same trap, there was clearly some additional hesitation delaying their hand in regard to the Hong Kong situation. Jack Cater privately acknowledged it was not easy to determine the level of response, because there was no way of judging how Beijing might react.

It was of course conceivable that the Hong Kong disturbances had commenced without Beijing's prior knowledge and permission, and were purely a product of local sympathies with rampaging Red Guards across the border. If that were true, the intention of our localised agitators might be to provoke the Hong Kong government into precisely the precipitate response that would compel Beijing to wrest control and terminate Hong Kong's continued existence as a British colony.

Uncertainty in Hong Kong was echoed in London, where the government shared our confusion over China's real intentions in regard to Hong Kong. Whitehall was as much at sea as we were in interpreting China's "verbal support" of the local leftists. Hence all the pussy-footing, including contingency plans for water rationing if China failed to deliver the water it was contracted to supply. Hence too the arrangements to hire tankers and draw water from Japan and other places in Asia. Together with preparations for food rationing if China closed the border and blocked the daily supplies of meat and vegetables.

When it was apparent that cross-border deliveries of food and water would continue, no matter what, it became equally conceivable that whoever held the reins in check back in Beijing—and my money was on that consummate statesman Zhou Enlai—might secretly share our wish to see this irritating little thorn plucked from our side. Interviewed years after the event by Wong Cheuk Yin, author of *The 1967 Leftist Riots and Regime Legitimacy in Hong Kong*, Jack Cater said "I had contacted Beijing, and it was quite obvious that Beijing, especially Zhou Enlai, did not like the troubles made by the leftists in Hong Kong."

At last convinced that China was unlikely to intervene directly in our internal affairs, we applied the firm hand the media demanded and the majority of the public dearly desired. In front of the Hilton Hotel, in full view of the overseas media representatives based at the Foreign Correspondents Club on its top floor, and right alongside our GIS offices at Beaconsfield House, the police were given the clearance to respond with force. Adding to the genuinely bloodied noses of the demonstrators who had done so much to provoke this retaliation was the fake blood theatrically applied by their make-up artists to enhance the effect.

Now that they had visible proof of the retaliation they had tried so hard to engineer, leftist reporters and photographers went to town with special supplements and with a hastily produced booklet entitled *Who is Guilty of These Atrocities?* Thanks to his contacts in the printing world—for Hong Kong is a small place with very intricate and potent connections—Mike Stevenson got hold of a copy of the latter while it was still in its print run. He set me down at a desk with a pair of scissors, a pot of glue, a typewriter and a stack of our photographs as opposed to theirs.

"Stick to the same heading, the same format and the identical layout," he instructed me. "Just exchange their pictures and captions for ours. I can find you a translator to work with you on the bilingual text. The two of you have just twenty-four hours to get this on the streets."

The translator worked as fast as I did at the same desk, providing Chinese versions of the slips of caption I passed to him straight from my typewriter. To substitute for the "aftermath" pictures of our policemen clubbing their demonstrators, I chose earlier photographs of those same demonstrators kicking our immobile ranks of restrained constabulary on their collective shins and sticking fingers in their eyes. On the back cover of the booklet we reproduced a pastiche of letters to the governor, expressing support for his administration and praising the courage and fortitude of our police.

Joining the tributes pouring in for the guardians of law and order was one from the *Far Eastern Economic Review* which commented, "Their superb mixture of forbearance and firmness in putting down hooliganism should be praised. Their correct attitude has cost them a comparatively high toll of injuries to their own Force, but has kept civilian casualties to a minimum."

The following day the two versions of *Who is Guilty of These Atrocities?,* so similar in appearance as to surrender their differences only to closer examination, went out to the news vendors through identical distribution channels, somewhat negating the effect intended by its original authors.

Speaking at a conference at the Commonwealth Office on June 29th 1967, Governor Trench claimed that ninety-eight percent of the general public supported the government in restoring law and order. It so happened that, according to the last census, ninety-eight percent of our population were Chinese, but Trench was not making any racial distinctions. Most Hong Kong residents, Trench added, were passive supporters who accepted and approved of what the government was doing without actually mentioning it. Neither did they voice their objections to the leftists. They kept their silence "because they were afraid that if Beijing really takes over Hong Kong, they would be in trouble".

With protest banners finally ripped down from the railings around Government House, and letters of public support still pouring in by the cartload—along with unsolicited gifts of cigars, wines and caviar—I happened to call with a draft press release requiring Trench's scrutiny and approval. I found him standing amid a pile of deliveries that gave the drawing room the appearance of being decked out for a premature Christmas Day. He removed a diminutive scarlet booklet attached to the neck of a bottle of VSOP brandy and held it up in an attitude intended to resemble the defiance of a typical product of the Cultural Revolution. Winking at me, he murmured "My own little red book".

Sir David Clive Crosbie Trench was certainly not lacking in courage. Serving as a district officer in the Solomon Islands when the Japanese invaded, he volunteered to be left behind enemy lines with a radio and a few loyal natives, to report on enemy shipping activity, much in the manner of French planter Emile de Becque in James Michener's *Tales of the South Pacific*. He had loved his life among the Melanesian islanders, and immediately before taking up the governorship of Hong Kong in 1964 had ended his Solomons career as High Commissioner for the Western Pacific.

He also possessed a marked sense of humour, as indicated by a tale he told of an episode on the eve of a major Hong Kong typhoon, when he attempted to call out of Government House only to find himself patched through on a crossed line. It was apparent from the subject of their conversation that the two parties he happened to overhear, oblivious of his presence on the line, were in the shipping business. They were discussing a vessel so old that one told the other, "Between you, me and the gatepost, I'm not bothered if she goes down at her moorings, so long as I get the insurance!"

Feeling constrained to interrupt, Trench cleared his throat. "Pardon me, but this is the gatepost speaking."

The line was immediately cleared so that he could proceed with his call.

Escalation

The next phase of the "struggle campaign" moved underground and resorted to acts of terrorism. Innocent bystanders started to die from crudely manufactured bombs. Sometimes—but not always—these devices were readily recognisable because they were left in public places or on street corners, in brown paper parcels, often with notes attached in Chinese, warning "patriots" to keep clear. Their nuisance value, in holding up traffic until bomb disposal personnel could be summoned to the scene, was enormous.

Any package, bag or parcel—whether or not discovered with a note attached—was deemed suspicious and placed under guard, pending investigation by explosives experts. On one occasion a cleaning lady at the Ocean Terminal went to recover her bag of sanitary materials from the corner of the arcade where she had left it, only to find it cordoned off and declared off-limits. The security personnel watching over it were unmoved by the bag owner's appeals and adamantine in their insistence that she must await the decision of the specialists.

I had commenced a feature article intended to assure overseas readers that Hong Kong was carrying on business as usual, despite the efforts made, by a very small and unloved group of malcontents, to undermine its progress. Unhappily I had chosen to entitle the article *What Makes Hong Kong Tick?* I realised, at the last moment, that this might convey the undesirable impression that we were all rushing around frantically looking for the time bomb that would blow us to smithereens.

Coupled with this bombing phase was an attempt to close down public transportation through organised strikes of leftist unions. Both ferry companies, the Star and the Hongkong and Yaumati, suffered major staff shortages as a result and struggled to keep their routes open. Buses too were running greatly reduced schedules and there simply weren't enough taxis to make up the shortfall. However, Hong Kong as ever quickly came up with improvised solutions, and owners of private cars operated *baakpai* services to transport commuters for modest fees. The police, with more important matters on their hands, turned a blind eye, for without these technically illegal operators many thousands would not have been able to get to work.

While general morale remained high—especially now that the authorities had gained the upper hand—this was also a period of increased exodus by the more nervous of our citizens, usually those of the wealthy minority who had most to lose if their worst fears were fulfilled. They had only to listen to the rumours coming out of China to envisage their fate should the red tide wash over our borders.

The rest of the populace demonstrated their contempt for the leftist cause through a collective boycott of all shops, department stores, banks and food outlets with mainland China connections. This entailed considerable sacrifice on the part of the lower-income majority, who had depended on the cheaper prices they paid for mainland supplies and merchandise, but it had been my experience, even back in Malaya, that when the Chinese launch a boycott the result is complete, unwavering and can quickly bring the ostracised party to its knees.

I was in effect a strike-breaker because I was unable to resist the cheap discount sales that the mainland department stores were compelled to advertise. Often I found myself the only customer on their vast, echoing floors, attended by staff who watched me warily in case I was a plainclothes detective from Special Branch.

To win new customers from the ranks of disaffected ex-patrons of the leftist establishments, traditional Hong Kong department stores like Wing On and Sincere were also lowering their prices and conducting a roaring trade. Unscrupulously playing both sides of the political fence, I shopped here as well, taking Mukti with me to where the prices were lower in uptown corners of Mong Kok and Shau Kei Wan, where we would often be the only non-Chinese visible in the streets. Wherever we went we met with the utmost courtesy and friendliness, enjoying a spirit of kinship and camaraderie that Hong Kong had not previously revealed.

But for us there was still nothing to compare with the pleasures of alfresco shopping at the stalls of illegal street hawkers, where one could browse through an extraordinary diverse range of products at ridiculously low prices. At Kowloon City, right under the final approach flight path to Kai Tak airport, I was once in the process of bargaining, for a rather attractive shirt that happened to be my size, when a hawker control squad launched a surprise raid. My vendor threw a sheet over his wares, grabbed the handles of his barrow and took off, but I wasn't about to let the opportunity slip from my grasp. I ran beside him, continuing a breathless exchange which went something like this:

"Three dollars."

"Eight dollars."

"Four dollars."

"Seven dollars."

"Five dollars. My last offer."

"Okay, okay. Five dollars." And he plucked the shirt from under the sheet and threw it to me, while I flung back a five-dollar note in exchange. We separated and ran off in different directions.

Mukti and I never felt personally unwelcome, leave alone threatened or endangered, amid those teeming hordes. It really was life as usual, no matter what the bombers might be up to. Scanning the Mong Kok traffic in Nathan Road for a chance to dodge between the cars and nip across the street, I watched a taxi slow to stop a few yards away from me. At first I thought the driver had misunderstood my intentions and was expecting to pick up a fare, but no, he already had his passenger aboard. He grinned at me through the windscreen to indicate that as a pedestrian I had the right of way, even though I was nowhere near a pedestrian crossing. I grinned back and insisted on waving him by. It was a kindly gesture but I wasn't looking for favours.

Any risk to which I, Mukti or anyone in the family might be exposed would be of the kind to which the populace as a whole were subjected. On one occasion Mukti was driving me along Clearwater Bay Road when we saw a whole slew of cardboard cartons scattered across both lanes.

"Look at that," said Mukti. "Some stupid driver has lost his load."

Too late to avoid scrunching over a couple of these packages, we motored on home, where I changed for a return to town to keep a dinner engagement. On the way back I joined the tail end of a small queue of traffic held up by a police barricade. Bomb disposal experts were blowing up the packages one by one.

At some point in all our lives we lose confidence in our immortality and begin to contemplate the possibility that we might die. Sometimes that happens in our childhood, just occasionally in our adolescence and more often when we are even older, depending on the timing of that first inevitable face-to-face encounter with death.

In my case, whether through delayed adolescence or some other reason, a certain sense of immunity had dogged me until now, quite late in my life. I attributed it to my certainty that I was marked for death by drowning—having come close to that specific form of termination on at least two occasions in my youth. So long as I wasn't in or near the water I thought I had a pretty good chance of surviving almost anything.

Sitting in that queue, waiting for the disposal of the last of those packages, I was made uncomfortably conscious of my mortality, of the fact that it didn't have to be death through water, of the possibility that any one of those packages might have borne my name.

When I mentioned to him the aftermath of that episode the following day, Mukti shrugged and grinned. "*Apa Allah mahu.*" Whatever God wills.

◆　　　◆　　　◆

Along with their policy of manufacturing home-made bombs, the urban guerrillas were now trying to amass firearms by seizing revolvers issued to policemen on the beat. At about two o'clock one morning I was awoken by a revolver shot directly above my bedroom. Rushing out into the darkened living-dining room, I collided with Mukti, coming from the opposite direction. He too had heard the report, which had awoken Asarah and the kids as well. We stared out at the carpark behind our apartment and spotted a Chinese police inspector, who lived with his wife in the flat above us, racing through it as if in pursuit of some unseen assailant.

Clad only in his underpants, he had in his hand the revolver whose gunshot we had just heard.

"I'm going out to see what it's all about," I said.

"I'll join you," said Mukti.

We made our appearance in the car park just as the inspector was returning from a clearly futile chase. "He got away," he muttered.

"What happened?" I asked.

"I woke up to find him trying to reach under my pillow, where I keep my gun. I got to it first and fired at him. I think I wounded him."

"He can't have got far," I pointed out, "or we would have heard a car."

We were joined by Tim Hodgson, who lived alongside me and was fairly highly placed in the immigration department. Tim suggested we split up and continue searching.

I chose to concentrate on the entrance lobby of the adjoining block, where I soon heard a faint moan from under the staircase. Investigating, I found a young man slumped in that confined space with his back against the wall. Blood was seeping through the fingers he pressed to his right side. I called out to the others, who came running.

The inspector immediately launched into an abusive tirade in Cantonese, and looked as if he were about to pistol whip the youth. I could understand his stress at being awoken in the middle of the night with his wife beside him and a strange man groping under his pillow, but he had already injured the intruder and there seemed no need for further punishment.

"Steady on," I murmured. "He's hurt enough and he can't harm you now."

The wounded man stooped forward with fear in his eyes and his arms out in a gesture of supplication. The inspector appeared to take pity on him, relaxing his guard.

"Watch out!" shouted Tim Hodgson. "He's going for your revolver,"

The youngster made a grab that missed by a wide margin and doubled him up in pain, so that he sprawled forward on the ground, groaning.

"I'll phone for an ambulance and alert your friends in the police," said Tim.

"I'll stay with him and make sure he doesn't get away," said the inspector. Turning to Mukti and me, he added "No point in all of us hanging around. Thanks for your help."

We left him to it.

◆   ◆   ◆

Tim Hodgson was a great man to have with you in a crisis, but also very adept at getting you into one you hadn't anticipated. Earlier he had invited Mukti and I to help him fetch his boat from Tai Po Market to Hebe Haven. It didn't look like much of a distance on the map, so we agreed, letting ourselves in for a saga that came near to a disastrous finale.

Tai Po Market lies at the western end of Tolo Harbour, the longest and largest inlet in the New Territories, while Hebe Haven lies at the western end of Port Shelter, the second largest inlet in the New Territories. Between them lies some of the most spectacular coastline in Hong Kong, rugged, rock-buttressed and formidable in a storm. This was the coast on which Brian Salt had chosen to wreck his government-purchased junk for the climatic typhoon sequence of *The Magic Stone*. It was also the coast where the Royal Hong Kong Auxiliary Air Force helicopter had rescued the crew of a wrecked freighter. I'd had the opportunity to admire its sheer cliffs and daunting aspect from the deck of the floating clinic on our voyage north to Sha Tau Kok, and I had thought then that I would not wish to tangle with it at close quarters.

We reached Tai Po in Tim's car, the idea being that I would later drive him back there in mine so he could recover it. It was an old, yet still serviceable and reliable vehicle. The boat, when we were ferried out it by one of the local sampan ladies, proved just as old, if not older, but that's where the resemblance ended.

"I've been having a bit of bother with the engine," Tim admitted. "I plan to have it seen to when I get it to Hebe Haven."

My heart sank. My maritime history had, at best, been ill-favoured. I'd had boats sink under me, run aground on shallow shoals, lose engine power and drift miles off course. And I still had that very real fear of drowning. But I didn't want to mention any of this to Tim. I preferred to look on the bright side.

We made reasonably good progress until we left the mouth of Tolo Channel and turned south past the island of Tap Mun. Then, somewhere beyond the promontory of Tanka Wan, the engine gave out, we drifted, rocks loomed and Tim sweated furiously over an open cowling. Mukti offered helpful suggestions while I disappeared into the cabin to consider how best to dispel my nausea and slow my palpitating heart.

The engine fired back into life, Tim put a safe distance between us and the looming shore and we proceeded on our southward journey for another twenty minutes or so until the whole cycle was repeated. This time I was relieved to note we had company; a distant Marine Police launch keeping an eye on us, much as a friendly sheepdog might watch over a stray goat that had wandered into its field. I caught a fleeting star of reflected sunlight I could only attribute to a pair of binoculars.

Again the engine struggled back to life and again we put a more determined gap between us and that *terra* all too *firma*. I noted that the police launch had decided we were out of danger. It had turned away and was no longer maintaining a parallel course.

The third engine failure was by far the longest and most worrisome. As the cliffs beyond Tai Long Wan towered ever higher above us I began to wonder when one was permitted to do the decent British thing by conceding that the time had come to stop making jokes and to start screaming.

When Tim pulled a hat-trick by sorting out even that hiatus, it was clear from his expression that he didn't retain much confidence in further miracles. Mukti waited until our skipper was turned away to shoot me a quick, head-shaking look that spoke volumes.

We sputtered on and rounded the tip of Long Ke to enter the channel that then ran between High Island and the Sai Kung peninsula (all of it now immersed under the High Island reservoir). Here, should the engine break down yet again, we were at least out of the swell and capable of fending off the rocks with a boat hook.

It did break down, and we did fend off the rocks with a boat hook, until rescued by a fast, slim yacht that took us in tow, keeping us at a considerable length from its trim lines, spotless deck and smartly attired, gin-swilling shipboard party, who returned to their bright and witty conversation, sparing us the occasional pitying glance.

◆　　　◆　　　◆

Despite being subjected to an ordeal which—had we known the full facts—we would not willingly have undertaken, Mukti and I found Tim a delightfully endearing character with some wonderful yarns to tell. We also respected his utter honesty and his willingness to risk his neck in challenging authority, should he suspect anything underhand. But like our other neighbour, the honest police inspector, Tim would pray the price for his firm opposition to corruption in any form.

Approached by a couple of subordinates in his department, with a proposition that would bring him a great deal of money should he assist in a certain problematic immigration case, Tim decided to play along with the invitation only to amass evidence he could bring to court. Rigged with a concealed tape recorder, he accumulated sufficient damaging proof—from a series of subsequent meetings—that achieved precisely that objective. But only at great cost to his career. Tim found himself sidelined and dead-ended, with no recourse but to request early retirement.

I thanked my lucky stars I had found my way into government through the tradesman's entrance, occupying a position where I could offer services nobody could conceivably consider worth paying for.

◆　　　◆　　　◆

With public support firmly and demonstrably on the side of officialdom, the government took steps to find and defuse the ticking clock that threatened the safety of the entire community. Information compiled by Special Branch enabled us to launch a series of raids on key centres where the bombs were being manufactured. The police provided the spearhead, with military units manning street cordons at ground level.

Sometimes our arrival would be resisted by force, but mostly not. Occupants would be herded together, squatting on the floor with hands over their heads, while the premises were searched for incriminating materials. In each case the general appearance of the rooms in which we found ourselves would follow a familiar pattern, with the PRC flag and portraits of Mao decorating the walls, together with big-character banners and caricatures of terrified white-skinned pigs and yellow running dogs being subjected to a variety of unspeakable indignities.

In the aftermath of one such raid on a communist school alongside Princess Margaret Road, I wandered through classrooms whose blackboards were covered in graffiti of a highly incendiary nature, which could only have been executed with the permission and encouragement of the staff.

Months earlier, before the troubles ever began, I had been conducting a visiting Australian television crew on a tour of Kowloon when we happened to be stuck in a traffic jam on our drive past this school.

"What's that?" asked the presenter of the documentary series.

"What it looks like," I responded. "The PRC flag."

"Why's it there?"

"It's a left-wing school."

"Can we take a look inside?"

"We're not supposed to. We don't want to antagonise them so we leave them pretty much to themselves."

Like a shot the presenter was out of the car with his cameraman close on his heels, shooting from the shoulder, followed by me in desperate and vain pursuit.

Once through the school gates we attracted immediate attention. The alarm was raised and staff and students came running towards us with arms outstretched and incredulous expressions on their faces. In the circumstances, the principal seemed more surprised than indignant. As if something about my distressed appearance indicated that I was the unwilling shepherd of this unruly party, he turned to me.

"Who are these people?" he asked.

"They're Australian," I replied, as if that, in itself, must surely explain their conduct.

Not unexpectedly, he refused to answer any of the questions posed by his would-be interrogator and simply pushed away the microphone rudely thrust under his nose. "If you don't remove them immediately, I'm going to report you to the education department," the headmaster informed me in a perfectly civil manner.

I apologised profusely for our unseemly intrusion, but it took an increasingly belligerent and menacing attitude on the part of the assembled mob of students to convince my fellow trespassers that there was nothing further to be gained by our continued presence.

Now that I was back, accompanying another party of intruders, this time conducting a nocturnal raid under changed circumstances, I found myself fascinated by the vengeful and vituperative nature of the slogans covering these walls of learning. Why did they hate us so much?

I paused in front of a blackboard bearing a chalked cartoon of diminutive foreigners fleeing before the advancing flood of the great proletarian revolution. Wasn't that a television camera one of them carried on his shoulder? And a microphone in the hand of another? And wasn't that me in their wake, looking especially worried and indecisive?

◆　　　◆　　　◆

Wherever possible, Mike Stevenson would be personally involved in both the planning and implementation of operations launched under this new retaliatory phase of our security measures. He would either take me along to provide back-up or, if he was too busy with other, more urgent priorities, I would be delegated to take charge of media arrangements. It was my task to compile and disseminate information and, once each strike target was secured, assemble and brief the press.

I found it extremely satisfying to be taking the initiative at last, rather than helplessly remaining at the receiving end, even though—because many of the raids were nocturnal—this meant spending nights away from home. Either I would be given a bed at the Stevenson household on Old

Peak Road, where I was thoroughly fussed over by Mike's wife Elizabeth, or I would doss down in some convenient police station bunk, awaiting the signal to move out in the early pre-dawn hours to some destination only revealed at the last moment.

The routine was to assemble our convoy in an area of town well away from the actual target zone, in order to create maximum confusion as to where we intended to strike. This was particularly important in the prelude to daylight raids, when word of our presence would quickly but misleadingly spread to every leftist "cell" in the vicinity. On one such raid, when our forces were gathering along Austin Road, Kowloon, in the vicinity of the Gun Club, an expatriate police inspector sharing my Land Rover suddenly realised he had forgotten to bring his "good morning" towel.

Cheap and readily disposable, those tiny little face towels were essential aids to coping with hot weather. Strung around our necks, they were used to mop up perspiration from our brows and keep it from running into our eyes. Having forgotten my own, I asked him where we might obtain replacements.

He glanced at his watch. "We've got plenty of time," he decided. "We won't be moving out for another twenty minutes. I'm going to buy one."

"I'll come with you," I said.

Alerted to suspicious activity among its tenants, we had already raided, some days earlier, a building that housed a large China products emporium at the corner of Nathan and Jordan Road. While we had no proof that the store itself was implicated, we had information that some of its personnel might be. Hence this address had been one of the first targets on our list. It never occurred to us its employees might think we were raiding them again.

With our standard-issue steel helmets and gasmasks slung from our shoulders, but minus our essential "good morning" towels, we trotted through the double doors of the department store and precipitated an immediate and simultaneous disappearance of staff on all sides. There wasn't a head to be seen above counter level.

Fortunately through years of familiarity, as happy and satisfied customers, with the layout of this establishment, we knew exactly where to go.

Sprinting down the aisles to the counters for haberdashery and clothing accessories, we picked up our precious "good morning" towels and left sufficient small change in their place to cover the purchase cost.

"Thanks," yelled my companion to the invisible store attendants. "And a very good morning to you too."

◆　　　◆　　　◆

While that particular emporium had figured among our initial targets, along with shipyards, communist schools and the headquarters of certain leftist trade unions, the general impression gaining ground through the public rumour mill was that we were concentrating on the "small fry" and avoiding the real nerve centres where the hard-core trouble-makers had holed up. Long suspected to figure among the latter was a cell located in the same building that housed the largest China products emporium in the colony, situated on King's Road, North Point.

This towering mass of a structure dominated its surroundings with an appearance of fortress-like invincibility. On one occasion I had stood in the empty traffic lanes of King's Road, watching our bomb disposal team checking out a suspicious package while police cordons at either end of the block held up all trams and vehicles in this normally busy thoroughfare. Canyon walls of densely packed tenement blocks loomed above us on both sides of the street, their windows crowded with the faces of residents impartially observing these proceedings.

They were so silent one could have heard a pin drop, but I half expected more than that. All it would take was one bottle, one empty tin can tumbling from those concrete cliffs of troglodyte dwellings to set off an avalanche of missiles that would send us diving for cover. But no, not even the proverbial pin.

One of the bystanders clustered on the sidewalk gave me a friendly smile, so I tried testing his grasp of English. Did anyone know who had planted this package?

With a thrust of his chin, he indicated the hulk of a building farther east, the one housing the department store. Everyone knew that was the stronghold of troublemakers in this locality. They used it as their sanctuary, secure in the belief we would never dare to follow them inside.

Overnighting again with the Stevenson household, I asked Mike which target we'd be going for this time. Hauling himself up to chin level on the improvised exercise bar he had fitted to one of the doorframes, he grunted "You should know better than to ask. You'll find out in the morning."

It was another of our pre-dawn assignations, assembled in the courtyard of the old Central police station on Hollywood Road. Located just below Victoria Prison—which ominously enough was the longest-standing structure in Hong Kong and already housed detainees we had picked up for inciting civic unrest—this reminded me of the ancient Georgian barracks in which I had been quartered at Woolwich, on the outskirts of London, during my two years of national service as a private in the Royal Army Pay Corps.

On the side directly below the prison stood a four-storey barrack block, erected in 1864, and opposite this was an office extension of similar height which, like the other blocks, had been added between 1910 and 1925. The entire complex was fashioned in classically imperial style, with broad balconies and high, pseudo-Grecian pillars fronted by an imposing columned façade facing out on to Hollywood Road. On the wall of the staircase above the main reporting centre hung the skin of the last tiger shot in the New Territories. This was a trophy described by G.A.K. Herklots in his book *The Hong Kong Countryside:*

> "In 1915, a tiger was shot by Mr. Burlingham A.S.P. in the New Territories, but only after it had killed Sergeant Groucher, and I believe it was reported to have visited both Hong Kong and Lantau island in its wanderings."

In the darkness of that ancient courtyard, echoing to the sounds of boots, broadcast radio communications and shouted commands, with Land Rover engines kicking into life, doors slamming and headlights lending a sense of drama to the occasion, we looked as if we were gathered for a hunt of another kind.

I shared the back seat of a Land Rover with Mike, the chill night wind whipping our faces as our transport column roared due east down the Hong Kong Island waterfront. My hopes were rising that this time it really was going to be that intractable tower block in North Point that had seemed the source of so much harassment.

A couple of Royal Air Force Westland Whirlwinds roared overhead, their bloated shapes silhouetted against the dawn-flushed sky. As we sped down Java Road, in parallel with King's Road, it became clear that these helicopters had reached their objective ahead of us. They were hovering over the roof of the building in question. It seemed for a moment that their whirling blades were scattering flocks of crows, until we realised those flapping shapes were articles of laundry left out on the roof to dry.

I glanced at Mike, who nodded. "They're carrying troops who will work their way down from the roof while the police go in at ground level, clearing floor by floor."

By the time we arrived, the ground floor of the emporium was already secured. I confidently pulled open the double doors at the main entrance and stepped in just as two voices rang out from opposite directions. One said "Not that way!" and the other said "Don't step on that!" I looked down to find that whatever welcome mat may have lain there had been pulled away. I was standing on an exposed wire mesh connected by cable to a wall socket.

"Well, at least you've answered one question," conceded the second of the two voices. This belonged to an engineer still kneeling in the position he had adopted before I abruptly resolved for him the issue of whether or not the grille was live. "Lucky for you they neglected to switch it on."

While the combined police-military contingents were working their way towards each other, compressing troublesome elements somewhere in the middle of the building, I received word of a surprising find in a block, known to be tenanted by leftist sympathisers, on the opposite side of the road. There a search party had stumbled upon a makeshift "hospital" on an illegally constructed additional floor, sandwiched between two of the structure's original storeys.

This medical centre was small but surprisingly well equipped. The ceiling was extremely low, so that anyone my size would have to stoop to move around, but it possessed enough equipment to carry out minor surgery if required. I recognised it from photographs I had seen in the pages of a leftwing newspaper, where an article had claimed its existence as a resource for the heroic patriots opposing colonial rule. When I first spotted this article I had contacted senior official in the government's medical services, advising them that it might be difficult for the authorities to track down injured troublemakers if they were being treated in unlicensed premises.

My warnings had fallen on disbelieving ears, for nobody in the health department could accept that it was possible to operate an illegal hospital anywhere in Hong Kong. I now had great satisfaction in summoning those incredulous officials to check out the proof for themselves. And I alerted the media to get there before them, so they would be subjected to another kind of grilling on their arrival.

The North Point raid had the salutary effect of demonstrating that the government was not prepared to recognise any area of Hong Kong as being "off limits" and therefore impervious to its measures to deal with the malefactors in our midst.

Virtually overnight, the Bank of China installed masses of coiled barbed wire on its roof to repel helicopters.

Pig on the Thirteenth Green

Unhappy that the Hong Kong public, instead of rallying to their cause, were antagonised by its violent consequences, our hard-core agitators now switched tactics again. Still bent on wringing more tangible support from reluctant Beijing, they upped the stakes in a calculated effort to bring the People's Liberation Army into the fray.

On July 8th 1967 they succeeded in provoking the ugliest incident so far at the quiet little border town of Sha Tau Kok, which I had visited under happier circumstances the previous year. Across that barely recognisable demarcation line, dividing the two sides of the main street, stormed some three hundred or more communist demonstrators. Chanting Mao slogans and waving copies of the little red book of the Great Helmsman's sayings, they began pelting the local police station with stones.

The police fired tear gas and wooden slugs to chase them away. Then a machine-gun stuttered into life from across the street. In a hail of bullets, five Hong Kong policemen died and a further twelve were wounded. No immediate reinforcements were sent to their aid because the police seemed paralysed with shock.

Sir David Trench being out of the colony at the time, Colonial Secretary David Irving Gass had assumed the role of Acting Governor. Gass, who would eventually follow Trench's earlier career path into the governorship of the British Western Pacific Territories, was a small, slightly-built man now confronted with a crucial decision that could brook no further delay. He arranged for a battalion of Gurkha troops to be rushed to the scene and for Police Commissioner Edward Tyrer to take immediate leave of absence.

From London, where Tyrer was ostensibly flown for talks with senior British officials on the security situation in Hong Kong, the Commonwealth Office announced that—for reasons of health—he would be unable

116

to return to Hong Kong and, at the age of fifty, had sought early retirement. The official statement read "The secretary for state has in the circumstances given his approval for Mr. Tyrer's retirement."

Tyrer had joined the police in 1945, immediately after the Japanese occupation. Rising steadily through the ranks, he had taken up his appointment as Commissioner in October 1966, just seven months prior to the Sha Tau Kok incident. He was replaced by Eates, who took charge in the knowledge that the police had forfeited their time-honoured lead in border security and would now have to play second-fiddle to the military.

Exactly who had commenced firing at Sha Tau Kok was never precisely ascertained. If the People's Liberation Army were involved the situation would have quickly escalated beyond the desultory sniping that greeted the Gurkhas once they moved in, so the supposition was that hotheads among the local militia had commandeered a machine-gun and engineered a crisis designed to force the PLA's hand. The evidence was that they had not succeeded.

The sniping continued for a while but ceased when it was clear the Gurkhas were under orders not to fire back. An uneasy calm descended on the area, but the message to the Hong Kong public was sobering: this was the first time since the communists came to power in 1949 that British and Chinese had faced each other across the border in an armed confrontation. Wong Cheuk Yin writes:

> "At the beginning, the Hong Kong government had been somewhat cautious about the clashes in Sha Tau Kok for fear of possible intervention from China. Later, when Jack Cater contacted the central leadership in China it was quite clear that Zhou Enlai had not approved of the incidents in Sha Tau Kok. According to Cater, Beijing told us to 'hold on' and that they would help. But then they were also in chaos. There were also riots and most of the provinces in China had serious problems. They could not do anything for us at that time.

> "Zhou had said in a meeting that 'as the struggle continued to escalate, it is really difficult to stop and we are already riding the tiger'. This confirmed Cater's remarks. Therefore, the Hong Kong government could conclude that the Sha Tau Kok incidents, though serious, were not an attempt at armed invasion of the colony as no regular units of

the PLA were involved. All these suggested that the incident was purely organized and executed locally by the Guangdong villagers in the immediate vicinity."

The night of the Sha Tau Kok debacle, I received orders from Stevenson that I was to report the following morning to the police-military headquarters located in the military camp at Sek Kong. Until further notice GIS would regard me as "our man on the border".

♦   ♦   ♦

Sek Kong was a throwback to earlier, less troubled times, and behaved as if those times were with us yet. It was a sprawling encampment of single-storey barrack blocks of the kind that had been in service throughout the tropics since long before World War Two. Attached to it was an enclave of officer's family quarters, a school and a *NAAFI* store operated by the Navy, Army and Air Force Institute, together with a cinema and an airstrip used mainly by light observation aircraft of the Royal Air Force. The whole constituted a world apart from the rest of Hong Kong. Life here was hermetically sealed and totally self-contained, until the events of 1967 projected Sek Kong into the unaccustomed role of coordinating the colony's first line of defence.

Reverting to that military environment, I was immediately plunged into nostalgic memories of my national service days at Devizes and Bulford camps in Wiltshire, where I had felt cocooned from the realities of the real world. I was given my own office off the courtyard that lay just below the police-military operations centre, typically abbreviated to PolMil for short, and I was granted honorary membership of the officers' mess, together with one of its rooms to myself. Had I wished, I could have accepted the offer of a batman, but already my precipitate elevation from the rank of private in my previous military career seemed pretentious enough.

Thank God I didn't have to wear a uniform, and could choose to don whatever form of civvies I wished, provided I turned up in a jacket and tie for our mess dinners. When not in uniform themselves, my fellow diners mostly wore blazers and cravats or regimental ties, smoked pipes, spoke with clipped Sandhurst accents and indulged in innocent horseplay of the endearing, Bertie Wooster kind. One of them went by the nickname "Bubbles". So attenuated was their connection to the rest of the territory in which they served that the Cultural Revolution might have struck them as a sort of bizarre *avant-garde* art movement. No matter what might be in store for Hong Kong, with such decent chaps beside me how could I ever feel vulnerable or endangered?

The mess secretary was Major Lawrence Pottinger, a small and deceptively solemn looking Gurkha officer with a deliciously wry sense of humour who would become a very close and dear friend and who, in his post-military career, would take on the role of Assistant Director of Protocol in the Hong Kong Secretariat.

Among other units, Sek Kong was the home of a Gurkha Signals squadron similar to the one to which my uncle Len had been posted at Seremban in Malaya ten years earlier. After the Sha Tau Kok incident this squadron set about installing a public address system at the ill-fated police station that had suffered such heavy casualties. They also equipped other border police stations with such systems, so that communist propaganda from China could be countered in the same way that we had reacted to it from the roof of Beaconsfield House.

Gurkha technicians deployed to maintain these facilities, as well as repair telephone lines along the border road, sometimes came under a barrage of heavy stoning from local dissidents. As the army took over more and more of the border posts from the police, so the squadron became more heavily involved in providing communications for the entire border area and the battalions deployed there.

My first border assignment was a story on how well the military were getting along with the police in manning the various observation posts lining the boundary fence. Most of these were little more than glorified concrete pillboxes located on high ground commanding wide prospects of the meandering stream dividing the northern New Territories from the considerably more mountainous terrain of southern Guangdong province. The only access to them lay along the fairly exposed border road that followed the course of this stream.

Not only the road, but the fields on the other side, seemed surprisingly deserted, for which I was grateful. In addition to my typewriter and telephone, I had been equipped with an office car, driven rather cautiously by Ah Lum, who was already one of the oldest employees in GIS service. Even older was our photographer, Gatlin Lin, who was always looking for a different angle and quite liable to throw himself on the ground and shoot from below; a manoeuvre that produced a disconcerting effect on many of his subjects.

Gatlin was a man with a mission. He saw this as possibly his last chance to make his name. Destiny had chosen him for this moment, entrusting to him the unique opportunity to be the only photographer on the spot when hordes of righteous mainlanders came pouring through the barbed-wire barricades. I believe he lived for what he saw as the last act of a dying empire, planning how he would smuggle his precious rolls of film out of the country before Hong Kong fell, so as to achieve international stature on the front pages of the world's press. This made him a good photographer if you wanted a flair for the dramatic, but not necessarily the right man for a standard news release shot of someone opening a clinic or handing out prizes at a school sports day.

However I had to admit he was an excellent cameraman for the sort of stories I had in mind, through which I sought to project an image of a thin red line stretched along a tenuous green frontier. But this angle didn't suit Mike Stevenson back at GIS. Mike preferred to play down the drama and reinforce the routine appearance of a border where, now that all the fuss had died down at Sha Tau Kok, nothing much was happening. His desired interpretation of events, of course, was the very reverse of what the opposition wished to achieve.

When we reached our final destination, at the end of that initial, unescorted drive south of the border, down Sha Tau Kok way, the town initially looked much the same as it had done on that first occasion when I disembarked from the floating clinic berthed at the far end of its pier. However the atmosphere was still tense enough for our military and police units, wherever possible, to avoid patrolling the main street, from the opposite side of which loudspeakers disseminated continuously recycled inflammatory broadcasts that may have contributed to the boredom and weariness—rather than hostility—we detected in the expressions of passers-by.

From the roof of a sandbagged observation post above the local fire station, Gatlin focused his telephoto lens on a straw-stuffed effigy of Governor Sir David Trench, hanging from a lamp pole at the street corner. Judging by the frustrated look in his eye, I could tell he would dearly love to be lying on the pavement directly below this, firing off typically Gatlin machine-gun shots from an unusual perspective. I left him to it and accompanied the local military commander on a stroll down the back lanes of the shophouses on our side of the street. Dogs and cats reluctantly interrupted their repose to clear a path for us. An elderly lady in a wide-brimmed Hakka hat, with a black cloth fringe around its edge, shuffled by, ignoring us.

Passing kitchen windows, we caught the reassuring clatter of mahjong tiles, and occasional snatches of Cantonese opera from transistor radios, insulating occupants from the repetitive onslaught of the propaganda dispensed across the road.

The photograph among my souvenirs that best sums up Gatlin's sense of theatre is one taken from the hill above the Man Kam To border crossing. He and I were accompanying Police Commissioner Eates on his first border inspection tour. We had earlier been briefed on the frontier situation by police at Ta Ku Ling station, the largest police installation along the border. All cross-border traffic had come to a halt following another unpleasant episode the day before, when one of our inspection parties, including district officer Trevor Bedford and battalion commander MacAlister, had been briefly held hostage by slogan-chanting farmers from the other side.

By the time we reached the hill overlooking the Man Kam To bridge, those farmers, and whatever additional supporters they had managed to summon to the scene, were charging the barricade our troops had laid across it. They wanted access to their fields on our side of the river and were enraged to be denied it simply because they had chosen to subject some of our officials to a bit of public criticism.

The Man Kam To bridge was one of those prefabricated metal structures, known as Bailey bridges, that army engineers were trained to throw across even quite large bodies of water at short notice. In ordinary circumstances, trucks from remote Chinese farms used this one to deliver supplies of vegetables and other produce for collection from the goods yard that lay below us. But today that goods yard lay empty and deserted, save for a solitary Gurkha soldier.

While Gatlin was busy taking photographs, Eates and I stood fascinated. It was like watching a rather unusual sort of cricket match. The Gurkha might have been wearing white flannels instead of an olive green uniform. He took long, loping strides towards the bridge and, with a lovely over-arm action, bowled another canister of tear gas into the screaming mob attempting to break through the barrier with a handcart. The latter, with damp "good morning" towels held to their mouths and noses, would grope through the clouds to retrieve the offending missile and hurl it back before the acrid fumes forced a temporary retreat that would end with a rally and renewed assault.

Gatlin has left me with a black and white print that perfectly encapsulates this scene, framed by two Gurkha soldiers standing on the slope directly below us, surveying the progress of the match like umpires. How long the stalemate might have continued is left to speculation because, shortly after this photograph was taken, a burst of gunfire started snipping branches off the pine trees not far from where we stood.

Somebody on the other side had got hold of another machine-gun, and I thought I could spot its location, in a depression by the river bank to the right of the bridge. Eates suggested we should get out of the way and leave the military to handle the situation.

The belligerent mood at Man Kam To was echoed at Lo Wu, where a similar burst of gunfire raked a goods train that had just crossed over with the day's deliveries of livestock for the markets of downtown Hong Kong. Unfortunately nobody—at the time—saw the connection between this and the subsequent discovery of a dead pig, killed by a Chinese-calibre bullet, on the links at the Fanling golf course. The result was a conundrum that left all of us at PolMil in Sek Kong groping for the least incredible explanation.

This was where a Sandhurst military background really paid off, through scientific exposure to ballistics and maximum velocities, with allowance for trajectories and following winds. Someone postulated that at the right angle, and with the right degree of tail wind, it was just conceivable that a bullet fired across the border might travel all the way down to the Fanling golf course, where it was the pig's sheer bad luck to be in the wrong place at the wrong time.

Yes, but what was the pig doing at the Fan Ling golf course?

Could it be some kind of mascot or something, allowed free range of the links when they were not actually in use by members?

Or could it have been shot nearer the border and, summoning its last reserves of strength, blundered on to the golf course to die on the thirteenth green?

Did anyone have a map to show precisely where it had been found?

We gathered around the large-scale wall map of the New Territories at the upper end of the ops room, with its little pins and flags to show where everybody was. Everybody except the dead pig.

The mystery was cleared up the following day when we received a report that workers at the Kowloon Canton Railway yards had discovered bullet holes in the sides of the goods vans, together with the fact that one of their pigs was missing. Questioning the Chinese delivery crew, they learned that the pig had been thrown out in the course of the journey so as to get rid of the potentially alarming evidence that it was shot with a Chinese calibre bullet. The train just happened to be passing the Fanling golf course at the time.

Detours and Diversions

To help boost public morale, the government allayed fears of any disruption to the piped water supply from China by bringing the new Plover Cove reservoir on stream, even before its freshwater storage had been thoroughly leached of all traces of salinity. There were a few grumbles about the water from the taps tasting rather brackish, but the gesture was appreciated.

Hong Kong Land, the property owners who had pioneered most of the principal public buildings in Central, announced plans for Connaught Centre, which was to be Hong Kong's tallest skyscraper, honeycombed with large, circular plate glass windows. Today, under its changed name of Jardine House, and unofficial description as the "building of a thousand assholes", this looks like a relatively small Swiss cheese in the shadow of much higher buildings that have followed.

Unquestionably the greatest stimulant to public confidence was the launch of Television Broadcasts Limited, immediately compressed into the acronym of TVB. Hong Kong had been supplied with cable television since 1958, thanks to the Rediffusion service introduced by its parent company in London. I had subscribed to its piped, black-and-white programmes since moving into Silverstrand, and Mazli and Mazlan were hopelessly addicted to its cartoons and serialised episodes of *The Man from U.N.C.L.E*, *The Avengers* and *The Prisoner*.

But most households could not meet the subscription costs of a cable service, so that when the first commercial wireless television station was introduced by TVB in 1967 it proved an instant hit. There were no licence fees to pay, and all one needed was an aerial and a receiver to obtain virtually non-stop gratification of the senses, suspension of critical faculties and general paralysis of all independent initiative. Television aerials sprouted everywhere, on rooftops, balconies, squatter shacks and fish-

124

ing junks. The battle for hearts and minds had been won the moment *Enjoy Yourself Tonight* aired its pilot presentation. TVB's founding fathers had hit on the right formula from the outset. They knew that the best way to build any sense of community was through shows like this, which reminded individual citizens they were *part* of that community.

Watching their favourite television stars indulging in slapstick humour, singing together, or making light of prevailing social issues, engendered a sense of identity and of mutual interest. For the first time one had the feeling of sharing in a wider commonality of experience. Hong Kong was beginning to look a lot like home. Enough to make one pray for another typhoon that would bring the city to a temporary halt—so long as TVB remained operational to entertain three million housebound viewers.

Established with a total staff of a mere two hundred or so, TVB is now the largest Chinese programme producer in the world, employing some five thousand personnel, including contract artistes and staff in overseas subsidiary companies. Its chairman is wily old Run Run Shaw, who turned his movie studios into a television lot and—well into his nineties—has stayed on top of the entertainment business.

Another milestone in 1967 was the inauguration of Lion Rock tunnel, burrowing through the Kowloon hills to provide a much faster road link between the metropolis and the New Territories. Sha Tin was still little more than a village surrounded by market gardens, but at least one could get there a great deal quicker now that it was no longer necessary to follow the meandering old route through the Shing Mun pass.

Nevertheless I preferred that old route, where I might pause to feed the wild macaques living around the water catchment. Construction of the Shing Mun reservoir had commenced in 1935, the year I was born, and completed, according to the legend on its plaque, in 1937 (*Nisi Dominus Frustra*, or God willing). *Nisi Dominus Frustra,* I thought to myself, we will get through this year too.

Less successful was the Shing Mun redoubt, a key but—in the event—futile link in Hong Kong's defences against the rapidly advancing Japanese Army in 1941. It failed to stem that advance because it was based on a World War One concept of largely immobilised and protracted warfare, waged from deeply entrenched positions. The Japanese simply swept it aside in their headlong southward rush down to the Kowloon peninsula. Today the old pillboxes and tunnels of the redoubt lie neglected and overgrown beside the Maclehose Trail, longest and most scenic hiking track in the New Territories.

A couple of bends past the reservoir lay the home of my friend John Howarth, a senior architect with the firm of Leigh and Orange who had produced, among other things, the plans for the Mandarin Hotel. Inaugurated in 1963, just two years before my arrival in Hong Kong, the Mandarin quickly disguised the fact that it was originally conceived as an office block, and rocketed to fame among the world's top ten hostelries, not so much for its fairly unpretentious appearance but for the quality of service it provided. Today the hotel still has its Howarth Suite, named after its designer.

John told me he had worked long hours, night after night, to complete the final design details that would meet the hotel's construction deadline, as a result of which he had become thoroughly disoriented on one of his nocturnal journeys home. The only cross-harbour route for cars and trucks in those days was aboard the Hongkong and Yaumati vehicular ferries, operating between the Hong Kong reclamation, in the proximity of the Macau ferry terminal, and a similar reclamation at the western end of Jordan Road.

On arrival at Jordan Road, John descended the ramp in his Rover saloon and, believing himself to be in Hong Kong instead of Kowloon, turned left instead of right. The car fell off the end of the jetty and quickly sank from sight, settling into the mud below and leaving just enough clearance for John to evacuate the driver's seat through an open window and stand on its roof, waiting to be rescued.

His home on the old Shing Mun Road was the most beautiful I have ever encountered in Hong Kong, but no trace of it survives. John engaged some of the last and best of the old village craftsmen who could still construct village homes in the traditional manner, from blocks of grey granite with pine rafters supporting overlapping tiers of decorated tile. He directed them to build three of these inter-connected structures at varie-

Detours and Diversions 127

gated levels down a gradient that also embraced a tiered garden with pagodas, arched walkways and the most magnificent prospects of the entire Sha Tin valley spread out below. It was *Shangri-La* in microcosm, complete with wind-chimes and Mozart suites, alternating with Sibelius symphonies and piped through the lawns via a discreet and unobtrusive hifi system.

Sharing the house with John was Godfrey Moyle, an old China hand with Jardine Matheson who had the Yangtze waters in his veins, along with a perpetual hint of nostalgia for his long years in Shanghai. Like so many others I met who had known that queen of cities in its heyday, Godfrey condescended to acknowledge Hong Kong as no more than the pale substitute for which he had been forced to settle because, in his lifetime, it would never be possible to return to his greater love. He influenced a poem I wrote entitled *Old China Hand*:

> "In avenues
> of trembling trees
> he sits and sees
> the Bund, rickshaws and pantaloons,
> the steamers ply,
> the life he knew,
> and the Yangtze flows
> in the cataract of his eye.
>
> "He gave his love a life ago
> to another port in another time,
> when careers were made in the coastal trade,
> when the black-tie palm court quartet played
> for the big hotels, for the social climb,
> where cadets and generals' daughters surged,
> where the waters of the world converged
> on old Shanghai."

When I first met him, John Howarth was busy designing another home for himself at Ronco, on the Swiss shore of Lake Maggiore. He let me look over his shoulder as he pored over the blueprints for this, explaining how he intended to install a private chair-lift to connect his property with the house he was designing for his friend Willie Tag, higher up the slope. Both

128   No Babylon

John and Willie urged me to become their guest when these properties were eventually completed, but I never found the time. I always seemed to have too much on my plate, and my spells of leave were too short to fit everything in. Besides, despite its undoubted beauties, and wonderfully rich history, Europe was not my scene. I was a creature of Asia, looking if anything further east, towards the Pacific, than over my shoulder to the west.

I was not alone in this orientation. Many of my friends, like Godfrey and Willie, had been in the east far longer than me, allowing it to permeate their blood. Willie was the doyen of the local German community that had moved into Hong Kong following the fall of Shanghai. Its other prominent members included Hans Siegel and Ernest Harnach, both of whom had represented German business interests well east of Suez since before the war. When that war broke out Ernest was on India's Malabar coast, working for the lesser-known pharmaceutical division of the great Krupp empire, which had established a formidable reputation through its manufacture of armaments.

Imprisoned as an enemy alien in a POW camp just outside Bombay, Ernest had earned the enmity of fellow inmates, many of whom were Nazi sympathisers, through his Anglophile leanings and his willingness to assist the prison staff. When the war was over and the other prisoners were repatriated, Ernest volunteered to stay on to help wind down the camp and complete its records.

Anyone who had in mind the Aryan prototype Hitler had idolized, and so conspicuously failed to resemble himself, would have been well advised to look closer on first introduction to Ernest Harnach. Although his tall and athletic physique, blond hair, aquiline profile and striking good looks made him appear the very model of pure-blooded Aryan breeding, Ernest loathed everything that holy grail of Nazi racism had come to represent. His best friends were drawn from among fellow expatriates in the German Jewish community or from the native populace of whichever country he had chosen as his home.

As it had been in India, where he was among those who discovered and nurtured the talents of the famed Indian dancer Ram Gopal, so it was in

Hong Kong, where Ernest developed very strong and lasting attachments among the Chinese. I believe our own close friendship arose from his discovery that I was an Anglo-Indian unashamed of my miscegenated origins.

He later urged me to accompany him on a holiday to Sri Lanka, where he had a second home in Colombo that he shared with an elderly Jewish friend. There I would find myself invited to dinner by Arthur C. Clarke, whose science fiction novels I had long and greatly admired. Ernest had met Arthur in the course of his house-hunting, thanks to the fact that the writer had earlier persuaded Prime Minister Mrs. Bandaranaike to allow foreigners to settle in return for their investments. Dinner with Ernest at Clarke's splendid old colonial mansion was a memorable experience. After the meal the three of us adjourned to the laboratory, where I had my first encounter with a desktop-sized personal computer, learning how small and compact this could be.

Clarke's cutting-edge example of the new technology was—naturally enough—named "Hal", in honour of the far bigger model that had figured as one of the principal protagonists in the joint Kubrick-Clarke production *2001: A Space Odyssey*. Arthur used it to demonstrate, on his small radar-scope monitor, how little green binary numbers could be programmed to dance around in an animated fireworks display. The computer, which was then almost certainly the only one of its kind in Sri Lanka, had been given to him by *NASA*, as a thank-you for Arthur's postulated theory of stationary satellites in fixed orbits—a theory that had since revolutionised the way in which the world communicated.

He took us upstairs to view his collection of giant-sized holograms, looming like ghostly apparitions in a black vacuum. I had never encountered holograms before, and remained mystified even when Clarke attempted to explain how they were fashioned. I did appreciate though that they would enable an entire museum to display three-dimensional exhibits that simply weren't there. It was my first exposure to a virtual reality world, and struck me as fitting that it should be revealed to me by one who had already done so much to expand the bounds of my imagination.

But I digress.

◆ ◆ ◆

Much as I preferred the detour of the old Shing Mun road, with its opportunities to linger over a *satay* lunch at the old Shatin Inn, it was seldom a practicable option in those days when I hurried back to Silverstrand for the brief spells of weekend leave that interrupted my Sek Kong sojourn. Stevenson had arranged for me to be issued with a special pass to use the Lion Rock tunnel even before its official opening, thereby greatly shortening the travel time both to my headquarters at Beaconsfield House and to my home.

Ah Lum would arrive with the car on a Sunday night, to collect me from Silverstrand at the end of an all-too-brief relaxation with Mukti, Asarah and the kids, and then find the shortest route through Wong Tai Sin to the southern end of the tunnel, still cluttered with piles of extracted rock. All the way through the freshly bored, two-lane passageway, lit only by our headlights, we would dodge heaps of cement, stacked wall-cladding and other construction debris, together with an occasional watchman flagging us down to warn us of potholes and low-slung electric cables.

Once clear of this obstacle course, Ah Lum would speed up on the straight, open and generally empty stretch of new highway leading down into Sha Tin itself. But one night I asked him—too late—to avoid hitting a very large python making slow progress across the traffic lanes. Ah Lum swerved to comply but couldn't avoid crunching over the tail end of the hapless reptile. I asked him to stop, and ran back to see if anything could be done to save this stricken example of protected wild life.

The python was looking a bit stunned from the unexpected experience of having its tail squished, but before I could figure out what could be done about it, I was joined by the driver of a public works vehicle that had followed us through the tunnel. His reflexes were far quicker than mine. He whisked out a pocket knife, flicked it open and seemed to know exactly what he was doing. With the fingers of his left hand he probed for a spot on the snake's spine, plunged in the knife, cut an incision about a foot long and extracted what must have been the reptile's gall bladder.

With head held back and mouth wide open, he dropped this bleeding organ into his gaping jaws and then grinned at me, rubbing his lower belly as if to assure me he anticipated a night of exceptional sexual prowess. Leaving me dazed by the roadside, he hurried back to his cab, impatient to test the efficacy of the potent aphrodisiac he had so providentially encountered.

The python lay perfectly still, its eyes glazing over.

◆　　　◆　　　◆

Just when it seemed that tension at the border was easing into monotony, a couple of unexpected diversions livened up the routine. A pair of off-duty Hong Kong policemen on a motor-cycle, unfamiliar with the road system in the border area, took a wrong turn across the Man Kam To bridge and were understandably "taken prisoner" by militia on the other side, who must have found this eventuality as difficult to credit as we did.

Then Inspector Frank Knight, who had earlier entertained me to an excellent curry lunch with some of the last serving Pakistani members of the force stationed at Fan Ling police headquarters, went to investigate an argument that had broken out just beside the Man Kam To bridge, became embroiled in this himself, failed to talk himself out of it and was hustled across the river to become another hostage in the hands of the those seeking to cause maximum discomposure to the Hong Kong authorities. In exchange for the three police personnel, these now demanded the release from detention of some of the ringleaders of the earlier troubles.

Meanwhile, infinitely more dramatic and disturbing events were taking place elsewhere. The planting of terrorist bombs in urban areas had, if anything, increased in frequency, with more sophisticated devices claiming greater numbers of victims. August 20th was marked by an incident that the *South China Morning Post* described as the most dastardly communist-inspired act to date. Two very young children, Wong Yee-man and Wong Siu-fan, were killed in a bomb explosion at North Point. The *Hong Kong Standard* assailed local leftists for provoking this tragedy, and the more extreme *Tin Tin Daily News* called for those responsible to be hanged.

The death of the two innocents was followed, four days later, by the callous murder of a popular radio talk-show host known for his fearless condemnation of those behind the unrest. In full view of horrified spectators, Lam Bun, thirty-seven years old, was doused in gasoline and set alight as he sat in his stationary car. Whatever lingering shreds of public support the instigators may have commanded were sundered in the aftermath of this shocking act, when they compounded their guilt by breaking silence to lay boastful claim to its execution.

The arrest of the editors-in-chief of three Communist newspapers in mid-August, coupled with the banning of their publications, gave a particularly militant group in Beijing a pretext for a full-scale Sino-British diplomatic confrontation. On August 20th, the same day that the Wong children were killed at North Point, the British chargé d'affaires in Beijing, Donald Hopson, received an "ultimatum" from the Ministry of Foreign Affairs, acting under coercion from Red Guard elements, to lift the ban on all Hong Kong publications within forty-eight hours, failing which Britain would be held answerable for the consequences.

Compliance with this demand—effectively tantamount to total surrender of all British authority for Hong Kong—was deemed out of the question. Two days later, Red Guards burst into the legation grounds and set its buildings alight. Hopson and his staff were beaten while evacuating the premises. Among these personnel was Hopson's advisor Percy Cradock, who would head the British delegation in the talks that led—almost exactly thirty years later—to Hong Kong's return to China.

Hopson had a very British sense of humour. In the build-up to the conflagration the Foreign Office in London received an interesting memento from the embattled legation. Hopson had cut down one of the straw effigies of Prime Minister Harold Wilson hanging from the walls of the mission building and had placed this in the diplomatic bag, together with the placard around its neck reading "Down with Wi-le Saxon!"

He later recounted, in official papers that have only recently been released, how the staff refused to be rattled, embarking on a surreal evening of entertainment while some twenty thousand angry demonstrators massed outside. "After dinner of tinned sausage and claret, I went to the first floor to play bridge while those of the staff who were not at work watched Peter Sellers in a film entitled, not inappropriately, 'The Wrong Arm of the Law'," Hopson recalled.

"At 10:30 p.m. I had just bid three no-trumps when I heard a roar from the crowd outside. The masses had risen to their feet and were surging like an angry sea against the small cordon of soldiers who linked arms three deep before the gates." But decorum was maintained amid the mayhem. "I only had time to throw on my jacket before the mob poured through and over the gate…" The staff of eighteen men and five women "were hauled by our hair, half-strangled with our ties, kicked and beaten on the head with bamboo poles. The girls were not spared the lewd attentions of the mob…So much for the morals of the Red Guards."

The Brits eventually managed to escape to the safety of other friendly embassy compounds; with Hopson concluding: "So ended our Armageddon." He reported the office a total loss. "My house was sacked and its contents, including my clothes, destroyed." But there was one crumb of comfort. "The signed photograph of the Queen survived, though slightly singed."

The maltreatment of Hopson, together with the manhandling of his consul in Shanghai, Peter Hewitt, would normally have provided sufficient grounds for any foreign power to break off diplomatic ties. But the British government avoided that step because, without diplomatic relations, Hong Kong could have been placed in greater jeopardy. Furthermore those British personnel still in China would have lost all remaining shreds of diplomatic protection. Most importantly, the British recognized the burning of the legation as the result of China's Ministry of Foreign Affairs falling temporarily under the sway of the Red Guards. The "wily Saxons" were taking the longer-term view.

◆　　◆　　◆

Tired of the cloistered atmosphere of the Sek Kong officer's mess, I had by now moved into the Sheung Shui Country Club. This delightful establishment, of which no trace now remains, was nowhere near as pretentious as it sounded, and was in fact less a club than a rather select holiday home. Here one dwelt in chalets spilling down a gentle hillside set just above and beyond the little market town from which the "club" took its name. Its principal buildings, converted from a private home designed by an architect and modelled on classical Chinese lines, formed a rambling assemblage of halls with tiled roofs and circular, moon-gate doorways, linked by courtyards and covered walkways with occasional filigree screens to confuse and discourage evil spirits.

The whole place was redolent of the principles of *feng shui* prescribed in the ancient Chinese art of geomancy, through which one sought to contrive a propitious and harmonious balance between man and nature. Elegant thickets of bamboo protected it on all sides, leaving the occasional gap to afford pleasing prospects of the river winding below. It caused me great pain when I returned some years later to revisit this peaceful and unspoilt retreat, only to find it unaccountably in ruins and the hill on which it had stood in an advanced state of excavation to make way for what would presumably become a crowded new resettlement estate.

During my Sheung Shui sojourn I was joined, briefly, by GIS colleague Gerry Xavier, while Gatlin Lin had been recalled to headquarters because of the decline in photo opportunities. Our principal duties were to escort local and overseas media representatives on trips to Sha Tau Kok, where we were confined to the rooftop of the fire station, and to a hill overlooking Lo Wu station. On one of these expeditions I had the pleasure of accompanying Larry Burrows, the famed photographer for LIFE magazine. I found him a charming man and was much saddened when he died covering the South Vietnamese invasion of Laos on February 10th 1971. During the unprecedented refugee influx of 1962, when China had briefly lifted controls and allowed thousands to pour across the border, Larry had captured some haunting images of those we had rounded up and repatriated.

Most days I would follow a routine that began when Ah Lum drove me to Sek Kong down quiet country roads, past villages that had not greatly altered in their distribution, size and appearance since the British conducted their first census of the New Territories following the grant of the ninety-nine year lease in 1898. None of these long-standing settlements rose as high as the tops of the acacias, sweet gums and groves of bamboo that bordered them. Some, like the Kat Hing Wai walled village at Kam Tin, were still buried behind embattlements of thick and ancient stone.

The forefathers of Kat Hing Wai, seeing British troops appear before their doors in 1898, had shut themselves in and barred their iron gates, claiming they had been told nothing about any lease. When they refused to come out, the troops broke down and removed the gates, which were presented to Governor Sir Henry Blake. On his retirement, Sir Henry took them with him and set them up in his home in Ireland. Not until May 25th 1925, after the villagers had petitioned for their restoration, were they welcomed back with a special ceremony of propitiation.

I would generally get to my office in the PolMil complex well before the others assembled for the morning briefing, which in those days was primarily concerned with the progress of talks to recover our missing police trio. The Hong Kong delegation to these discussions, comprising district commissioner Kenneth Kinghorn, his deputy David Akers-Jones and the government's assistant political adviser, would be conducted across the Lo Wu bridge to a flag-bedecked hall on the other side, where the meetings would commence with readings from Chairman Mao's quotations and then get down to the principal issues. These involved compensation for crops on our side that had been left untended as a result of the Man Kam To bridge closure, removal of barbed wire from certain fields and of course the question of precisely who was going to be included in the exchange of detainees.

The returning delegation would board a waiting helicopter at Lo Wu which flew them direct to Hong Kong Island, where they reported to the Governor. Integral to the debate on how Hong Kong should respond to the demands was a committee that met at PolMil under the chairmanship of Brigadier Peter de C. Martin, commander of 48 Brigade. Because its members were drawn from the police, army and New Territories administration, this committee was given the acronym PAGENT and would survive the more immediate issues to formulate longer-term policy for dealing with illegal immigration, strengthening of the border fence and replacement of the Bailey bridge at Lo Wu with something more efficient and durable.

Brigadier Martin was another of those infected with the incurable British propensity for turning gravity to levity. He came up with a design for an exclusive necktie with which all of us involved might commemorate those exceptional times. It consisted of successive layers of thin red lines, white-skinned pigs and yellow running dogs on a green background. I never found the courage to wear mine in public.

One morning I arrived at Sek Kong to find a familiar but bedraggled figure standing barefoot in the PolMil courtyard, in animated discussion with two military officers who seemed at a loss to know how to deal with him. He was Frank Knight, the police inspector who had been abducted at Man Kam To and who formed a key component of the package deal we had just concluded with the Chinese, after much prolonged and laborious discussion. Despite his prodigious girth, he claimed to have escaped through a window from the hut where he was being held prisoner. He had literally walked out of China without anyone noticing. From the sidelong glances the military men were exchanging I suspected they would dearly love to smuggle him back before his absence was detected.

Although Frank had flown the coop, greatly diminishing the opposition's bargaining hand, the talks continued and led to an agreement whereby our two missing constables were to be returned at Man Kam To, in exchange for those detainees who were to be released from our custody and who would be handed back at Lo Wu. Precisely why this simultaneous interchange was to take place at two widely separated points along the border I have never been able to fully understand, but my task was to observe the transaction at Lo Wu station.

Stevenson provided me with a photographer and impressed upon me that I was to keep him concealed from view. It had been agreed by both negotiating parties that there was to be no photographic coverage of the exchange, so that our record was merely a precaution, "just in case" the other side went back on their word. I duly positioned myself with our cameraman behind the stationmaster's office on the platform at Lo Wu, and was busy briefing him, on how careful he must be to remain under cover, when I noticed that we were being overheard by a policeman standing nearby and clearly in charge of the five or so men accompanying him.

I asked the constable why he was there and who were the men with him.

"They're the prisoners we're exchanging," he smilingly assured me.

Who by now had heard every word of my instructions to our photographer.

It had been agreed that the exchange would take place at precisely five pm. Kinghorn was in charge of the Man Kam To end of this operation while Akers-Jones was handling the arrangements at Lo Wu. The two were in touch through those bulky walkie-talkie radio sets of the "Roger, over and out" variety that were employed for two-way communications in those days. Punctually at five o'clock Kinghorn came on the line to inform Akers-Jones that the word was "go". Akers-Jones, assuming this was intended to alert him to some last-minute code word that would signal the precise moment of the exchange, nodded and continued pacing the platform.

Those on the Chinese side must have fine-honed their own two-way communications because shortly afterward Kinghorn came back on the line to ask what was happening, since our policemen had already been returned and the party who had surrendered them were becoming unaccountably restive. The same heightened tension had become apparent at the far end of the Lo Wu bridge, where a joyous homecoming reception had been prepared by a large crowd impatiently awaiting their own returnees.

The hiatus resolved, and the exchange duly completed, we breathed a collective sigh of relief at the close of another chapter in those strangely disturbed days along the seismological fault zone between two separate and distinct cultures.

Beyond the Watershed

By the close of 1967 it was clear even to the most radical of left-wingers in Hong Kong that they had lost their battle to topple the government. However their frustration served only to exacerbate the ruthless hard-core elements, who refined the sophistication of their booby-trapped bombs to trick the sorely-taxed disposal teams manned both by the police and the army. Over a seven-month span these had responded to some nine thousand incidents. At least one military ammunition examiner was killed during this period and another seriously injured when run over by a Chinese motorist while kneeling to dismantle a suspicious package on a traffic island.

The early improvised explosive devices had been manufactured by stripping the black powder from firecrackers and adding a triggering mechanism, but the later ones incorporated photo-electric cells and other systems that could defeat all but the most practised and experienced experts. These took a cruel toll, and the sheer vindictiveness of their creators lingered on years after the "struggle" had petered out. As late as the early 1970s, one particularly brave police officer, Norman "Bomber" Hill, who had survived many previous attempts on his life, lost both hands and suffered extensive facial injuries as the result of an especially nasty contraption he had been called upon to deal with in the grounds of the Central Government Offices in Lower Albert Road.

In the spring of 1968 the New China News Agency requested a meeting with governor Trench and Jack Cater to discuss issues of the "struggle" and to "restore the stability" of Hong Kong. But Trench felt stability had already been restored. "We knew earlier that the local Communists' campaign had been haphazard and misdirected; and there was a good deal of evidence that they had been dissatisfied with the amount of assistance they received from across the border," Trench reported to the Foreign Office.

"It was clear that they steadily lost support. Now, their 'struggle' has little effect on the daily life of the colony…Do we really need to talk? Is there anything we need to discuss? I do not think so."

Given the gradual resumption of political order and internal stability, the government had begun to direct its attention to speedy restoration of the economy. Trench said, "At present the principal threat to the colony appears to be the risk of long-term economic stagnation caused by reluctance to invest. If the policy of reviving trade with Hong Kong is pursued, it will become more difficult subsequently for the Communists to revert to the aim of making the colony an 'economic desert', and to encourage terrorist activities that might have the same effect."

But this reversion to earlier, largely external priorities was viewed with concern by those who felt the administration was neglecting a golden opportunity to build upon the goodwill demonstrated by the great mass of the people it governed. Surely it would be foolish of the government to slide back into the attitude that had prevailed throughout colonial history—based on the belief that the Chinese had no interest in the way Hong Kong was administered and that there was accordingly no need either to inform them or to seek their advice and consent.

The events of 1967 had caused what had hitherto seemed a transient population to earnestly re-examine their perception of Hong Kong, which suddenly appeared less a temporary abode and more a place worth fighting for and holding on to. By failing to recognise that fundamental shift in the groundswell of public opinion, we risked losing all the good that this otherwise ill wind had blown our way. Fortunately we woke up to that danger just in time, and the whole relationship between government and the people became closer and more intimate than it had ever been before.

If only that eccentric old John Pope Hennessy had lived that long! Certainly 1967 marked a watershed in my own attitude towards the territory. I divide my Hong Kong experience into three distinct eras—the two years that preceded 1967, the next thirty years leading up to the handover, and the decade that has followed our return to China.

To enhance public participation in public affairs, the government began appointing committees to advise on its various policies, their members comprising individuals with established expertise or familiarities in the appropriate fields. By 1980, more than a hundred and fifty advisory bodies would be established, forming a comprehensive network through which to sieve policy initiatives and legislative proposals. *Government by consensus* was the catch phrase of the new order, and *bridges of communication* were the construction task allotted to its newly established wing of public relations, which became an integral component of Government Information Services. Heading this wing was Major David Ford, who had come out on secondment from the army in the later months of 1967 and was later joined by fellow officer Bernard Renouf Johnston, better known as "Johnnie".

Growing numbers of citizens took an interest in this promising trend. Letters of considered political opinion or earnest criticism appeared with greater frequency in the readers' columns of the *South China Morning Post,* which were no longer the chief reserve of an expatriate minority or the principal organ of its discontent.

Gearing, perhaps a little belatedly, for Hong Kong's self-evident transition from a small trading port with an agricultural heartland to a major manufacturing centre with an increasingly affluent, educated and expectant populace, the government also instituted a chain of city district offices. Serving as training ground for its most promising young cadets, these provided points of personal contact through which the administration could descend to grassroots level and apply an ear to any rumblings of dissatisfaction.

Increasingly there was a semblance of a hitherto preoccupied bureaucracy almost anxious to bare itself to scrutiny, willing to listen, eager to respond. Some departments went so far as to appoint their more personable officers to follow phone-in radio talk shows that might touch upon their portfolios. Instant accessibility to responsive civil servants became the goal, if not the norm. It didn't all happen overnight; some of it might not materialise for a few more years, but 1968 was ground zero for this explosive and brand new epoch.

Meanwhile, I had to adjust back to a more routine role in GIS. With Bill Fish gone to the Trade Development Council, and new expatriate recruits—including Adam Lynford and Peter Iliffe-Moon—arriving to share the burden of writing feature articles and taking care of a new magazine we had launched, there was a vacancy for a publications editor to take charge of all other publishing requirements. With this assignment came promotion to the rank of principal information officer, and an opportunity to undertake new initiatives. Catering to the newly awakened appetite for more information on the workings of government, I launched the first of a series of fact sheets describing the role and services of each of its departments, for free dissemination through the newly inaugurated city district offices.

As a thanksgiving for the way in which Hong Kongers had rallied together through the dark times we had just survived, the administration also went for the trusted "bread and circuses" recourse favoured by Roman emperors. In December 1969 the first Festival of Hong Kong was staged, with a crowded week of programmes including musical and sporting events, exhibitions, youth rallies and special displays. Succeeding Roy Wraight as GIS's new art director, Arthur Hacker arrived just in time to design the festival logo, a kind of giant beach ball in alternating orange and white stripes that adorned banners all over town.

With Hong Kong resuming "business as usual" I took a week off to visit neighbouring Macau, sailing there overnight in the stubby old ferry *Fat Shan*. I had a cabin to myself and leaned on the rails outside when we departed just before midnight, slipping slowly past the glowing incandescence of Hong Kong Island. Chinese novelist Li Feigan, writing under the pen name Ba Jin, described just such a night, much earlier that century, when his ship threaded a course through Hong Kong harbour and a friend summoned him from his cabin to view the spectacle:

> "There were lights on the mountains, on the streets and on the buildings. Each light was like a tiny star, but to me they seemed brighter and more splendid than stars. In their dense array they resembled a mountain of stars, shining endless beams of light in the night sky. The night was soft and still. Not a sound was to be heard from the shore; Hong Kong seemed to have shut its great mouth. Yet when I gazed upon that

scintillating mountain of stars, I could hear the lights whispering to each other."

The lumbering progress of the *Fat Shan* put me in mind of the movie *Ferry to Hong Kong*, made in 1959 and based on the real-life case of one those unfortunate stateless persons, denied entry to any country, who drift in limbo, either stranded in airport terminals or aboard vessels endlessly travelling between inhospitable destinations. In the fictional movie scenario, the victim of international administrative bungledom is a fugitive from Vienna, played by Curt Jurgens, condemned to eternal shipboard life on a ferry shuttling between Hong Kong and Macau. As a reporter for the *Malay Mail* in Kuala Lumpur, I had interviewed my hero, Orson Welles, on his way back to Europe after portraying the captain of this rundown ferry. It proved to be a disappointing B movie, and clearly a film he wished to put out of his mind as soon as possible, although he had taken the opportunity to privately obtain movie footage of himself running through the ladder streets and alleyways of Hong Kong, with a view to some other purported movie of his own that—like too many of his ventures—never saw the light of day.

At five in the morning the cabin attendant awoke me to announce that we had berthed in Macao. I went on deck to find us tethered alongside a jetty where murky figures moved by the light of ill-spaced street lamps. I had an hour in which to freshen up and vacate my cabin before going ashore with my passport, visa and single suitcase. A taxi conveyed me along the Praya Grande, still looking much as it had when resident artist George Chinnery rendered it in countless sketches and paintings dating from the pre-Hong Kong era of Britain's desperate efforts to gain a toe-hold on the China coast. My destination was the Hotel Bella Vista, a crumbling but gracious old hostelry overlooking the Praya Grande, where I was allocated a second floor room where the vista was bella indeed.

Despite the rude shock of the spillover from the cultural revolution two years earlier, Macau had remained a delightful, easygoing backwater, seemingly caught in an endless siesta, light years removed from the ceaseless pace and energy of Hong Kong. Its prospects for expansion were curtailed by a totally inadequate electricity supply. The power generators

Beyond the Watershed   143

working at peak load were providing only about two-thirds of the actual consumption needs. Consequently, the Lisboa Casino Hotel, then at the heart of the monopoly on gambling held by Stanley Ho and his empire, had invested in one group of generators and had ordered another, yet were still unable to open more rooms due to insufficiency of power supply.

Factories couldn't function normally as they had power for only part of their equipment and that too was unstable, constantly putting their equipment at risk from the impossibility of ensuring an acceptable voltage level. Elevators in high-rise buildings were not functioning properly; newly constructed flats and offices could not be used as the power company couldn't wire them up. Telecommunications and hospital equipment suffered serious disturbances, air conditioners in homes and offices were unable to perform according to specification, fluorescent tubes could not be turned on and incandescent bulbs were weakly lit. Engineers described the situation as "chaotic".

Not until a total revamping of the power infrastructure in the eighties was Macau able to embark on the boom that has since made it one of the most incongruously motley communities in Asia—part historical heritage, part adventure-land theme park and part Asiatic Las Vegas. I sometimes feel an irrepressible urge to smuggle myself back there and blow up a generator or two.

One always returned to Hong Kong, even then, feeling one had been away years rather than a few days. It was hardly possible to turn one's back without spinning around to see a building that wasn't there before. As further proof of the fact that we had turned another corner, it was announced that Hong Kong would be taking part in its first world Expo, scheduled to open in Osaka, Japan, in 1970. Grahame Blundell, previously employed by the Rank Xerox organisation to promote its latest photocopying machines with flying visits to key European capitals, was recruited to coordinate the design and preparations for the Hong Kong pavilion. Grahame was like no one I had ever worked with before. He was a dyed-in-the-wool showman, part Serge Diaghilev of the Ballet Russes, part Barnum & Bailey circus impresario. His mind was like a box of fireworks to which somebody had accidentally applied a match.

He engaged architect Alan Fitch, who had designed City Hall and Statue Square, to come up with an effective concept for the pavilion. The challenge was to best express the idea of Hong Kong in an eye-catching way that would differ from all others and command attention in a global arena where far bigger exhibitors were showcasing entire countries and continents. Competition was fierce. The Osaka showgrounds at Senrei Hills, miles out of the city centre, would end up with ninety-five international pavilions and thirty-two Japanese pavilions spread across eight hundred and fifteen acres. There would be five entrances and parking for twenty thousand cars and one thousand five hundred tour buses, as well as eighteen information boards, five types of female guide (in colour-coordinated uniforms), a hundred and ten clocks, nineteen post boxes, twenty-nine guard stations, a hundred guard boxes, two hundred and fourteen restaurants and snack bars, fifteen food inspectors, four hundred wheelchairs, seventy thousand copies of a special guide book for those using these wheelchairs (with another ten thousand copies in braille), fifty closed-circuit remote-control TV cameras, one thousand four hundred baby strollers, ten thousand umbrellas, one hundred emergency phones, seven thousand telephones, one thousand two hundred special Expo guard corpsmen, a free dental clinic and strategically placed first aid stations.

The Japanese had thought of everything. They simply forgot to inform their customs officials, who would play havoc with the importation of exhibits and enrage all exhibitors with impracticable and unreasonable demands. This was somewhat surprising in view of the fact that Japan's first participation in an overseas exposition was in London more than a hundred years earlier, in fact way back in 1861. The first official Japanese pavilion was displayed at the Paris Expo in 1867 and the first participation of Japan's Meiji government in an international exposition was at Vienna in 1873.

The Mikado, Gilbert and Sullivan's best-loved operetta, was the result of Gilbert dropping in on an exhibition of Japanese culture that was visiting London in 1885. He purchased an elaborate Japanese sword, which he mounted over the doorway to his study. Frustrated by the slump in popularity that the so-called Savoy operas were experiencing at the time, he was bent over his desk, lost for the inspiration he craved for the next production, when the sword's mounting broke, causing the weapon to fall to the ground like an omen carefully precipitated by a diligent muse. Gilbert claimed that this trivial incident prompted him to write his comedy about a Japanese executioner.

Japan had initially submitted a bid to host an international exposition in 1940, to commemorate the 2600th anniversary of the country's foundation. Its government invited the world's leading composers to contribute specially commissioned works for this event. Richard Strauss responded with a piece entitled *Festmusik zur Feier des 2600-jährigen Bestehens des Kaiserreichs Japan* (Op. 84), which did neither the occasion nor Strauss himself much credit, and is almost forgotten today, while Benjamin Britten contributed what has proved the finest of all his orchestral works with his *Sinfonia da Requiem, Op. 20.* Unfortunately the Japanese considered this too gloomy, reduced their planned celebrations to low priority and decided to wage war instead.

In the long-delayed aftermath of that disastrous miscalculation, Japan was now set to become only the third nation to host a category one exposition since that global conflict so mysteriously and ominously presaged by Britten's seminal musical threnody. The overall exposition plans for Senrei Hills were finalised by thirteen architects in January, 1968. The layout resembled a tree in bloom with a central "symbol area" as the trunk. The monorail, moving sidewalks and seven sub-plazas—all of them painted white—symbolized the "boughs", and the colorful pavilions represented the blossoms of one gigantic cherry blossom tree. Unfortunately the sheer scale of all this symbolism meant that it would only become apparent from the air, if you were privileged to fly over Senrei Hills in a satellite, hot air balloon, airliner or helicopter.

But how was Hong Kong going to make an impact at this first international exposition ever to be held in Asia, which would attract an eventual total of sixty-four million visitors? Alan Fitch came up with a design for a relatively low, flat-topped roof, surrounded by water. The roof would serve as "deck" space where, twice a day, thirteen large, bat-winged sails were to be ceremoniously raised and lowered, reminiscent of a fleet of traditional

Chinese junks either setting out for or returning from their fishing grounds. To avoid the possibility of a sudden and violent gust of wind catching the sails at full mast and lifting the entire pavilion into the sky—embarked on an aerial voyage in majestic, Jules Verne fashion across to the other side of the Senrei Hills—it was necessary to come up with a porous material to substitute for the sailcloth; something suitably russet-coloured and authentic-looking but impervious to all but the strongest typhoon squalls, of which we should expect plenty of warning.

Looking for somewhere to live during the prolonged preparations for this pavilion, Grahame came out to lunch and was greatly taken by the ambiance of Silverstrand. So he applied for it on the next quartering list and got exactly the flat he wanted in the block next door to mine, just in time for the arrival, from Finland, of his fiancée Lisbet. Small, gamin-like and much younger than Grahame, combining the looks of Elke Sommers and Brigitte Bardot, Lisbet was his equal in her intellectual range, sense of humour and love of life. They were about as perfectly matched as any couple I had ever met and I was honoured to be best man at their wedding.

One of our first outings together on Lisbet's "familiarisation" tour of the colony included a visit to the large China Arts emporium in newly-built Star House, opposite the Tsim Sha Tsui terminal of the Star Ferry. In those early days, immediately following the disturbances of the year before, this was still suffering the sharp decline in business engendered by the massive boycott imposed by the local populace, so that we were virtually the only customers in the establishment. I had long hankered after the artifacts directly inspired by the Cultural Revolution, and was especially attracted to the tableaux exquisitely carved in wood or ivory, depicting Red Guards either marching in triumphant unison or vigorously opposing the "reactionary elements" they saw as a threat to the reforms on which they were engaged. The care lavished on these singular works of art was as great as any to be found on the most elaborate of traditional subjects such as flowing-robed gods and goddesses, crouching tigers and cloud-hidden dragons, yet I sensed this was a fleeting and ephemeral art form that would never be repeated.

Beyond the Watershed   147

Lisbet admired them too, but this admiration was undermined by a particular piece which—characteristically—showed a pair of diminutive and terrified imperialists put to flight by an angry posse of righteous peasants, armed with scythes, pitchforks and the ideological convictions inspired by their little red books. Something about the expressions on the frightened faces of the fleeing foreigners triggered Lisbet's hilarity, which at the best of times was never far from the surface. She was reduced to helpless gales of laughter, so infectious that Grahame and I were swept away by them ourselves.

From the corner of my eye I caught the outraged looks on the faces of the staff, who appeared to be edging towards us as fast as I was trying to herd my companions towards the door. We made it to the exit in time and I have regretted ever since that we never stood our ground long enough for me to purchase the piece in question, for today—aside from a plethora of Mao badges—it is seldom possible to encounter the best of those by-products from that extraordinary hiatus in China's history.

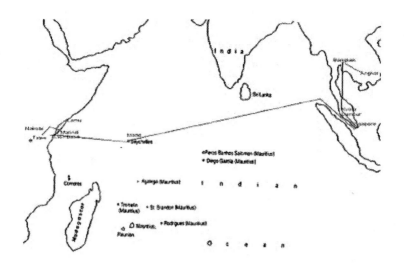

A map of my voyage home in 1968–69

Before the Killing Fields

At the onset of winter in 1968, having completed my three-year contract with the Hong Kong government I was offered—and accepted—another. But first I intended to make maximum use of the six-month spell of home leave to which I was entitled, in those days when the administration still permitted such enormous paid vacations on the grounds that much of that time would be taken up by the ocean voyage home and back. Never mind that by now relatively few were bothering to travel by sea when, for the equivalent cost of a sea passage, one could fly to an infinitely greater variety of destinations en route.

I planned a protracted itinerary that would begin with Cambodia, and take me on to Bangkok, Kuala Lumpur and Singapore, where I would board a cargo ship for a crossing of the Indian Ocean to the Seychelles and then on to Mombasa in East Africa. The ruins of Angkor, the sea voyage and a tour of the game parks of Kenya and Tanzania were the three lynch-pins of this odyssey.

Like many others, I had fallen under the spell of Angkor long before I ever got to visit it. Buried in the jungle, and sunk into ruin and mythology long before its supposed "rediscovery" by Henri Mouhot, it encapsu-lated—more effectively than any other residual trace of a once-great civili-sation—the romance of all of history's dead and forgotten ages. Percy Bysshe Shelley's poem *Ozymandias of Egypt* dates from 1818, long before Mouhot gazed in stunned silence at the two hundred enigmatic faces of Avalokitesharva, but it expresses no less forcefully the awe engendered by such encounters. One need only substitute a wasteland of sand, for the tangled forest giants that embraced the crumbling towers of the Bayon, to ponder the ephemeral nature of all man's works:

"I met a traveller from an antique land
Who said:—Two vast and trunkless legs of stone
Stand in the desert. Near them on the sand,
Half sunk, a shatter'd visage lies, whose frown
And wrinkled lip and sneer of cold command
Tell that its sculptor well those passions read
Which yet survive, stamp'd on these lifeless things,
The hand that mock'd them and the heart that fed.
And on the pedestal these words appear:
'My name is Ozymandias, king of kings:
Look on my works, ye mighty, and despair!'
Nothing beside remains: round the decay
Of that colossal wreck, boundless and bare,
The lone and level sands stretch far away.

My eagerness to visit Angkor was first ignited by Brian and Moyreen Tilbrook, who had paid so many visits there, starting with Christmas 1962, that on the basis of their varied experiences they already qualified for description as anchorites. On one of those visits, Brian was incensed to find, affixed to a door in the Auberge du Temple, the label "Lord Jim", which he took to be an arrogant presumption on the part of its current very transient incumbent. He quickly learned that many other doors in the establishment bore the same label, identifying the accommodations reserved for the crew and cast of the film of that title, based on Joseph Conrad's classic tale which would use Angkor for some of its key settings. So large was the entourage for this production that Columbia Pictures constructed a commodious extension to the hotel, which they subsequently donated to its management.

Brian gave me one of the paintings he had executed on his first visit, sketched in the unkempt precincts of Ta Prohm, left largely in the jungle's embrace and much as Mouhot had first chanced upon it. At Angkor, said Mouhot, "there are ruins of such grandeur that, at the first view, one is filled with profound admiration, and cannot but ask what has become of this powerful race, so civilized, so enlightened, the authors of these gigantic works?"

My own visit to Angkor was further foreshadowed by a marvellous film shot in the early sixties by my friend, Hugh Gibb, maker of independent documentaries on obscure aspects of Asia which were screened by BBC television. Hugh told me he had received considerable assistance in his Angkor endeavours from Norodom Sihanouk, Cambodia's wily, cultivated and energetic head of state, who had expressed keen interest in the project because he too was a prolific film-maker, producing, directing and setting music for no less than twenty-eight of his own films, many using Angkor as their subject matter.

Sihanouk intrigued me almost as much as Angkor. Here was a man who had obtained Cambodia's independence from France, abdicated in favour of his father, Norodom Suramarit, founded a political party under the name of the People's Socialist Community, swept to power as prime minister with eighty-two percent of the votes cast, proclaimed his country's neutrality at the first Afro-Asian conference of Bandung and cocked a snoot at America when that giant entered the imbroglio in neighbouring Vietnam. He seemed half lovable clown and half consummate gymnast, dancing on his lone high wire without a safety net above Asia's political arena. Should he fall, one anticipated he could never survive.

He did fall, and he did survive. Unlike Humpty Dumpty, he put himself back together again, piece by astonishing piece.

On March 1970, little more than a year after my visit to his capital at Phnom Penh, he was deposed in the course of an official visit to the Soviet Union, when he became the victim of a coup d'état engineered by Lon Nol and Sirik Matak, who would plunge the country into a bloodbath and annihilate a third of its population on the killing fields. From his exile in China, Sihanouk would work tirelessly to overcome the perpetrators of that slaughter, treading as thin and perilous a tightrope as he had ever dared until, on September 24th 1993, he would be unanimously elected both Cambodia's king and its head of state for life. Exhibited at a round-about on the banks of the Tonle Sap river, when I was in Phnom Penh, was the wreck of an alleged American spy plane which Sihanouk had arranged to display as a reminder that Cambodia would brook no interference with its internal affairs. The plane was clearly incapable of rising, phoenix-like, from its ashes to fly again. But Sihanouk rose from his, and is still flying.

Fascinating though Phnom Penh was, with its palaces and temples, it wasn't old enough. I flew on myself, to lodge at the Auberge du Temple, opposite the gates of Angkor Wat, whose serried stupas and spires rose like the gibbosities of some gigantic astronomical device, ensnaring and deciphering the auguries encrypted in the last rays of a dying sun. White-jacketed, tuck-trousered hotel staff, their young and cherubic faces glowing in the twilight, provided a latter-day reincarnation of a Bayon fresco as they decked the trees in the hotel grounds with fairy lamps in preparation for the coming Christmas.

Grahame and Lisbet Blundell were due to fly out from Hong Kong to join me on Christmas Eve, but for the moment I had to myself that whole sprawling temple complex, embracing some sixty distinct structures dating back to the ninth century and earlier. I would replay for my friends the role that the Tilbrooks had played for me, and indeed others had played for Mouhot, who was not the first to stumble across these ruins. Before his time, there had been rumours and even tangible reports of the existence of a mysterious ancient kingdom in Cambodia. D.O. King, an English explorer, had made an expedition to the Angkor region, returning to lecture on his travels, and to report that only one temple of the ancient Cambodian capital remained. E.J.F Forrest, another English explorer, visited the region in the 1830s or 1840s. From documents that survive, he too appeared to have had some knowledge of the temples.

So why did Mouhot get all the credit for seeming the first to stumble across that lost citadel? Primarily because he wrote more evocatively, for a wider audience, illustrating his account with lively sketches, and partly because he had died in the jungles of Laos before that account was published, so that—like Angkor itself—he appeared to address his readers from beyond the grave. *Encyclopedia Britannica* describes him as the French naturalist and explorer who "alerted" the West to the ruins of Angkor.

Of all those ancient relics, none impressed me more than the exquisite red sandstone jewel of Banteay Srei and the gray-green wreckage of Ta Prohm, tossed and scattered as by the upheavals of a subterranean dragon, turning in its sleep. The latter's remaining walls, arches and turrets were seized in the talons of giant trees, and smothered in their roots as though drowning in the molten wax of giant candles. But glad as I was to have Angkor briefly to myself, I was delighted when Grahame and Lisbet arrived to join me. Together we travelled yet farther afield on many modes of transport, including hired bicycles, *motodups* (motorcycle-rickshaws) and, one evening of romantic excess, atop stately elephants traversing the distance from Angkor Wat to the Bayon.

On the evening of December 27th 1968 we were returning to our hotel from Siem Reap, sharing one of those motorised pedicabs, when we saw a pinpoint of light slowly traversing a rich backcloth of stars. We had been following by radio the mission of the *Apollo 8* spacecraft, which took off atop a Saturn V booster from the Kennedy Space Centre on December 21st, with three astronauts aboard—Frank Borman, James A. Lovell, Jr., and William A. Anders—for a historic mission to orbit the moon. As it travelled outward on its lunar trajectory the crew had focused a portable television camera on earth so that, for the first time, humanity had seen its home fixed in the great universal order of things; a lovely but tiny "blue marble" suspended in the blackness of space.

Now that winged messenger was returning, in readiness for its "splash-down" in the Pacific Ocean, and we were seeing it from the perspective of an extinct civilization, whose survivors still believed the holy Khmer rabbit *Pouthesat* lived on in the moon after surrendering his life to feed his friend *Preah Ean*. No other moment in that brief visit did more to mark us as strangers in an antique land.

Not two years later, in the aftermath of the carnage the Khmer Rouge wreaked in that lost world, I would feel compelled to look back and recall the passive faces of those inhabitants with whom we had come into con-tact—the pedicab drivers, hotel employees, women who had served us drinks and snacks at wayside stalls—wondering which, out of every three, had died in the genocide of the killing fields.

◆   ◆   ◆

From Siem Reap I travelled to Bangkok in a battered turbo-prop Vis-count of Burma Airlines, flying on auto-pilot and buffeted all over the sky in heavy turbulence while its captain and co-pilot sat facing each other, unshod feet up on their respective armrests and smoking cheroots. After a few days with Thai friends, revisiting familiar scenes in their fast-expand-ing, traffic-constipated capital, I flew on to Kuala Lumpur to stay with my former colleague and flat-mate Gerry Jackson.

The old offices we had shared in Pudu Road were no more. All three newspapers, the *Straits Times, Malay Mail* and *Berita Harian,* had moved to their new combined headquarters at Jalan Riong in Bangsar, so Gerry had shifted to a modern, two-storey dwelling overlooking them from a rise nearby. With him was cook and houseboy Khairuddin, still "the perfect Jeeves" but as critical as ever of Gerry's gargantuan appetite and lifestyle, together with his insensitive expectation that Khairuddin should continue serving him foods that good Muslims were not supposed to cook.

Before proceeding on leave I had sent Mukti, Asarah and the boys ahead of me to stay with Mukti's parents at Kampong Ijok, on the wind-ing old road to Kuala Selangor. There I joined them with a rented car for a tour of old haunts at Pulau Pangkor and the Cameron Highlands. But this time I sensed all was not quite as it had been before I left Malaysia four years earlier. There was a curious, indefinable tension of the kind that presages a typhoon, when the air is uncannily still and you wait for it to start stirring in a different direction.

In Singapore I boarded a Royal Interocean Lines freighter bound for Mombasa via the Seychelles. This Dutch shipping company, in common with the Norwegian Asia Line, was still accepting small numbers of passengers for its limited cabin accommodations; a concession designed primarily to provide the crew with company rather than the passengers with a less hurried mode of transportation. Once through the Malacca Straits, pausing only at Penang, it was a long, slow, leisurely voyage across a large expanse of open water until we reached that other port Victoria in Mahe, the Seychelles. Here they were just laying the foundations for the archipelago's first airport, pending which its only links with the outside world were by sea, through irregular arrivals of freighters such as ours—on average, barely more than once a month.

Here too, thanks to the impossibility of getting the timing right, I just missed my brother Paul, whose two-year contract with the Seychelles government, as its only information officer, had expired three months earlier, culminating in precisely the kind of East African game park safari that I proposed pursuing myself. Paul and Mary had fallen in love with these sleepy little mid-oceanic islands and their multi-racial population. They wrote me that they greatly regretted the decision to decline a second contract—dictated by the absence of adequate educational facilities for the three children, Nicholas, Kate and Jeremy.

Paul's former secretary, a Seychellois girl possessed of that remarkable beauty displayed by so many of their miscegenated ancestry, learned of my arrival and presented herself as my tour guide, driving me all over Mahe and pressing herself upon me with such ardour that I felt the time could not be far off when I must cool her enthusiasm with a declaration of my true sexual orientation. Her husband was manager of the island's only tea plantation, set on the slopes of its central highlands. She took me to meet him and from his cautious reaction I judged he was weighing me up as another potential threat to an already endangered marriage. I wondered if she had made the same overtures to Paul, and whether these might have accelerated the departure of my monogamous and happily-married brother, so patently in love with the woman to whom he would remain unswervingly faithful throughout his relatively short life.

Despite the unabated attentions of my self-appointed companion, I found time to savour the charm and beauty of Mahe, the friendliness of its natives and an atmosphere that struck me as very reminiscent of some backwater in the Caribbean. We lunched near Beau Vallon at Le Northolme, the hotel where my brother's family briefly resided on their first arrival in the Seychelles, and where others who sojourned at various times included authors Ian Fleming, Somerset Maugham and Noel Coward.

During his spell in the Seychelles, Coward wrote his only novel, *Pomp and Circumstance,* a comic delight set in a fictitious colonial insular possession that is making preparations for its first-ever royal visit and falling over itself to get things right. When he checked out at the end of his stay, the manager of Northolme asked the famous playwright whether he might put up a sign reading, "Noel Coward Slept Here". "Certainly," Coward replied, "if you'll add one word: fitfully."

From Mahe our ship sailed on to Mombasa, where I booked into a charming old-world hotel whose manager was so outrageously gay that local voluptuaries would gather at his table on the terrace every evening to sip tall cocktails, decorated with little umbrellas, and whistle at likely-looking lads passing by in the street below. This extravagant behaviour produced a centrifugal dispersal that scattered other diners to tables on the outer periphery, but the hotel's reputation survived, and its occupancy rate remained high, largely on the strength of its excellent food and service.

In the tiny museum of Mombasa's lovely old Fort Jesus, regarded as one of the finest examples of 16th century Portuguese military architecture, I was astonished to discover a large collection of Chinese pottery. Much of this had been traded along the coast by Arabs, following an expedition, under famed Admiral Zheng He, that brought twenty thousand Chinese sailors and soldiers across the Indian Ocean to Zanzibar, some eighty years before Columbus set sail to prove that the world was round.

Hiring a Volkswagen, I motored north to the six-hundred-year-old ruins of Gede, a Swahili settlement long overgrown by baobabs and tamarind trees, giving it the appearance of a miniaturised African Angkor. Then on to Malindi, where Portuguese navigator Vasco da Gama anchored his caravels in 1498, picking up the Swahili guide who would steer him across the Indian Ocean to the first European landfall on the coast of India.

From Malindi I risked the back roads, stopping several times to dig myself out of ruts and sand traps with the help of local villagers, and entered the great sprawling expanse of Tsavo game park via its Buchuma Gate. Among the world's largest wildlife sanctuaries, Tsavo was established in 1948 and covers more than twenty thousand square kilometres of bush and scrub. It is easy to get lost there, and one's drive is constantly interrupted by the impulse to pause and photograph ostrich families, giraffe duos and herds of zebra and gazelle, or make way for foraging elephants, wreaking massive destruction on sparse vegetation.

When the latter drew uncomfortably close I kept a wary eye on the bulls, which would pause with raised heads, coiled trunks and ears outstretched to sniff the air from my direction, as though daring me to poach their magnificent tusks. I found it did not help to leave both Volkswagen doors wide open in a head-on situation, for this would give the car the appearance of a mocking reflection of that belligerent attitude and cause the bull in question to investigate further, on one occasion prompting my quick reversal and a hasty retreat beyond harm's way.

Somewhere in the middle of Tsavo East I stopped to spend the night at a game lodge by the side of a lake haunted by water birds and ringed by herons, ibises, secretary storks and crowned cranes. Seated in a deckchair outside my chalet, to watch the last of a magnificent sunset sketching the fading silhouettes of flame trees, I became aware of a deep subterranean rumbling, like the onset of an earthquake, which I traced to a family of hippos heading in my direction. I vacated my chair in a trice, dragging it back into the chalet and closing the door behind me just as, through the window, I watched those behemoths rush by at a speed faster than I'd expected of their size and girth, trampling over the spot where I'd sat.

Returning to Mombasa, I headed by air for Nairobi in a plane that was left circling the latter's airport for the best part of an hour because President Jomo Kenyatta had just returned in style from an official overseas visit and was taking his time inspecting the guard of honour. His recently published biography, *Suffering Without Bitterness,* had described his nine-year prison sentence on charges of leading the Mau Mau rebellion.

Staying at the Stanley Hotel, I decided to make an exception to my rule against travelling with tour groups by booking to join a party of four on an extended safari that would cross the boundary with Tanzania and cover the game parks of Amboseli, Masai Mara, Serengeti and Ngorongoro. Seated throughout that extended journey on the unforgiving front bench of our Land Rover, beside our Tanzanian driver, I repeatedly played—at his request—my cassette tape of a Philips recording of the *Misa Criolla,* which sounded to him so African in its tempo that he couldn't accept its South American origin.

By the time I returned to Nairobi I'd had my fill of wild life, staggering scenery and unconventional menus. Even the beauties of Ngorongoro's stupendous crater, swimming in dawn mist through which popped an occasional giraffe head, were not enough to detain me a moment longer. I cancelled my onward booking to Khartoum, whence I had planned to travel overland to Cairo, and instead flew directly back to England and a reunion with my parents.

I was with them at their home in Hastings when we watched in stunned silence the television coverage of race riots that had broken out in Kuala Lumpur, on May 13th 1969. It seemed that thousands of Malays, assembling for a rally to celebrate another victory by UMNO (United Malays National Organization) in the latest elections, had decided to exact revenge for earlier Chinese taunts that this time they might lose their privileged place at the top of the polls. Chinese on motor scooters and in cars were attacked and either wounded or killed, and before long, patches of the city were engulfed in widespread rioting, looting, and bloodshed. When the fires died down, some two hundred were reported dead with many more seriously injured. In the aftermath of the riots, the government imposed emergency powers, suspended the press and parliament, and established a National Operations Council which would ultimately function as a *de facto* government for the next two years.

I had earlier arranged to interrupt my journey back to Hong Kong, first in Malta and then in Athens, where I would meet up with Gerry for a holiday through the Greek isles. Now this unexpected turn of events in Malaysia seemed so fraught that I put through a long-distance call to Gerry to ask if I should cancel those plans and expedite my return via KL instead, in order to recover Mukti and the family and take them back with me to Hong Kong. He said the situation was already under control, and he had received word that Mukti and family were safe in the *kampong*. He suggested I stick to my original itinerary.

So I proceeded to Malta, to stay in Valetta with my Uncle Len and Aunt Zena, who were stationed there for Len's latest posting with the Royal Signals. They took me all over the island, and helped me in my house-hunting errands on behalf of Nigel Watt and Grahame Blundell, both of whom had asked me to investigate the availability of affordable properties. Based on my recommendations, Nigel bought an old farmhouse near Mosta and Grahame purchased another even older dwelling at Zabbar that had once served as a stronghold contributing to Malta's defences against Napoleonic invasion.

At Athens I met up with Gerry for a week on the Aegean coast, sailing with him from Piraeus to Hydra and travelling by coach to Mycenae and the ruined palace of Agamemnon, after which we flew back to KL via Singapore.

Only then did I learn from Mukti the full story of his experiences on that fateful May day a month earlier, hitherto kept from me to avoid needless anxiety. He had set out from Kampong Ijok on the afternoon of May 13th, accompanying the village *ketua kampong* (headman) to take part in the UMNO victory celebrations. They had no inkling of any trouble until they reached Circular Road, in the vicinity of the palatial home of Selangor's *Mentri Besar* (chief minister), Harun Idris, located just to the north of Kampong Bharu. They saw a car burning in the middle of the road and learned this had had been filled with Chinese, waylaid and set alight in their vehicle by Malays. A policeman directed them into the chief minister's home, where—along with several other Malays who had been herded into the premises—they found themselves effectively stranded by the sudden curfew that descended on the city.

The curfew was still in place when, on the night of May 14th, Malaysia's Deputy Prime Minister, Tun Abdul Razak, arrived for a meeting with Idris to discuss the situation. Mukti went up to Razak and complained that he and others from the Kuala Selangor region lacked the means to return home to their families, who must by that time have become extremely worried about them. Razak arranged for Mukti to put a call through to one of the few shophouses in the vicinity of Kampong Ijok in possession of a telephone, through which Mukti alerted his relatives to collect him and his companions in a convoy of trucks early the following morning.

Mukti reassured me that the troubles had been restricted largely to KL and its immediate suburbs. Racial tensions had not penetrated most out-station areas, where the situation was a great deal more relaxed. He invited Gerry and me to the wedding in Kampong Ijok of his younger brother Shariff, where we found, among the guests scattered at tables in the garden, a sizeable group of Mukti's Chinese friends from the local town of Batang Berjuntai. These drank Anchor beer straight from the bottle and clapped Mukti on the back to applaud his skills in Cantonese.

Nevertheless, much as I still loved it, this was no longer the country I had known during my eight years with the *Malay Mail*. The old, easygoing *tida apa* (never mind *lah*) attitude had gone. Something fundamental had changed. The trust was no longer there and would take a long time to restore. I persuaded Mukti that he and the family should return to Hong Kong even before I managed to secure new quarters to replace the flat we had been required—by my terms of service—to surrender at Silverstrand. I would arrange to put them up in a boarding house till we could move into whatever might take its place.

I went to Hong Kong's old Kai Tak airport a week later to watch their plane land, standing alongside a large assembly of middle-aged "White" Russian refugees in the terminal's "waving gallery". The Russians were a hangover from the exodus driven out by the Soviet revolution fifty years earlier. They had sought sanctuary first in China, mainly around Shanghai, and had then joined the mass migration into Hong Kong in the early fifties. Dressed in peasant attire straight out of a Fyodor Dostoeyevsky novel, they were at Kai Tak to bid farewell to friends departing for resettlement in America.

When I met up with the family in the arrivals lounge I found Mazli and Mazlan—now aged eight and six respectively—disconsolate at losing their pet mynah, which Mazlan had tried to smuggle aboard their Malaysian Airways flight in his carry-on bag. While the plane was taxying for take-off, the youngster had been unable to resist taking a peek to see if the bird was comfortably settled. Though it may have been up to that point, it immediately sought the opportunity to escape, flying up and down the economy cabin and raising shrieks of alarm from fellow passengers convinced it was a bat.

Retrieving the errant avian with some difficulty, the boys had been forced to surrender it to the cabin crew. Friends and relatives from Kampong Ijok, still hanging around at KL's Subang airport to watch the plane take off, were astonished to see it return to the terminal, where a broadcast announcement requested them to take delivery of the mynah.

Moon Dust, Shipwrecks and Landslides

I found a room for the family in one of the many boarding houses in Chungking Mansions, fittingly situated near the anus of Kowloon's gastrointestinal tract down Nathan Road. The several towers of this dingy complex, each seventeen stories high, had gained an unsavoury reputation for drug dealing, prostitution and gambling. At street level they formed an intricate maze of narrow arcades, in which you were accosted by touts for the numerous tailors' shops competing for business. To gain access to higher floors you crammed yourself into small, overcrowded and unreliable lifts that conveyed you to warrens of bordellos, alongside cheap and much-frequented Indian restaurants with exotic names, posing as gymkhana clubs and curry parlours.

Later Chungking Mansions would become a hideaway for illegal immigrants from Africa, Nepal, Sri Lanka, Bangladesh, Pakistan and India, subjected to frequent raids by immigration officials who—along with the rest of Hong Kong's administration—seemed unable to achieve any lasting change in this ghetto's unrepentant atmosphere of "anything goes". Only recently has the installation of more efficient management services, and a better security system, led to such a renaissance for Chungking Mansions that old-timers can now only sigh with nostalgia for the bad old days.

While still living at Silverstrand, I had befriended a recently-arrived trio who trekked through India in search of alternative religions and ended up in Hong Kong to replenish their depleted financial reserves. Ross Haig, together with John and Trea Wiltshire, had booked into a Chungking Mansions boarding house, but were disappointed with the lack of facilities to prepare the classical Christmas dinner they had promised themselves after months of culinary deprivation. Since I was invited to join the Tilbrooks at their home in Kennedy Road, while Mukti and family were spending Christmas Eve with their own friends, I offered my apartment as the venue for the joint Haig-Wiltshire celebrations.

Laden with a fake Christmas tree and large quantities of festive fare, including hams, cheeses, Christmas pudding, boxes of crackers and chocolates and of course the obligatory turkey, the threesome were descending one of Chungking Mansions' few escalators when the frozen turkey, rotund and slippery in its plastic wrapping, popped out from under John's arm and went hurtling down the moving stairway, across the length of the arcade, down the steps and over the sidewalk into the traffic lanes. There it was hit by a passing bus and rebounded into the gutter. Shedding strands of tinsel and trailing coils of decorative lights in hot pursuit, John managed to recover it while Trea offered first-aid to an elderly American tourist, overcome by the spectacle of a dead turkey making its posthumous getaway.

Fortunately, my adopted family's residence at Chungking Mansions was hardly longer than the term to which Ross, John and Trea were subjected before they moved to alternative, safer and more comfortable accommodation elsewhere. Ross and Trea had found work writing for the *South China Morning Post* and John had joined the publicity wing of the Trade Development Council. Compelled once again to compete for the paucity of accommodation reserved for bachelor civil servants, I was awarded a tiny apartment on the fourteenth floor of Green Lane Hall, at the top end of Blue Pool Road in Happy Valley.

Until driven away by fatal fevers they attributed—in those unenlightened days—to noxious miasmas emanating from the swamps, Hong Kong's earliest colonial settlers had chosen to live in Happy Valley, which constituted the only sizeable stretch of lowland along the island's north shore. An ancient cemetery on the western flank of this ironically named defile still testifies to the brief life-spans of those borne off by malaria. Hong Kong's second governor, Sir John Davis, sought to ingratiate himself into the favours of an ill-disposed populace by securing funds to drain this valley—ostensibly for health reasons but in reality to indulge their obsession with horse racing, thereby replacing one fever with another.

Moon Dust, Shipwrecks and Landslides   163

Set in the middle of the Happy Valley basin, and founded in 1846, within four years of Hong Kong's inauguration, the Jockey Club had become the world's wealthiest racing establishment. My flat vertiginously overlooked this expansive arena, whose surrounding amphitheatre of high-rise buildings was bathed on race nights in the incandescent glow discharged from high-energy stadium lighting. On those occasions some of my neighbours at Green Lane Hall—mostly policemen—would sit out on their balconies with race cards, binoculars and telephones on extension cords, dialing in their bets.

The move into our new home coincided with the date chosen for man's single greatest technological achievement of all time, when a human would first set foot on another celestial body. My first task therefore was to set up a small black-and-white television receiver in the living room, angle its antenna out the window to pick up a usable signal, and have the kids keep an eye on the screen while Mukti and I were shunting crates and boxes through the front door.

Summoned by the boys, Mukti, Asarah and I joined them around the set to watch blurry images relayed from the moon's surface via NASA's Kennedy Space Centre, some six hours after the actual landing had taken place at 4:17 p.m. Eastern Daylight Time on July 20th 1969. We watched Neil Armstrong take that "one small step for man, one giant leap for mankind" which all thinking men hoped would presage a new future of planetary expansion for the human race. Little did we know then how quickly that hope would die, and how far that epochal event would fade from human memory until it now seems a barely recollected dream.

It so happened that the sky over Happy Valley that night was so clear and still that a waxing crescent moon hovered like Allah's proverbial fingernail over the luminous bowl of Happy Valley. I looked up at it and said "That's where they are night now, Neil Armstrong and "Buzz" Aldrin, walking about on the moon's surface and kicking up those little clouds of dust." Asarah joined me at the window, switching her gaze from the moon to the TV screen and back again. She shook her head in disbelief. "Where's the dust?" she asked. "Why isn't it falling on us?"

164   No Babylon

It saddens me now, thirty-five years later, to see how much stupidity has accumulated, thicker than moon dust, over the intervening years. A search of the Internet, for details of the moon landing, brings up an astonishing web of ignorance and downright malicious deceit, with sites devoted to such abysmal misinformation, based on incomplete research and manipulated facts, as "The Moon Shots Were Faked" and "Was the Moon Landing a Hoax?" At times like these it seems the intelligence quotient of the human race is regressing in inverse ratio to our ability to compute the data we process.

I am reminded of the conversation Ernest Harnach and I enjoyed as dinner guests of Arthur C. Clarke in 1975, when we discussed with him this very eventuality that, through inadequate follow-up, the world's wonder at Armstrong's "giant leap for mankind" would diminish to the point where, if anything, it would seem a giant leap backwards into ennui and cognitive decline. Clarke, whose vision had prompted the collaboration with Kubrick that produced *2001: A Space Odyssey*, was more pessimistic on that score than we were, and I believe has since been proved right.

Among my neighbours at Green Lane Hall was Frank Brett, an executive officer with the urban services department who had been born in Hong Kong before the war and educated at the King George V school. His father was in the marine department, on leave with his family in Australia when the Japanese simultaneously invaded Pearl Harbour, Hong Kong and Malaya. Recalled to Hong Kong, Brett senior sensibly left his family in Sydney and, shortly after reporting for duty, was imprisoned in the Argyle Street POW camp for the duration of the occupation. He was among those who survived that gruelling experience, returning to Australia to collect his family and then serving on in the marine department until his retirement.

Frank, who would eventually retire to Australia himself, occupied an apartment on the tenth floor, directly below mine. He was a great music lover, owned one of the largest record collections I had ever seen, and was extremely generous in loaning these, to imbue in me the same eclectic taste for Stravinsky, Richard Strauss, Wagner, Dvorak, Sibelius, Carl Neilsen, Bohuslav Martinu, Leos Janacek and Francis Poulenc, with diversions into

Schoenberg, Berg and Webern on the side. He also collected obscure original cast recording of Broadway musicals, which constituted one of the two greatest contributions Frank made to my musical education, the other being an absolute obsession with the symphonies and song cycles of Gustav Mahler.

My balcony at Green Lane Hall commanded a sweeping panorama of the whole of Happy Valley and the harbour beyond. On a site just beside us the Jockey Club was busy erecting new air-conditioned stables for its horses. But other than that there was nothing to mar the unbroken vista. Sitting out on this balcony one weekend afternoon, taking advantage of the light to work on one of my acrylic paintings in the German expressionist style I favoured at the time, all of them treating enigmatic subjects drawn from deeply Freudian themes, I was visited by Frank with another stack of records he was willing to loan me. He took one look at my rendering of a titanic pillar of stone, rising in vaguely human form from Amazonian jungles and circled by a miniscule biplane, and then directed his gaze at the crowded basin below, with its racecourse ringed by high-rise residential blocks.

"I don't think you've quite got it," he murmured.

Behind Green Lane Hall were the then largely uncluttered slopes of the island's mountainous spine, cleft by the Wong Nei Chong Gap that led to Repulse Bay, Stanley and the whole of the southern seaboard. A short sharp ascent of the high ground to the east of this gap led to some well-worn trails and footpaths that followed the contour lines encircling these uplands. These were generally named after past dignitaries who had frequented them, and my favourite was Sir Cecil Clementi's Ride, linked to a similar bridle path named after his wife, Lady Clementi. I so often strolled along this trail, pausing to enjoy the magnificent scenic vistas it unveiled, that I composed a poem in honour of its trailblazer:

"Dear Sir Cecil, though hardly lesser,
where other governors gave us roads
left us a modest little ride.
Lady Clementi too, God bless her,
no doubt with Sir Cecil by her side,

spurning the usual social graces,
trotted her mare in unlikely places,
blazing a trail for us would-be-thinners
to work off the guilt of our Christmas dinners.
However at other times of the year,
the weather is far less clement I fear,
So that genteel expatriates turn aside
From the rigours of Cecil Clementi's Ride."

◆　　　◆　　　◆

By the spring of 1970, Gerry Jackson had moved from KL to Tokyo, to establish a Japanese office for the *Straits Times*. Since Grahame and Lisbet Blundell were by now based at Senrei Hills, outside Osaka, I accepted invitations to visit both homes, and consequently embarked on a love affair with Japan, which I shared with Gerry but not with the Blundells, who had been at the receiving end of the worst of Japanese bureaucracy in the preparations for Expo 70.

So marked was the general hostility developed for the latter, among virtually all exhibitors at the Expo showgrounds, that when I accompanied the Blundells to a reception at one of the larger pavilions, the host stood on stage and addressed an audience of well over a hundred guests, declaring "I'm very happy to inform you all that there isn't a single Japanese present at this gathering tonight." A burst of applause and loud cheers greeted this assurance.

Notwithstanding all its preceding trials and tribulations, Expo 70 proved a great success and the Hong Kong pavilion drew large crowds, especially keen to watch the raising and lowering of the junk sails. Leaving the latter's management in good hands for a brief spell of relaxation, Grahame accompanied Lisbet and myself on an outing to Kyoto, Japan's earlier capital and so steeped in priceless historical treasures that American bomber crews had been instructed not to target it on their wartime raids. Suspending their aversion to Japanese officialdom, the Blundells succumbed as readily as I did to Kyoto's glorious temples and gardens and joined me in my hunt for souvenirs in the crowded little alleys of quaint shops and minute eateries serving distinctive Japanese delicacies.

From Osaka I caught the relatively new and astonishingly fast *Shinkansen* "bullet train" to Tokyo, where I tracked down Gerry at his home in Higashi Gotanda, conveniently located near the circular Yamanote Line, whose clockwise trains are known as "*soto-mawari*" (outer circle) and anti-clockwise trains as "*uchi-mawari*" (inner circle). Gerry was renting a house built by one of Tokyo's wealthiest families in the prewar years, when it had been fashionable to incorporate a European-style drawing room into an essentially traditional home. The result was a fascinating contrast, where a semi-Victorian parlour was attached to an utterly Japanese main building with *tatami* mats for floors and white rice paper *shoji* screens for walls. In those fragile surroundings I felt Gerry and I should emulate the cartoon ballet dancers from Disney's *Fantasia*—the hippos and ostriches in their tutus, learning to move around on our points with great care and delicacy.

Gerry suggested a trip to Shimoda, a coastal resort on the Izu peninsula southwest of Tokyo, and David Friend, who taught at historical Waseda University, volunteered to accompany us. One of the elder *gaijins* of Tokyo's expatriate community, David was something of an authority on things Japanese, and an indispensable guide to those new to the country. But like all seasoned foreigners who had spent any length of time in Japan, he employed his love for his adopted home as an argument in defence of his freedom to criticise its imperfections.

Seated on *tetami* mats in our very traditional Japanese *ryokan* inn, over-looking the rooftops of Shimoda's picturesque little fishing port, all three of us uncomfortably cross-legged in our uniform hotel *kimonos* of blue on white, I listened to the complaints of my companions, deploring yet more aspects of Japanese idiosyncrasy. It was not so much a discourse as a contest, in which each opponent awaited a lull in the other's monologue to interject the opening salvo of a riposte which—as often as not—bore no relation to what had just been said.

The match was interrupted only when our middle-aged room attendant, her hair swept back in a bun well clear of her severely dark brown *kimono*, pushed back the *shoji* and, still on her knees, levered herself and her tray, by carefully practised stages, into the room to serve our supper. She set before us not so much a meal as an exquisite work of art; a tableau in which a miniature fisherman, wrought from dough and miscellaneous vegetables, had snared for us the *sushi, soba, tempura* prawns, *udan* noodles and other delectables that looked far too beautiful to eat.

Acknowledging our muttered exclamations of appreciation with a smile and a slight nod of her head, she left Gerry and David struggling to regain supremacy for their resumed soliloquies, which I contrasted with the Nippophobia I had found in the Senrei Hills. I noted an immediate and striking difference; whereas these privileged residential grumblings were voiced more in sorrow than in anger, the others had most decidedly reversed that order. Japan, I felt, was not a country that would care much either way, for it had never set out to be universally loved or understood. Much as it might depend on its trade with the outside world, it wanted—indeed needed—to keep itself at one remove from the rest of the planet; like the clam, in Japanese mythology, whose sealed lips caught the intrusive *kappa* by his toe.

If these islands bore any similarity to another country I had known, that resemblance could not be found elsewhere in Asia but in an archipelago of similar size on the far side of the globe. Rotate the atlas one hundred and eighty degrees and I would find its mirror-image, sitting off the coast of Europe in the identical relationship to that continent as Japan bore to the rest of Asia. Which was why the Japanese, despite baseball and hamburgers, saw their nearest western echo in Britain rather than in America, for they recognised in the British character something of their own reticence and reserve, a similar sense of values and tradition, not to mention a corresponding conviction of their innate superiority.

◆　　　◆　　　◆

The early 1970s brought to Hong Kong a chain of disasters in rapid succession, providing grist to the mill of author James Clavell, who would use at least two of these for his book *Noble House.* The new decade dawned promisingly enough with the arrival in Hong Kong waters of the giant ocean liner *Queen Elizabeth*, formerly the proud flagship of the Cunard line. She had been purchased at auction in 1970 by Taiwanese shipping tycoon C.Y. Tung, father of the man who would become the first head of state of post-colonial Hong Kong in the aftermath of the 1997 handover.

Together with GIS colleagues Keith Robinson, Jonathan Lange and Peter Iliffe-Moon, I went on board at Tung's invitation to report on the renovations that were transforming this fading maritime glory into his dream of a learning centre that would tour the world. It was to be staffed by the cream of academia, tutoring hundreds of international students under the name *Seawise University*, derived from his own initials. Talking to him, it was impossible not to be infected by C.Y.'s enthusiasm for this venture. Unlike his fellow Hong Kong shipping magnate and rival Sir Y.K. Pao, I found C.Y. a man of warmth and ready accessibility, living proof that one could achieve the summits of success without losing one's essential humanity.

In touring his floating colossus, however, I wondered why he had chosen to engage an army of workmen with unmistakable leftist inclinations to bring his Taiwanese ambitions to their ultimate fulfilment. Everywhere we went, from the bridge through the cluttered grandeur of the saloon and ballroom to the engine room below, the metal-encased air reverberated with drills and welding equipment and reeked of hostility, as though a massive resentment was building up against a great deal more than our barely noticeable presence in all that cacophonous expanse.

During the night of August 16th 1971, the colony was hit by one of the most intense and violent typhoons in its meteorologically recorded history. Maximum wind speeds of Typhoon "Rose" were only slightly lower than those of Typhoon "Ruby" in 1964 and Typhoon "Wanda" in 1962, occurring during the night whereas the earlier hurricanes had swept by in daylight. Because the GIS newsroom was always manned on a shift basis for emergency situations, I headed one of the earlier teams while wind strengths were still building up to hurricane force during the evening of the 16th. We were already receiving reports of ships breaking from their moorings and careening directly towards the western anchorage, which was straddled by the immense length of the erstwhile *Queen Elizabeth*.

With storm anchors holding at both ends, that majestic vessel miraculously survived blow after blow as these smaller craft impacted against her hull before being swept on to destruction along the coast of Lantau Island.

Our shift was relieved just before increasing gale or storm signal number nine was hoisted at 9.10 p.m., at which point "Rose" was plotted some fifty miles south-southwest of the Royal Observatory. With colleagues who were also coming off duty, I shared a lift home along deserted, rain-drenched and wind-buffeted roads in a government Land Rover. I found Mukti and Asarah working hard to mop up the rain seeping through the tiniest gaps in window frames, and worried that the glass of the French windows on to the balcony was going to fail, despite the web of adhesive tape we had criss-crossed over the panes to reinforce their resistance.

Hurricane signal number ten was hoisted at 10.50 p.m. as the eye of the typhoon continued to move northwards at ten knots. The air in our sealed flat began to pulse with the hum of a dynamo as wildly vacillating pressure levels ripped the atmosphere outside. At about 1.52 a.m. on August 17th the edge of the typhoon's eye passed close to the west of Cheung Chau Island. By daylight the worst was over. Strong gusts still flayed the windows but it was by now safe enough to step out on the balcony to see the extent of the damage. The sounds of tinkling glass being swept up in neighbouring apartments assured me we had fared better than others, but the sight that first caught my eye from the car park below was a Mercedes-Benz saloon inverted on the roof of a Volkswagen alongside. Some freak blast had tossed it up like a coin and left it in this curiously vulnerable position, swaying like a boulder poised on a pebble.

The roads were still so clogged with debris that I found it safer to walk back to the office, where statistics on the extent of the damage were still coming in. Tragically, fatalities and damage to property had proved the worst since Typhoon "Wanda" in 1962. Over thirty ocean-going vessels had run aground or suffered collision. Some three hundred small craft, including about a hundred pleasure craft, were sunk or damaged. Three of the fourteen hydrofoils on the Hong Kong—Macau run had suffered severely and a total of six Hong Kong & Yaumati ferries had beached while sheltering in Kowloon Bay. Worst of all, the *Fat Shan*, the charming old ferry on which I had made my first trip to Macau, had capsized with the loss of virtually all its crew, while the *Lee Hong*, another ferry laid-up at the time, was also submerged. A chalked tally on the blackboards updated in our GIS newsroom showed total fatalities from Typhoon "Rose" stood at a hundred and ten confirmed deaths, most resulting from the loss of the *Fat Shan*. Of the ninety-two people on board that vessel, there were only four survivors. Elsewhere, two hundred and thirty-six persons were injured, of whom ninety had to be hospitalized.

Jonathan Lange and I were assigned to go up with one of our cameramen in an Auxiliary Air Force helicopter to survey and photograph the worst of the damage around the harbour. Even hours after the storm has passed the air remained so disturbed that I wondered our pilot had volunteered to fly. We were tossed all over the sky, so unpredictably that it would have been impossible to hover over the worst of the wrecks at close quarters, for fear of being drawn into the rigging. I looked down at the *Queen Elizabeth* and marvelled that so huge a target had escaped more or less unscathed, despite al the knocks she had taken from the less fortunate drifting helplessly into her and then ending up on the rocky shoreline of Lantau. Most of those thirty or so more significant wrecks were spread in a great swathe of destruction along the harbour's western periphery, dwarfing the diminutive but infinitely more tragic *Fat Shan*, whose inverted tub of a hull was visible beside the entrance to the treacherous Kap Shui Mun channel.

◆　　　◆　　　◆

Subsequent disasters sparked off government-appointed commissions of inquiry with such regularity they seemed in danger of becoming an annual fixture. The first of these commissions, appointed in November 1971, examined the causes of a horrifying flash fire the previous month aboard the giant "Jumbo" floating restaurant undergoing refitting in Aberdeen harbour. Seventy-one people were killed and sixty injured in this calamity.

Less than three months later, on January 9th 1972, the victim of another fiery inferno was no less than the *Queen Elizabeth* herself, freshly fitted out in her new all-white colours. I couldn't credit my eyes when Mukti drove me round a bend in Magazine Gap Road, on my way to work, to reveal that beautiful ship engulfed in smoke. Nearing completion, in readiness to sail for Japan where she was to be dry-docked in preparation for her maiden voyage as *Seawise University*, she had been set alight in a clear case of arson. Fires had broken out simultaneously at several locations on different decks, and fire doors had been jammed open to hasten the spread of flames licking hungrily off the fresh paintwork. With fire-suppression systems still incomplete, there was nothing to stop the blaze consuming the luxurious wooden interiors and causing the superstructure to melt and cave in on itself.

Fireboats did their best to quench the gathering conflagration, guilty of the same careless miscalculation that had put the giant *Normandie* on her side when—almost exactly thirty years earlier, on February 9th, 1942—that ocean liner too caught fire in New York Harbour. As more water was poured on to both vessels to try to extinguish the flames, the sheer weight of the inundations caused them to list to starboard, so that they ended up half submerged on their sides.

Ironically the revolutionary lines of the *Normandie,* largest ship in the world when she was launched as the pride of France at St. Nazaire on October 29th 1932, had exerted a profound influence on the design of the *Queen Elizabeth*. In order to see what made the *Normandie* as great as she was, Cunard had smuggled one of their people on board, disguised as a grocery clerk on the passenger manifest. His findings resulted in a design for the *Queen Elizabeth* that differed markedly from that of her earlier running mate, the *Queen Mary*.

In her capsized state, the *Seawise University* was deemed a total loss. The decision was taken to scrap her where she lay. However, before the salvage crew moved in, she would have one last role to play, featured as the secret Hong Kong headquarters of MI6 in the James Bond movie "The Man with the Golden Gun".

Moon Dust, Shipwrecks and Landslides   173

◆   ◆   ◆

Another massive post-mortem exercise was conducted in June 1972 "to inquire into the circumstances in which disasters causing loss of life occurred during the rainstorms between June 16th and 18th 1972, with particular regard to those at Sau Mau Ping and Po Shan Road". "Black Sunday", June 18th began with the collapse of a forty-metre-high embankment overlooking the Sau Mau Ping Estate in Kowloon. News broadcasts reported heart-breaking scenes of stricken residents digging with their fingers through a tide of mud, screaming in anguish for missing relatives. Seventy-one lives were lost in that avalanche.

That evening I was again heading an emergency shift in the GIS news room, gathering and disseminating information on the search for survivors, when a call came through that struck me as so improbable I decided it needed verification. By then Brian and Moyreen Tilbrook had moved into a very high tower block on Po Shan Road, in the vicinity of the location that figured in this report. I called them in the hopes that they might be able to amplify the extraordinary details jotted down on my note pad. Moyreen answered the phone, astonished to find it was working. The whole block had been without power, water or telephones for most of the day, due to disruption of utility supplies through soil subsidence. It was immediately clear from her voice that she needed to unburden herself of the horror she had just witnessed, even more than I needed to probe its particulars.

She had heard a muffled roar that drew her and Brian out on the balcony, along with virtually all their neighbours on floors above and below. From that vantage point they watched the disintegration of an entire slope alongside their apartment block, triggering a mud slide that gathered volume and momentum until it swept across Po Sham Road and on down to Kotewall Road below. There the insupportable weight of this accumulation sheared the foundations of a twelve-storey building, which first toppled backwards and then collapsed in a pile of rubble. "I couldn't believe it," said Moyreen. "It was there one minute, lights blazing, and gone the next, in complete darkness."

I alerted those emergency personnel who had not already heard of this latest calamity and then hung on, past my shift, to log any information that could be gleaned from search parties working through the night, with whatever lighting and excavating equipment they could summon. Although there were some astonishing miracles, in which survivors were dug out from the wreckage relatively unharmed, another sixty-seven lives were lost at Kotewall Road to add to the fatalities at Sau Mau Ping.

Elephant's Ovaries and the Honourable Picnic

Hong Kong was undergoing an acceleration of its ceaseless metamorphosis. The seventies were the "MacLehose decade", an era more closely identified with a particular governor than any other in Hong Kong's history. Given the changing habits and inclinations of the public, their nascent interest in public affairs and even their burgeoning tastes for supermarkets and fast foods, it was perhaps inevitable that this tall, patrician figure, representing a throwback to an earlier, unmistakably gubernatorial and distinctly more authoritarian style, should be dubbed "Big Mac".

The choice of Sir Murray MacLehose as the colony's twenty-fifth governor was a departure from tradition. His predecessors had generally earned that appointment through long service in the ranks of the administration, whereas Sir Murray came from a diplomatic background. His career had earlier brought him into much contact with the Chinese, aided by some knowledge of their language acquired during a spell in Malaya. He even had prior experience of Hong Kong through a posting as political adviser under Sir Robert Black. When Sir Murray returned to Hong Kong in 1971, to take up his first governorship, he disembarked at Queen's Pier in high style and full plumed-hat regalia, striking a magisterial figure alongside his diminutive wife.

My first exposure to this august presence was not encouraging. I went up to Government House, as I had done many times when Sir David Trench was still in office, bearing a draft speech for his consideration. As I opened the door to his secretary's office an enormous mastiff rose on its back legs to plant its paws on my shoulders and look me challengingly in the eye. The effect was so unexpected that I must have boggled, for behind this man-sized canine stood tiny, prim-looking Lady Maclehose, who turned to call out over her shoulder to the secretary at her desk. "There's a terrified young man here," she announced, "with a piece of paper in his hands."

The piece of paper proved unacceptable to her husband, who had very firm ideas on what he wanted to say and how he wanted to say it. My pathetic little draft simply didn't measure up. While I stood silently in front of his desk, he excised such large chunks of it with his blue pencil that in the end he abandoned the effort and dismissed me. That was the first and last speech I drafted for Big Mac, and indeed virtually the first and last time I encountered him at close quarters, but for attending the annual dinner at the Government House ballroom which he and his wife would later institute as patrons of the arts.

I did not envy whoever would have to work at closer quarters, and yet among those that thrived through this association was David Ford, who had been on the point of returning to England at the end of his attachment to the GIS public relations division when Sir Murray singled him out to succeed Nigel Watt as our director. The two hit it off from the first. While Trench had begun the process of wider consultation, MacLehose placed greater emphasis on grass-roots opinion as the starting point of the governing process, and Ford was there to give this new policy maximum exposure. It soon became apparent that our new broom not only swept cleaner and faster but reached into deeper corners.

Sir Murray appointed advisers from a wide spectrum of society, including those with working class backgrounds. The elevated heights of the Legislative Council were no longer the preserve of the big *taipans* of industry, but could also be attained through the extensive network of government consultative committees. The administrative machine itself came under the microscope when he engaged a team of management consultants, the McKinsey Company, to examine its workings and make recommendations for improvement. This led to a massive reorganisation designed to separate the formulation of policy from its execution, redistributing an intricate web of responsibilities by placing government departments within the portfolios of policy secretaries.

Elephant's Ovaries and the Honourable Picnic   177

Because this initiative presented an opportunity to tap into the process of policy formulation, conducting a pre-natal probe into the ovaries of the elephant before it gave actual birth, Ford set out to learn everything that was going on. His objective was to receive early warning of any embryonic legislation that might prove contentious and difficult to present to the public. And with so much in the fallopian tubes, it was quickly apparent that, in those cases where he could not attend policy meetings himself, he would require the help of someone based in the secretariat. I was transferred from my editorial duties for yet another attachment, but this time to a very different front line. I became GIS's first secretariat press officer, sitting in at policy meetings on a wide range of issues and then briefing Ford on possible public relations implications.

Of all the new policy secretaries, I worked closest to Jack Cater, who had done such a terrific job of handling the spillover from the Cultural Revolution. He was not destined to remain long in that capacity, for Sir Murray would soon single him out to head the newly established Independent Commission Against Corruption. I enjoyed working with him, admired his acumen and was sorry—when the time came—to turn down his invitation to leave government service for secondment to the "untouchables" he would lead into the crusade against corruption.

More than anyone else, it was Jack Cater who had correctly assessed the changing mood of the Hong Kong public, their awakened sense of a cohesive, if still embryonic community. And it was he who did much to instigate the formation of the city district offices that were now tapping the grass roots of public opinion and proving valuable training grounds for our new breed of locally-born administrators, the generation who would eventually take over the reins of post-colonial Hong Kong.

Much else about Hong Kong was changing too. The cheongsam was steadily disappearing as young women adopted western attire. Young men were barely recognizable under tonsorial extravagance in their high-collared shirts and bell bottom trousers, dancing to the rhythms of such Beatles-inspired groups as Teddy Robin and the Playboys. Hong Kong was letting its hair down.

My brief stint at the secretariat, enjoying fairly extensive access to the corridors of power, could not have come at a more timely juncture in the context of the changes that were taking place as a result of the McKinsey reorganisation. This was a period when "localisation" of the civil service became a more pressing issue, when a whole new generation of talented, home-bred administrative officers was recruited into a structure previously dominated by expatriate personnel. These bright young Chinese cadets, many of whom would scale the highest ranks of the administration, were full of zeal, laden with promise, brimming with suggestions and fun to work with. I was privileged to join them as observer at their round-table discussions on policy proposals, where it seemed at times that ideas were flying faster than the speed of thought, or at least a great deal faster than my capacity to keep up with them. I made many friends in those days who, in years to come, would remind me how powerful was this little village in which I had accidentally—but also providentially—made my home.

Fortunately for me my presence in a small backroom annexe to those corridors of power went largely undetected by the media at large, for my task was to report personally to David Ford and the GIS directorate, brief them on whatever I had gleaned and leave them, and their public relations wing under Bernard "Johnnie" Johnston, to follow up whatever PR issues might arise. However I did not escape the attention of enterprising Ranjan Marwah, a "star" reporter of Grahame Jenkins' *Star* newspaper, who would bluff his way past the reception desk at the central government offices and—relying on the fact that we were both of Indian origin—"drop in for a chat".

Tall, good-looking and full of charisma, Ranjan would sit, half twisted around on the far side of my desk, leaning towards me and dominating the conversation, his bright eyes flashing around the room as if seeking further stimulus for his discourse. Unknown to me, they were taking in much more than that, for Ranjan had acquired the knack of reading typescripts upside-down, at a distance of more than a metre. Only when I began to see headlines in the *Star* that could only have resulted from such clandestine perusals did I learn to clear my desk by sweeping every document from sight the moment he put his head round the door.

The crisis of 1967 had reminded the government of Hong Kong's vulnerability and increased our determination to be better prepared the next time things went wrong. To hone our reflexes for any such an eventuality, we organised periodic "security exercises", based on incredibly convoluted scenarios. These threw the book at us by simulating unlikely conjunctions of whole chains of disparate circumstance, any one of which would have taxed our endurance to the limit in a real-life situation.

Quite typically, a direct hit by a typhoon would leave us short of food and power, with major communications disrupted, a public outcry arising from our failure to make adequate provision for homeless survivors of a landslide, a political crisis looming over some delicate border issue, and terrorists hijacking an incoming airliner bearing the head of state of a fictitious island state in the Indian Ocean. All compressed within a period of thirty-six hours, during which most of us would lead schizophrenic lives with one foot in the "no duff" real word and the other in this orchestrated nightmare.

Manning a temporary "exercise headquarters" housed in the central government offices' basement, we were equipped with closed-circuit telephone lines and most of the impedimenta that would be installed in a genuine "ops room". Here we were barraged with messages relaying the most improbable developments, while all around us phones rang, typewriters clattered and serious-looking gentlemen frantically scrawled statistics illegibly updated in chalk on inefficiently erased blackboards. I have seen grown men, including senior civil servants, crack under such pressure. I watched one shift commander, with a receiver to his left ear, blindly reach for a second shrill telephone with his right hand, which instead encountered his unfolded spectacles and thrust these against his right ear. "Hello, hello," yelled this harassed individual into his left eyepiece.

Another shift commander, about to step down after a harrowing twelve-hour spell at the helm, was informed he could not leave the building because of a sniper posted in the bell-tower of St. John's Cathedral.

"I'm not leaving by the back door," he replied. "I'm going out the front. And don't tell me he can cover that from the bloody bell tower."

"We have reason to believe there's another sniper in the tree in the front yard." By which the caller was referring to the ancient arboreal survivor of countless previous administrations that still spread its cockatoo-infested branches over much of the secretariat forecourt.

"I don't believe it," snapped our shift commander. "You couldn't be so incompetent as to leave him there. And if you were I'd go out the window."

It was not the only occasion when we came close to mutiny in the ranks.

◆　　◆　　◆

In the autumn of 1972 I was due for my second spell of home leave, and planned to make this my first circumnavigation, flying east across the Pacific, Canada and the Atlantic and returning across Europe and Asia. Gerry again invited me to stay with him at Higashi Gotanda, and extended this invitation to Mukti, knowing of the latter's eagerness to visit the country whose language he had been compelled to learn as a schoolboy during the Japanese occupation of Malaya.

By now the two boys, Mazli and Mazlan, aged eleven and nine respectively, had switched from the Rosary Hill English School in Stubbs Road to the Quarry Bay school run by the English Schools Foundation, where we hoped to improve their proficiency in what had become their first language. However in those days none but the highest echelon of civil servants could retain their government quarters while away on home leave, which effectively meant that we must surrender our accommodation in Green Lane Hall, awaiting my return to Hong Kong six months later and my renewed hunt for our next home. It was tedious having to disrupt the boys' education for such a protracted hiatus; but we had no option but to send them home to Kuala Lumpur with their mother.

We saw Asarah and the boys off on a direct flight to KL, put all our effects into storage, surrendered the flat at Green Lane Hall and moved in

Elephant's Ovaries and the Honourable Picnic 181

briefly with John McDermott, a waterworks engineer I had known since Malaya, whose apartment overlooked the site of the Kotewall Road disaster. There we were kept awake until late at night by continuing excavations of that extensive collapse, a constant reminder of its toll in human life, which had exacted a high price to presage the improved soil-stabilisation measures that would follow.

Hong Kong's first cross-harbour tunnel had just been inaugurated, replacing the vehicular ferries that hitherto provided the only link between the island and Kowloon, but a more direct and tempting means of conveyance to Kai Tak airport was offered by a newly-launched helicopter service. Paying just twenty-five Hong Kong dollars a head, we checked in our baggage at the heliport in Harcourt Road, on the central waterfront, were flown in minutes across the harbour and deposited on the taxi-way at Kai Tak, for priority clearance aboard our Japan Airlines jet.

This was the inaugural flight of JAL's direct service from Hong Kong to Kagoshima, at the southern tip of Kyushu, in the southwestern extremity of Japan's island chain. We were given to understand that virtually all the bigwigs of Kagoshima Prefecture were turning out at their airport to honour us with a VIP welcome. The only trouble was—as we learned halfway through the flight—a force ten typhoon was hovering off the Kagoshima coast.

In the circumstances we assumed that the official ceremonies would be postponed so as to allow our plane to make a safer landfall elsewhere, but no, this was not how the Japanese did things. An order had been given and must be obeyed. Come hell or high water, we were to land at Kagoshima. The first approach was nerve-wracking enough, with our wings visibly rising and falling in the volatile air currents like the pinions of a distressed pelican as we staggered in from the sea through blinding rain. Overhead lockers began to open and spill their contents while we were alternatively batted from left to right and up and down, sometimes traversing all four directions in a fraction of a second. We could hardly hear ourselves scream.

Having cleared the end of the runway, with which our undercarriage was about to make contact, our port wing suddenly plunged downward at such a sharp angle that I could have sworn it sheared the grass. Seated by the window on that side of the plane, I caught a brief glimpse of the official reception party, wrapped in raincoats and leaning into the wind under the tattered remains of their umbrellas and reception stand awnings, cheerfully waving at us through the deluge.

With that attempt aborted, the plane began an ominous and unmistakable circuit for a second try. I clutched at the sleeve of a passing hostess, who was risking decapitation to assure herself we had survived so far. "Please, please," I begged, "tell the pilot not to land here." She smiled patiently and patted me comfortingly on the hand, responding with the self-evident explanation that "They wait for us!"

The second attempt was even scarier. We bounced once—or at least some unspecified part of our aircraft made contact with the runway—before we were hurled skyward again, this time all of us shrieking in unison and threatening that—if we lived through this—we would collectively sue Japan Airlines. Somehow this information must have communicated itself to the cockpit, for the pilot came on the air to apologise for the fact that we would have to fly on to Fukuoka, at the northern end of Kyushu, whence we would be returned to Kagoshima by overnight express train.

On the last leg of that prolonged journey, having changed trains at Kagoshima for the final relatively short run to the coastal resort of Ibusuki, Mukti and I were joined in our compartment by a sad-looking, middle-aged gentleman on whom Mukti decided to try out his long-disused Japanese. The man immediately lost his careworn expression and took on the rapturous appearance of a sinner reprieved at heaven's gate by a totally unforeseen miracle.

"What did you say to him?" I asked Mukti.

"I told him we were supposed to fly to Kagoshima but landed at Fukuoka instead."

"Why does he look so happy?"

"I think he says he works for the Ibusuki mayor's office. And the mayor was one of the officials waiting for our plane to land at Kagoshima."

Elephant's Ovaries and the Honourable Picnic   183

I might have expected as much, for this largely mimed exchange of information had been accompanied by much wavering and vacillating of extended arms unsuccessfully attempting to drop outstretched palms onto carriage upholstery. Oh God, I inwardly thought. Gerry had repeatedly warned me never to become embroiled in the Japanese tradition of the *honourable picnic*. "Once they get their claws into you, they'll never let go. You're their honoured guest, and they will see to it that every moment of your time belongs to them as they fête you, wine you and dine you into your honourable grave. Hospitality knows no excess like that of the Japanese."

He quoted to me the case of David Tambiah, one of our colleagues in the *Straits Times* organisation who had been sent to Tokyo on an official visit to check out a printing press. From the moment of his arrival at the old international airport of Haneda, David had been commandeered by the owner of the printing works, desperate to impress upon him how valued he was as a potential customer. Subjected to two days of unremitting entertainment, force-fed Japanese delicacies, befuddled by unwanted quantities of alcohol, serenaded by *geisha* girls and never returned to his hotel room until well past midnight, David was determined to dig in his heels when his escort arrived to collect him on the third morning. He refused to open the door.

The emissary went down on his knees at the keyhole. "Please to come with me," he begged. "Our boss makes great plans for you. A morning in Ueno Zoo. Afternoon at *kabuki* theatre. Evening at French restaurant with…"

"I'm not coming," shouted David emphatically.

"But I will lose my job."

"Tell him I'm ill."

"But I will lose my job."

"Tell him you couldn't find me. I've already checked out."

"But I will lose my job."

It was simply inconceivable to the Japanese that anyone would spurn their munificent generosity, and our companion in the railway carriage was already assuring Mukti that a municipal vehicle would be around to collect us at noon.

I instructed Mukti to thank him for his kindness, which regretfully we would be unable to accept, not only because of the weather but because we were staying well outside town, in the Ibusuki Kanko hotel. The weather was no problem, we were assured. The Ibusuki municipality would be proud to entertain its distinguished visitors, who had come all this way to honour their humble prefecture.

I consoled myself that, the way the wind had continued to rise as the typhoon hovered offshore, there could be no possibility of fulfilling this threat, since it looked as though by noon the eye of the hurricane would be directly overhead. Meanwhile we would refresh ourselves in the Ibusuki Kanko's justly famed "jungle baths", the largest indoor bathing complex attached to any hotel in the world. Housed under a glass-domed roof large enough to accommodate a Zeppelin-sized airship, this collection of fifty-nine separate baths, all of varying temperatures and mineral consistencies, was spread among tropical gardens and linked by meandering, cobblestone paths under coconut palms and vine-laden trees.

It was an eerie experience touring these with my little *fundoshi* towel while the glass panes rattled from the howling winds outside. There hurricane-spawned waves crashed on a beach in whose medically-recommended black volcanic sands—on a clear day—hotel attendants would normally bury you up to your therapeutically-immersed neck. Most other bathers in those sexually-integrated baths that gray, storm-besieged morning seemed to comprise the entire personnel of a typical Japanese business organisation, collectively enjoying, in the buff, a typical company vacation in which all staff were expected to share, along with their families. I paused to watch a bevy of nude and attractive young secretaries subjecting their equally naked boss to the humiliating ritual of repeatedly bowing, with nothing more than his handkerchief-sized towel in front of him, as each of them separately bowed to him in succession.

At noon I received a call from the front desk that a car from the mayor's office was waiting to pick us up. I toyed with the idea of disregarding it, but could hardly pretend that I had not received it, since apparently the call was put through in the presence of whoever had arrived to collect us. I went in search of Mukti, who stressed that it would be the height of bad manners to decline such a gesture.

We dutifully presented ourselves to our beaming acquaintance of the night before, who delivered us to the mayor's office. There we found a sizeable chunk of municipal worthiness in the form of prefectural officials and staff, all gathered in the conference room to greet us. Apparently we were the only passengers they had been able to track down from the manifest of yesterday's flight, so all the hospitality that had been planned for that occasion was now concentrated upon Mukti and myself.

An interpreter explained the carefully planned itinerary ahead of us, which would include a motorcade to all the prominent beauty spots and places of historical interest throughout the prefecture.

In the circumstances it seemed thoroughly irrelevant, and of course positively ungracious, to point out that by this time there was virtually no other traffic on the road, that the township was battened down for the full impact of the typhoon, that large chunks of vegetation were already blowing away and that, even if our motorcade managed to keep to the rubbish-strewn roads, we were in dire danger of being struck by flying debris. We set off, in blinding, terrifying conditions, accompanied by the mayor and our interpreter, who pointed out through streaming windows to indicate some vague manifestation of a blurred presence in a smear of rain-shrouded panorama, informing us that we were currently passing this or that landmark feature. I dared not ask questions for fear we would linger for closer examination.

At several points we stopped to make perilous dashes through the rain to selected buildings of allegedly historical interest, including temples and private homes whose guardians and occupants reluctantly responded to our hammering at their doors. They admitted our soaked presence in the belief that we must be orphans of the storm, only to watch in profound surprise as our guide embarked on explanations of the principal features of their premises.

From Kagoshima, once the typhoon subsided, we caught the train back to Fukuoka and across to the main island of Honshu, where we transferred to the *Shinkansen* for our greatly accelerated progress to Miyajima. There we visited the island Shinto shrine of Utsukushima, with its famed red "floating torii" gate standing in the sea and its aggressive herd of resident deer. These nudged us impatiently on the hips and buttocks if we failed to respond with sufficient alacrity to their demands for food. One tourist, generously dispensing deer fodder from a large paper bag, was so besieged by the belligerent animals that he took flight with what looked like a substantial cohort of the herd in hot pursuit. We wondered how long it would take him to realise that his safest recourse was simply to drop the bag.

Our next stop was Hiroshima, to tour the Peace Park and its museum to the victims of the first atomic bomb. Akin to the experience of visiting the holocaust museum at Auschwitz, or Phnom Penh's Tuol Sleng museum to the thousands who died in the great Cambodian genocide, the exhibits only hinted at an enormity too great for the imagination to comprehend.

After a brief stay with Gerry at Higashi Gotanda, Mukti and I went our separate ways—he returning on a direct flight to KL to rejoin his family at Kampong Ijok and I catching my first jumbo jet to Hawaii. As if to make up for scaring the pants off me at Kagoshima, Japan Airlines upgraded me to first-class.

Honolulu was too modern and too ersatz Hong Kong for my taste. I chose the less developed and less tourist-ridden island of Molokai and booked into a beach motel at its capital of Kaunakakai. My taxi driver introduced himself as the local mayor. A refreshingly far cry from his dignified counterpart in Ibusuki, this one was the delightfully laid-back heir to a classic Hawaiian song with words and music by R. Alex Anderson. The only difference was that this Mayor of Kaunakakai wasn't cockeyed, and therefore didn't quite measure up to the lyrics:

"He wore a *malo* and a coconut hat;
One was for this and the other for that.
All the people shouted as he went by;
He was the cockeyed mayor of Kaunakakai."

Although lacking the skinny mare his alleged predecessor had ridden, this engaging latter-day office-bearer not only placed his taxi at my disposal but, in the words of the song, "he made her buck and he made her fly, all over the island of Molokai". We couldn't traverse the steep descent to the historic leprosarium on the north shore, so I had to content myself with a distant view of the colony where Father Damien had devoted his life to the untouchables living in enforced isolation on that remote, hostile and largely inaccessible coast. The saintly man had provoked such envy and calumny from local Presbyterian and Congregational churches that Robert Louis Stevenson felt compelled to spring to his posthumous defence in a rebuttal of the claims made by a Honolulu Presbyterian, the Reverend C. M. Hyde. Stevenson called Hyde a "crank" and wrote:

"When we have failed, and another has succeeded; when we have stood by, and another has stepped in; when we sit and grow bulky in our charming mansions, and a plain, uncouth peasant steps into the battle, under the eyes of God, and succours the afflicted, and consoles the dying, and is himself afflicted in his turn, and dies upon the field of honour—the battle cannot be retrieved as your unhappy irritation has suggested. It is a lost battle, and lost for ever."

From Molokai I flew on to the archipelago's main island of Hawaii itself, to tour the ever-changing lava fields at the ever-restless summit of the earth's most massive and active volcano. Rising more than four kilometres above sea level, Mauna Loa was the pride of the Volcanoes National Park, first established in 1916. On display were the results of seventy million years of volcanism, tectonic migration and evolution—the very processes that led to Hawaii's creation through titanic upheavals from the sea. I began to comprehend something of the scale of that prolonged but intermittent series of eruptions, as the earth's plates moved over a fixed hot spot on the ocean bed, which produced one of the planet's most spectacular island chains and eventually contributed the fiftieth state to the USA.

Demoted to my customary economy class in a distinctly pre-jumbo domestic airliner, I flew on for my first landfall on the parent continent, arriving in San Francisco at the tail end of the hippie revolution, when "flower" people in pyrotechnic apparel with flared trousers were still handing out blossoms to passers-by and every street corner had its resident musician. Like exotic birds, the latter employed violins, saxophones, tubas and other instruments both to harvest small change and sound off their territorial display calls to keep rival claimants at bay.

Attending an evening performance of the musical *Godspell*, based on the gospel according to St. Matthew, I joined fellow theatregoers spilling out on to the sidewalk during the interval to applaud and reward a couple of energetic young street performers. This boy and girl team treated us to such a stunning display of tap dancing, in an updated version of the Ginger Rogers-Fred Astaire style, that we were half-inclined to ignore the bell summoning us back to the auditorium for the second half of the show we had paid much greater sums to see.

From San Francisco I caught a Greyhound bus to Seattle, seated alongside a barefoot, mop-haired young black who paid me the compliment of assuming I was a fellow hippie and taking me into his confidence. He proved remarkably well-informed on the social mores of every township through which we passed, briefing me on the relative severity or laxity of local law enforcement, the prevailing attitude to strangers and the best places to go for handouts. I regretted not bringing a notebook to jot it all down.

Most of our eight hundred-mile journey was accomplished overnight, through a prolonged tunnel of darkness interrupted by neon-lit strip malls of gas stations, soda fountains, quickie restaurants and fast food outlets where diners spilled over their bar stools like sagging hamburgers supported on toothpicks and coming apart at their fillings. I began to detect a monotonous rhythm to this endless repetition of the same constants in a limited range of variables, like the visual equivalent of a pop tune that has outstayed its welcome and will not be dislodged from the mind. I remembered Leslie Howard, Bette Davis and Humphrey Bogart in their 1936 movie *The Petrified Forest,* much of it set in an early version of those many service stations we traversed in the course of that night. The only difference was that now the forest was a petrified urban landscape.

Snatching a quick breakfast in Seattle, I caught another bus to Port Angeles, on the north shore of Washington State, overlooking the Juan de Fuca Straits that separated America from Canada, the land of the free from the land of the decorously restrained. A ferry ride conveyed me to Victoria, British Columbia, a sort of mini-London theme park filled with nostalgic reminders of a supposed "motherland" on the other side of the world. It was odd, I mused, that Paul had chosen to emigrate here. He had come from one Victoria, the capital of Mahe in the Seychelles, and I from another in Hong Kong, founded just one year before Victoria BC.

Here I discovered Victoriana of every recherché species; including flags bearing almost as many union jacks as maple leaf emblems, and was stopped in my tracks by bright red double-decker omnibuses, pseudo-British "bobbies" with their policemen's helmets and truncheons, even ersatz beefeaters in full Tower of London regalia. How, I wondered, could genuine, loyal Canadians suffer all these spurious tributes to an origin known to only a few of their forebears? Had they no sense of pride? The province would eventually adopt the slogan "Super, Natural British Columbia", tempting me to remove the comma and conjoin the two adjectives. It was positively eerie how desperately those who dwelt in that uniquely beautiful landscape contrived to make it look like somewhere else.

On the back of a car bearing British Columbian registration plates I saw a bumper sticker that read "Thank God I'm British". How come some red-blooded Canadian didn't shoot, out of hand, the ungrateful, disloyal "landed immigrant" behind the wheel?

As I got to know the province better, I came to recognise why it was the only one in Canada bearing the archaic prefix "British". It seemed to me that Victoria was the concentrated quintessence of its Britishness, and that the rest of BC had long been surrendered to Columbians. Red-necked warriors of the latter tribes encircled this wilderness outpost aboard four-wheel-drive trucks, with chainsaws rattling and Alsatians yelping in the back, awaiting an opportunity to sack and pillage bookstores, tea parlours and other bastions of Great Britannic respectability.

But the background scenery, so immediately, patently and unapologetically un-British, was stunningly beautiful, and the midsummer temperature deliciously halcyon. With the air so balmy I could forgive everything else for being so too. And awaiting me at the ferry pier were my brother Paul, his wife Mary and their three children Nicholas, Kate and Jeremy, then in their mid to early teens. With them was my mother, who had courageously embarked on her first-ever flight across two oceans—one of sea and the other of land—to be reunited with all of us in the town where Paul and family had chosen to make their home.

Paul's spell in the Seychelles had reinforced his ambition to pursue a career in the last reaches of imperial twilight, but beyond the restrictive confines of the British Isles. In that too, as in so many other respects, we were of one mind. I had chosen Hong Kong and he, equally by default, had chosen Canada. Clearly his choice had suited the entire family. The kids were in school, Mary was housekeeping their charming rented cottage in an open tract of suburban farmland and Paul had joined the staff of the *Times Colonist* newspaper. There he rapidly established a reputation as leader writer and was winning applause from loyalist Canadians for attacking the pretensions of those who continued to fly the union jack in preference to the maple leaf from their front lawn flagpoles.

I could see why life on Vancouver Island would seem so attractive to them. On the map this elongated, upended detachment from the continental land mass stretched way below the forty-ninth parallel, like a plummeting airship about to collide with the land mass south of the border in Washington State. Its physical separation from the rest of Canada engendered an unmistakable insularity, accompanied by an endemic air of superiority in its inhabitants which extended right down to the parochial level. My brother and his family would later move to the rural Victorian suburb of Metchosin, whose horse-breeding, orchard-growing rustics, on their plots of no less than the prescribed minimum of four acres, scoffed at the adjoining, more crowded neighbourhood of Colwood. Paul would have a hand in designing an emblematic tee-shirt which misquoted the Bible (Matthew: 22) by claiming "Many are Colwood but Few are Metchosin".

I too fell in love with this uniquely beautiful and bucolic tract of Canadiana, so vastly different from the geography and climate which predominated in the bulk of the provinces to the east of the Rockies. Had I known of its existence sixteen years earlier, when I was accepted as a landed immigrant headed for London Ontario, I might not have been persuaded at the last moment to change my mind and settle for Malaya instead.

After two weeks in this arcadian pastorale, my mother and I bid farewell to the family and headed by ferry for the provincial capital of Vancouver, where we boarded a Canadian Pacific express train for Banff, in the heart of the Canadian Rockies. Not since our overland crossing of the Indian subcontinent from Calcutta to Bombay had either of us enjoyed such a protracted train journey, and never before had we experienced such luxury set against a scrolling backdrop of spectacular vistas.

We booked into a hotel set beside deep woods near Banff's famed hot springs, where I left my mother to write postcards on the back porch while I went in search of the restaurant for breakfast. When I returned I found her still seated on the porch, where she described with some excitement the pleasure of observing a large black bear emerge from the trees to investigate the contents of a rubbish bin at the foot of the steps. The bin still lay where it had been overturned and thoroughly rummaged, a few feet from where my mother had maintained her enthralled vigil.

"Bears are dangerous and unpredictable," I reminded her. "Why didn't you go inside?"

"I didn't want to disturb him. He wasn't interested in me and besides, he looked so cute."

From Banff we caught a bus to Calgary and then flew to Montreal, where we enjoyed a few days of French cuisine and culture before flying on to London. I was delighted to find my father a man reborn. He had taken a new lease on life, reverting to his favourite hobby and turning it to profit by constructing a huge model railway layout as a feature of the paid attractions provided on Hastings pier.

However he and my youngest brother Robert were growing discontented with their home at 1 Old Harrow Road, stuck beside a busy intersection subjected to ever increasing volumes of the main traffic flow from London and points north. We went house-hunting and I saw my parents settled into a small but charming prewar bungalow in the village of Three Oaks, off the main Hastings to Rye road that I had regularly traversed on my rounds as district reporter for the *East Sussex Express and County Herald*.

The New Deal

On returning to Hong Kong at the end of my leave, I was once again braced for surprises—because rapid change was the nature of this unquiet colony, forever busy reinventing itself. But this time the changes were, if anything, more immediately apparent and more marked. It was not just a question of visible alterations to the basic geography, with massive reclamation projects pushing the waterfront ever further into the harbour, or to the skyline, with its prominent new landmarks. Nor was it merely confined to the style and appearance of the populace in general—the young men with their beatnik haircuts, the women bursting out of their chrysalid *cheongsams* into mini skirts and pompom hairdos. It was the unmistakable sense that Hong Kong had "arrived", that it had finally thrown off the last vestiges of its transient refugee mentality and become a community.

Just as President Roosevelt had offered post-depression America its "New Deal" when he came to office in 1933, so MacLehose had set about modifying Hong Kong's notions of itself and where it stood. He had in him more than a touch of the zealous reformer. As if paving the way for the bigger act to follow, when he would grapple with the long-endemic problem of corruption that permeated almost every level of Hong Kong society, he began with an assault on two fronts—a faster pace of resettlement, to eliminate the eyesore of squatter shacks cluttering our hillsides, and concerted action to solve the other, perhaps even more readily visible problem of inadequate urban hygiene. Under his direction, we began to clean up our act.

Sir Murray personally led cleansing squads to dispose of litter on beaches and in public parks. He had become the primal force behind the *Clean Hong Kong Campaign*, which would serve as spearhead to successive publicity drives that would deluge the populace with more and more posters, television messages and print media, urging responsible civic behaviour. The phrase *Lap Sap Chung* had entered the local argot, to designate and alienate those citizens so anti-social in their behaviour as to merit scorn and ostracism.

GIS was in the forefront of the *Clean Hong Kong Campaign,* and our creative director, Arthur Hacker, had come up with its defining symbol, creating a cartoon litterbug called *Lap Sap Chung.* A masked villain of the good old-fashioned *boo-hiss* species, with a bloated green body covered in red spots, a phallic snout, fanged teeth and a forked tail, this character resembled a mutated mixture of Dracula, Satan, an alien from outer space and Britain's wartime "gremlins". *Lap Sap Chung* was the "public enemy number one" we were supposed to hate, but many thought him so lovable they wanted posters and little *Lap Sap Chung* buttons to wear on their lapels, not as badges of dishonour but as endearing and enduring souvenirs. An early poster for the campaign—and one which prompted the greatest demand—showed him looming, gigantic and Godzilla-like, above the city skyline, poised to trash the metropolis.

Because Nigel Watt, in his new role as co-ordinator of television and entertainment licensing, had the foresight to secure a guaranteed minimum proportion of airtime for government messages in each hour of commercial television broadcast, we were afforded an avenue for free public communication that most other administrations would kick themselves for failing to secure. *Lap Sap Chung* virtually pioneered this crucial medium. His advent coincided with the further rapid inroads of broadcast television services into every home in Hong Kong, so that, even though his anti-social behaviour was not to be emulated, he became an instantly recognisable icon of both the New Deal and the new age.

Most of our television messages—or announcements of public interest (APIs) as we called them—were simplistic in the extreme, produced on a shoestring and punching their message home with a minimum of tact and subtlety. Ted Thomas, briefly drafted into our ranks to contribute to our "think tank", was inspired to borrow a truckload of pigs headed for the abattoir and release then on Repulse Bay beach, where their foraging through the spilled contents of litter bins was supposed to represent the anti-social behaviour we must collectively reject. Perhaps our most memorable API from this time portrayed two neighbouring housewives sharing a public balcony in a typical resettlement block, each of whom, while the other was distracted, would surreptitiously sweep the rubbish from her front door to the one alongside—until both realised that this selfish conduct wasn't getting them anywhere.

Grahame Blundell had been placed in charge of all of our department's publicity services, so that I was given the option of returning to my former role as publications chief or taking charge of the newly established campaigns office. I chose the latter, heading a team of really versatile young GIS recruits who worked with great energy, enthusiasm and commitment, relishing every new challenge that came our way. The *Clean Hong Kong Campaign* was followed by the *Fight Crime Campaign*, the *Anti-Narcotics Campaign*, the *Anti-Smoking Campaign* and, eventually, the *Environmental Pollution Campaign*, the promotional funds for all of which were placed at my disposal and directly under my control. The various departments involved would have to come to me, cap in hand, to persuade me that their pet programmes were worthy of inclusion in our list of priorities.

While television remained our most effective means of communication, we supplemented this with posters, special events and a mobile street theatre. The latter, mounted on a converted goods truck and equipped with a collapsible stage, its own generator and sound equipment, toured housing estates and factory areas, conveying our messages in the context of variety programmes that employed the services of up-and-coming talents, many of whom would later pursue prominent careers in the entertainment business.

I persuaded Bill Yim, one of Hong Kong's many gifted cartoonists, to join our mobile theatre team and devise a family of glove puppets, loosely based on the *Muppets* whose worldwide popularity had far exceeded their origins in American television. He came up with the *Yimmies*, for whom we wrote little one-act playlets, all of which had one or more of our topical campaign messages at their core. These peripatetic street players attracted large followings but also provoked occasional negative reaction, as in the case of a resettlement estate resident whose letter was published in one of our leading Chinese newspapers, complaining of the noise made by the "compulsory entertainment" imposed on her neighbourhood.

With the beginnings of community awareness and a civic mentality implanted in the public conscience, engendering a wholly new and potent force of public opinion—often vociferously expressed—MacLehose felt it was time to crack down on the much more pressing problem of corruption, so long endemic in the body corporate that no previous governor had tackled it for fear of stirring up a hornets' nest. People were sick of ambulance attendants demanding "tea money" before picking up patients, firemen soliciting "water money" before turning on the hoses, even hospital amahs asking for tips to provide patients with bedpans or glasses of water.

Offering bribes to the right officials had long been a necessary preliminary to applications for public housing, schooling and other public services, and corruption had spread its tentacles not only throughout the administration but into the business sphere as well. However it was particularly conspicuous in the police force, where corrupt officers covered up vice, gambling and drug activities. Hong Kong's beloved crusader Elsie, still known by her married name of Elliott because she had not then become the wife of Andrew Tu, had fought long and hard to expose these evils, but only found a willing ear when MacLehose took office. Recommending Elsie for a C.B.E., Sir Murray murmured to her as he pinned it on her breast "For great courage and achievement".

To give him his due, much of the initiative for a cleaner police force came from its new Commissioner, Charles Sutcliffe, whom I had admired for his cool command of anti-riot operations back in 1967. He dispensed with and disbanded the formidable "tigers" behind the rackets, the staff sergeants who—with all the force of a mafia—had controlled corruption within the ranks. These were replaced, under a different ranking structure, by newly-recruited and carefully vetted "station sergeants". Sutcliffe's big break came through a routine enquiry from a Canadian bank, into the account of Chief Superintendent Peter Fitzroy Godber. Sutcliffe was astounded. How had Godber amassed so much money? He launched an inquiry whose results rocked not only the police, but all of Hong Kong.

The scandal had yet to break when I sat with Godber on a committee exploring options for a publicity campaign to tackle juvenile crime. I had run into him earlier, in 1967, when he was in charge of the training programme that prepared young police recruits for anti-riot duties. I was impressed with his skills then and I was again struck by the contribution he made to that committee. As luck would have it, we had both attended Hastings Grammar School within a few years of each other, Godber being a little older than me. Little could I guess, as we cheerfully reminisced about treasured old form masters we had known and loved, that he was already plotting how he might escape from the colony before his case exploded in the media.

Godber's flight from Hong Kong, the international manhunt that this triggered, and his return in handcuffs to face trial, were all elevated to landmark prominence as the first resounding triumph of the new Independent Commission Against Corruption, launched by MacLehose in February 1974. But I still deplore the fact that much of the evidence against him was secured by deals ensuring that fellow officers of lesser professional stature and competence, just as much part of the web of corruption as he was, got off virtually scot free—including one who publicly admitted having enlivened his constabulary days, while on beat patrols in Welsh villages, by urinating through letterboxes.

◆　　　◆　　　◆

Because of increased wages and job opportunities, it had become impossible to find anyone willing to undertake domestic service, so that Hong Kong's more affluent families began looking overseas for their help with the kids, the cooking and the household chores. The Philippines, where corruption was rife on a greater scale, and where the Spanish-traced aristocracy had such a stranglehold on the economy that the native masses were kept in permanent penury, provided the main source of this imported labour. Thousands of English-speaking, hardworking, unfailingly cheerful Filipinas were pouring into Hong Kong, desperate to supply services well below their often highly-trained professional abilities because these offered far higher salaries than they could earn at home.

Mukti and Asarah befriended many of these new arrivals, sometimes bringing them back to our flat for a meal and a rare chance to enjoy domestic relaxation in surroundings where they didn't have to cook the meal and wash the dishes themselves. It pained me to meet young wives and mothers separated, by force of economic circumstance, from husbands and children, making the best of what Hong Kong had to offer and saving every cent they could to send home to their families.

Statue Square became their principal rendezvous. After attending Mass at the Catholic Cathedral in Caine Road, or at St. Joseph's Church in Garden Road, they would spill down the hillside into Central, transforming each Sunday into an impromptu Mardi Gras celebration. Eventually the transport authorities and the police surrendered Central district to these weekend festivities, closing off Connaught Road as a pedestrian precinct that connected both sides of Statue Square into one crowded alfresco enclave, part marketplace, part picnic ground and virtually all a microcosm of our neighbouring archipelago in the South China Sea.

Anyone acquainted with that polyglot archipelago might recognise that different areas of this weekend fairground became the territorial focus of different island communities. Traversing Statue Square meant effectively crossing a miniature configuration of the Philippines, missing only its terraced rice fields, volcanoes and palm fringed beaches but redolent of its music and culture. Everywhere guitars were strumming, choral groups were practising for their next concert and dancers were trying out their folk routines to taped music recorded on squeaky cassette players.

Through this joyous assembly strolled families of Cantonese with cameras and straight faces, bemused and bewildered to find their city centre commandeered by this friendly invasion but not begrudging the Filipinas their one chance of the week to get together with friends and appease some of their inevitable homesickness. The presence of these less privileged economic migrants provided further proof, if any were needed, that Hong Kong was elevating itself above the level of its third-world neighbours and establishing the comforting "underbelly" any upwardly mobile commu-

The New Deal 199

nity must acquire as an inevitable adjunct to growing affluence and wellbeing. The Cantonese, if nothing else, are an essentially accommodating people, instinctively ready to accept, in a live-and-let-live symbiosis, anyone willing to share their lot.

This same tolerance was extended towards another major group of new immigrants, in this case Indonesian Chinese who had failed to resettle successfully in China during the wave of Chinese nationalism that swept their ranks in the aftermath of the communist takeover of China. The Indonesian Chinese had always been a divided community, the earlier *peranakan* settlers, principally of Hokkien descent, having become far more Indonesian in their language, culture and sensibilities than the later wave of *totok* migrants—mainly Hakka and Cantonese—who were attracted to the archipelago purely for economic gain, and determined to preserve their Chinese ethos.

Even before Soekarno's downfall in 1965, following an attempted coup d'etat by the Indonesian Communist Party, relations between China and Indonesia had been—at best—erratic. In 1955 Indonesia and China signed an agreement on dual citizenship, which allowed Chinese living in Indonesia to hold both Indonesian and Chinese passports. In 1958 Indonesia approved a citizenship law which stipulated naturalization. The following year both countries agreed to a repatriation process for 140,000 Chinese descendants. While most of these were *totok* who had never fully accepted Indonesia as their home, a significant proportion were *peranakan,* who quickly learned that life in China could never make up for the loss of their adopted homeland. China might be in their genes but Indonesia had long claimed their hearts.

In 1967 Indonesia's diplomatic ties with China were frozen, abruptly halting the process of repatriation. Countless thousands were rendered stateless. Thousands of others, already in China, had failed to acclimatize and were longing to return to the only country in which they felt truly at home, and where they were now no longer welcome. China permitted these unsuccessful returnees to leave, but Indonesia would no longer receive them back, so they crowded into whatever sanctuary would accept them, Macau and Hong Kong being high on their list of options.

Mukti and Asarah, long deprived of the company of those who spoke their native tongue, now found themselves surrounded by stateless Indonesian Chinese who shared their tastes, their attitudes and most especially their language. We entertained large groups of them and made lifelong friends amidst this transient community, as a result of which I would later be accepted into the homes of those of their relatives who had remained behind in Indonesia.

◆　　　◆　　　◆

For this, my third three-year contract with the Hong Kong government, I was allocated a flat in Hillside Mansions in Cloud View Road, overlooking the area known as North Point, towards the northeastern end of Hong Kong Island. As soon as I settled in I summoned Mukti, Asarah and the boys back from Malaysia so that the parents could resume their interrupted employment and the children their disrupted schooling. Ironically, while our new residence was ideally placed for commuting to Quarry Bay school, both Mazli and Mazlan had by now graduated to the parent institution at Island School in Borrett Road, which would have been vastly more accessible had we remained at Green Lane Hall. Mukti drove all of us on the long daily trek westwards towards Central, dropping his sons off first, in their regulation school uniforms, and then delivering me to Beaconsfield House.

Directly alongside our block in Cloud View Road was Braemar Hill reservoir, which had originally been developed to supply water to the Taikoo sugar refinery and had once come to the rescue of the government back in the early twenties,. On June 24th 1920 the Colonial Secretary, A.G.M. Fletcher, reported to the Finance Committee of the Legislative Council that there was a drought in Shau Kei Wan, as a result of which "the water ran dry and the Taikoo sugar refinery kindly assisted government and connected pipes to our mains from their reservoir."

Not that it was an especially substantial body of water. I could stroll around it in a quarter of an hour at a fairly relaxed pace and, if I chose, then continue across the island's watershed along trails leading to the much larger Tai Tam reservoir on the island's south side. For outdoor enthusiasts, the location was ideal, with direct access to some of the best walking trails in Hong Kong. But there were drawbacks, not least in Hilltop Mansions' exposure to the brunt of any winds from the eastern quadrant, whence sprang the worst of the gales during our numerous typhoons.

Braemar Hill reservoir has long disappeared, giving way to yet another gigantic complex of tower blocks that have screened Hilltop Mansions from the worst of these blasts. But while we were there, our tenth floor flat was on the block's most vulnerable corner, and my bedroom had windows on both sides of that corner. During one not especially fierce typhoon the window on the east side blew in, scattering shards of glass across my unoccupied bed and drenching the room from the almost horizontal rains falling at the time. I rushed to close the bedroom door, so as to limit the extent of the damage, but it slammed shut in my face. I then set about rolling up my mattress, which I strove to insert through the broken pane as a literal stop-gap measure.

In the midst of this struggle the windows on the other side of the room blew outward as a result of the rapidly fluctuating air pressure, momentarily sweeping me off my feet. Fighting my way back to the origin of this turmoil I somehow succeeded in jamming the void with the thoroughly soaked mattress, by which time Mukti and Asarah had forced their way into the room to see what had become of me. Between us we spent the rest of the night mopping up the floor, until the storm abated enough for me to telephone the quartering office and report the extent of the repairs necessary to restore the flat to serviceable condition.

Within months of my mother returning to England, after spending with us the first of her Hong Kong excursions, I received a phone call informing me my father was once again seriously ill and not expected to survive. This was the second call in five years that had sent me scuttling back to England to join the vigil at his bedside, but this time I arrived too late. He died of a stroke, at the age of sixty-three, even before I boarded my plane. My one consolation was that his last two years were the happiest he had known since returning to England, because somehow *The Labur-*

nums, that tiny bungalow I purchased for them at Three Oaks had reminded him of India.

Paul flew back from Canada for the funeral, so that all three sons joined our mother for the service at St. Mary Star of the Sea. Since Dad had never left the Anglican faith, and had only hovered on the fringes of Catholicism for Mum's sake, this was followed by burial in the grounds of the lovely old Norman church of Guestling, which called to mind Thomas Gray's *Elegy Written in a Country Churchyard*. So withdrawn had my father become in his later years, and so close about him had he pulled the cloak of humility to smother inherent talents that had flowered only on distant Indian plains, that we had despaired of him ever reviving his true potential. One particular stanza of Gray's poem fitted him very well:

"Perhaps in this neglected spot is laid
Some heart once pregnant with celestial fire;
Hands that the rod of empire might have sway'd,
Or waked to ecstasy the living lyre."

Habitually grief-ridden by any separations, Mother took the finality of this one especially badly, since she would now have only her youngest son Robert to keep her company in that little cottage, still filled with so many memories of Dad. I resolved that I would make it up to her on my next home leave.

◆   ◆   ◆

Shortly after my return to Hong Kong I became immersed in preparations for the first-ever visit of a reigning British monarch. Accompanied by the Duke of Edinburgh, Queen Elizabeth II was due to arrive in May 1975, en route to Japan to pay a State Visit to Emperor Hirohito. I had last seen her when she was still a princess and I was a student of Hastings Grammar School, assembled with thousands of other children, all of us armed with little paper union jacks, on the grounds of the old Hastings Cricket Club, to cheer her as she was driven past, waving at us from the back of a Land Rover. Her brief Hong Kong sojourn, all those many years later, was the pretext for a crowded programme of activities of the kind so deliciously described by Noel Coward in his one and only novel *Pomp and Circumstance*.

The *pièce de résistance* was to be a grand parade up Nathan Road, Kowloon. I joined David Ford and Grahame Blundell in the inter-departmental team organising the arrangements, and my particular task was to put together sufficiently diverse participating groups for the Nathan Road procession. This would be our last chance to stage such a cavalcade in Nathan Road, which was imminently due for extensive excavation by the cut-and-cover method to make way for Hong Kong's first mass transit railway. Following its restoration, the resurfaced thoroughfare would be divided down the middle for its multi-lane traffic flow.

The viewing platform for the royal party was a covered dais on the western side of Nathan Road, near the entrance to what was then the newly vacated military camp of Whitfield Barracks, which had long been home to British, Indian and Gurkha troops serving in Hong Kong and—during the Japanese occupation—a detention camp for military prisoners of war. We used the deserted barracks and parade grounds to muster components of the procession in their allotted marching order—military and police bands, various community associations, educational establishments, elderly citizens' clubs, athletic associations, practitioners of *kung fu* and martial arts, dancers from a local ballet school and, of course, the traditional lion dancers that must accompany any local festivity.

Finally, as the showpiece of the entire promenade, we had a royal yellow dragon rippling its gigantically elongated mane, virtually a full block in length, with five-toed feet flashing auspiciously in all directions. It had been my secret desire to substitute, in place of the baggy-trousered men half concealed beneath its undulating silken coils, a troupe of high-heeled, fishnet-stockinged chorus girls, kick-stepping their way through synchronised choreography straight from a classic Busby Berkeley Hollywood routine. Though this was clearly neither the time nor the place for such carryings-on, I confided my guilty would-be extravaganza to Richard Hughes, author of *Borrowed Place on Borrowed Time* and doyen of the Hong Kong press corps, who was seated beside me in the viewing pavilion.

Dick, bless his heart, was large, rough-hewn, uncompromisingly forthright and legendary in the compass of his reportage on all things Asian, but was nevertheless the most accessible and charming of companions, who would treat everyone—no matter what their age and seniority in the ranks of the local media—as if they were at least as knowledgeable as he was. He applauded the idea, which appealed to his anything-goes Aussie unshockability.

Another of our most respected senior China watchers was Anthony Lawrence, whose portrayal as a Far East correspondent, on a vintage cover of the *Radio Times*, had contributed to my earliest pre-arrival expectations of Hong Kong. The picture remains vividly fixed in my mind—Anthony reclining in a deckchair under an umbrella on Repulse Bay beach, a rather elderly portable typewriter poised on his knees. I had thought to myself that if that sybaritic scene genuinely portrayed the life of a Far East correspondent, it differed markedly from my experience as a newspaper reporter with the *Malay Mail* in Kuala Lumpur. Distressingly, however, Anthony had assured me, almost as soon as I first met him, that it did not. The photograph was staged.

I was talking to Anthony, somewhere near the middle of the ballroom floor in Government House, when we were introduced to the Queen, who had found space in her busy itinerary to meet with the local media. I engaged her attention for only the briefest of split seconds before she concentrated her full focus on Anthony, who was obviously known to her from his coverage of Far Eastern affairs, concerning which she proved very enlightened. She engaged him in a debate on a matter which was then only just beginning to loom on our horizon, but which appeared to cause her some concern.

Her arrival in Hong Kong had followed closely on the fall of Saigon on April 29th, 1975, when America withdrew ignominiously and completely from the old noncommunist capital of South Vietnam, leaving it at the mercy of North Vietnamese tanks. The day she and Prince Philip set foot on Hong Kong soil a Danish ship, *MV Clara Maersk*, sailed into the harbour bearing three thousand nine hundred refugees picked up at sea from a small, overburdened and imperilled vessel, the *Truong Xuam*.

Already we had received our first ship-borne refugees fleeing Vietnam, representing the merest trickle of what would eventually become a seemingly unstoppable flood. Her Majesty voiced grave misgivings regarding the consequences. She told Anthony that she thought Hong Kong would prove extremely vulnerable in its exposure to the main outward thrust of the diaspora she believed would shortly ensue. I was impressed at the time, but more so when her prediction was all too ominously fulfilled three years later.

Shamelessly Shirtless in Galle

The Royal Visit brought me to the end of my third contract and yet another spell of home leave, commencing with a fortnight in Sri Lanka, escorted by my dear old German friend Ernest Harnach. He drove me on the grand tour, starting with a stay in the historic Queen's Hotel at Kandy and taking in to the rock fortress of Sigiriya and the ruins of Polonnaruwa, where our palatial room at the local lakeside resthouse had once been occupied by Queen Elizabeth during her circuit of the colonies in 1954.

When Ernest left to fly back to Hong Kong, I caught a train down to Galle and booked into the New Oriental Hotel, one of the most charming I have ever chanced upon. Its antecedents could be traced back to 1863, when a consortium of British businessmen acquired an imposing, three-storeyed, former Dutch garrison building standing at the junction of Church and Middle Streets and commanding views of the harbour. There these investors set up a European-style hostelry, patronised by clients in transit from the weekly passenger ships and other vessels passing through this formerly busy port. But Galle's steady 20th century decline as a port of call had applied a tourniquet to the hotel's patronage, which was somewhat scant when I was there in 1975.

It was perhaps this scarcity of guests that caused the then owner, Nesta Brohier, to take me under her wing. A descendant of prominent Dutch Burgher family, the Ephraums, who had been associated with Galle for more than a century, Nesta was born in the establishment's room number twenty five. She admitted the hotel was haunted by the ghost of her grandfather, Albert Richard Ephraums, whom she had once seen ethereally perambulating past the foot of her bed.

Nesta personally conducted me around Galle, and will forever be associated with my memories of that charming old fortress town and its crumbling ramparts. She dreaded the advent of the "new tourists" from

Germany, creeping down Sri Lanka's western seaboard from Colombo, principally because their women behaved disgracefully by exhibiting their breasts in public. She later told me, in the course of a visit to Hong Kong, that she had posted her oldest Singhalese retainer at the door to the dining room to keep watch for the approach of topless females. If he saw one he would immediately start removing his threadbare khaki tunic, telling her "Oh Memsahib, I am so sorry to see you have no shirt to wear. Please to accept my humble shirt." This was usually sufficient to send the offending female back to her wardrobe.

The "grand old lady of Galle Fort" lived on until a few months past her 90th birthday in 1995, marked by a grand anniversary party in her honour staged in the hotel's dining room. Guests arrived from Colombo in the "Viceroy Special" steam train, to be met at Galle station by beflagged three-wheelers that conveyed them up the hill in relays.

From Colombo I flew across the straits to Kerala in the southwest corner of the Indian peninsula, landing at Trivandrum, known as Thiruvanathapuram before that mouthful defeated pronunciation by Anglican tongues. Thiruvanathapuram took its name from the abode of the sacred snake god "Anantha" of ancient Indian mythology, in whose serpentine coils Lord Vishnu found rest.

With high levels of academic attainment and low levels of employment, communist-governed Kerala boasted the most educated and career-frustrated populace in all India, and lovely old Trivandrum was at the heart of its discontent. It was not uncommon to find street sweepers with university degrees, denied their aspirations as effectively as the storm clouds, stacked in seeming immobility off the Malabar coast, denied us the monsoon everyone craved. From my hotel room in what was once a lovely old palace, situated on a prominence overlooking the three crescent bays of Kovalam beach at the southern end of one of the longest virtually uninterrupted strands in the world, I watched each morning as fishermen braved the heavy pre-monsoon swell in their slender longboats against the leaden backdrop of all that suspended deluge.

Seeking to outstrip the arrival of the rains, I boarded a Fokker Friendship at Trivandrum airport to head further up India's western seaboard to

Cochin. The airport authorities were attempting to conform with a worldwide trend towards greater airport security, following the contagious phenomenon of aircraft hijackings that had begun with terrorist acts designed to draw attention to the plight of homeless Palestinians. A complex of atap huts had been erected alongside the modest terminal building, housing what seemed like a military battalion specifically tasked with searching the dozen or so passengers due to board this once-weekly flight. After running this gauntlet I was decanted into a supposedly sterile zone to await the boarding call. There, in true Indian humanitarian fashion, an aperture had been set into the atap wall to permit us a last loving embrace with those we were leaving behind.

Cochin is sometimes described as the "Venice" of the Malabar coast, but aside from its antiquity, and the fact that it straddles a series of waterways, it has nothing in common with that Adriatic resort. I was booked into the old Malabar hotel on Willingdon Island, where the view from my window would frequently be augmented by the lanteen sails of rice-laden barges, whose sweating crews would strain at their punt poles to work these heavily burdened vessels around the point. A mere ferry ride away was Fort Cochin, another relic of those accreted layers of past imperial sojourns that—from Galle to Goa—lined this littoral of the Arabian Sea.

Fort Cochin reputedly testified to an even earlier influence, for here I found—still in regular use—giant fishing nets of unmistakably Chinese design, ancient but still efficient, and supposedly introduced by the traders from the court of Kublai Khan. Huge cantilevered nets on a system of pulleys, ropes and weights were lowered into the water at high tide, then pulled out after a few minutes, trapping the fish within. This operation continued on through the night, with oil lights dangling over the nets to attract the fish.

Thanks to Ernest Harnach, I had an introduction to a local tea auctioneer who took me under his wing and introduced me to Cochin society. An ideal opportunity for such a social encounter presented itself in the form of a garden party at the residence of one of Cochin's most prominent families, where I met the cream of the local community and never heard—from any one of them—even the merest trace of a Peter Sellers

"Indian" accent. If I closed my eyes I might have been at a soiree in Knightsbridge or Twickenham, for not only was the discourse distinctly English upper middle class but its subject matter was equally cerebral. Few of them had ever left India, but it seemed they either didn't need to or hardly cared to, for everything befitting their status in life was readily available either from Bombay, Delhi or Calcutta, to which they regularly commuted in voyages to the outer peripheries of their social galaxy.

It was an experience simultaneously stimulating and depressing, for the world they inhabited was as far removed from the masses thronging any of those cities as the Antarctic from the Equator. And this, I felt, was the core of the Indian dilemma, the continuation of a caste system based not on religion but purely on class distinction; the survival of the Victorian Raj in some kind of time-warped parallel universe, untouched by the realities of Indira Gandhi's crisis-ridden governance. It was not that they were unaware of those realities, for much of their conversation was devoted to her latest efforts to muffle the press, whose criticisms she so patently found unendurable. It was just that it seemed to strike them as no more than a source of amusement, as irrelevant to their lives as a crocodile would seem to a penguin.

From Cochin I journeyed on to Bombay for a spell of high colonial self-indulgence at the famous old Taj hotel on Apollo Bunder. This stood in all its magnificent ostentation of turrets and cupolas alongside the even more elaborately arched Gateway of India, which I had last seen when my family departed from the sub-continent for self-imposed exile in England in 1946. I expected to be flooded with nostalgia, but it all seemed so long ago that my mind failed to make the necessary connection. Instead I gazed empty-eyed at what had never been more than an extravagant attempt to conceptualise an impossible dream. And I wondered why, after all these years, I should still remain fixated on that long-defunct imperial delusion. Was I the only one still dreaming?

Next on the itinerary was Rome, where I arrived a day earlier than my mother, picking her up at the airport and installing her in our modest but comfortable little demi-pension, serving as a base for our expeditions to various churches. I felt that Mum, still stunned by the death of my father a year earlier, was in need of religious solace. Our timing could hardy have been better. While exploring the interior of St. Peter's, we were astonished to see Pope Paul VI, seated in a sedan chair and beaming a little cherubic smile, borne aloft through the nave like a spectacular monstrance, scattering blessings with little waves of his hand. I had last seen him in November 1970, when he made a brief stopover in Hong Kong in the course of a Far Eastern tour that also took him to Iran, East Pakistan, the Philippines, Australia, Samoa, Indonesia and Sri Lanka. On that occasion I had been responsible for producing a souvenir book of his visit, most of it devoted to an account of the open-air Mass he commemorated in the Government Stadium in So Kon Po, Causeway Bay.

A train ride away from Rome, we checked into a room with a view in an old Florentine hotel, commencing a week-long visit to the birthplace of the Renaissance. We both fell under the spell of Florence, compared with which Milan seemed a dismal aftermath, despite our ascent to the cathedral roof and visit to Leonardo da Vinci's sorely decayed mural of the Last Supper. The latter seemed sentenced to perpetual restoration, following years of neglect which led Henry James to call it 'an illustrious invalid' and Aldous Huxley to describe it as 'the saddest work of art in the world'.

From Milan we embarked on another train ride to Basle, Switzerland, to commence a week-long cruise down the river Rhine. Having become a recent convert to Wagner's *Ring* cycle, I could hardly look upon those waters without envisaging Teutonically proportioned, sub-aquatic Woglinde, Wellgunde and Flosshilde taunting the gnomish Alberich until—to my mind—he quite justifiably avenged himself by stealing their precious Rhinegold.

This being the last of my prolonged, six-months spells of home leave, I resolved to use much of it refurbishing *The Laburnams*, the home I had bought for my parents three years earlier. I caused my mother extreme distress by scraping old wallpaper off the asbestos panels that constituted the basic materials of this largely prefabricated dwelling, which had seen its first metamorphosis back in 1924, long before *Mesothelioma* and *Asbestosis* became recognisable diseases. Halfway through these proceedings, I broke off from the plastering and carpet-laying to collect Mukti from Heathrow airport. He too had been recently bereaved by the premature loss of his mother, so I decided to cheer us all up by hiring a small motor home for a trip to the Lake District and the Scottish Highlands.

It was a crowded holiday, not just in terms of distance covered but in the accommodations we shared. Mum and my youngest brother Bob, then aged 33, slept in the main body of the vehicle, I slept in the 'loft' over the driver's cab and Mukti slept in the cab itself. Mukti and I took it in turns to drive.

When I got back to Hong Kong in the late autumn of 1975 I found that, thanks to Grahame Blundell keeping an eye on the quartering lists in my absence, I had been allocated a spacious apartment on the first floor of Olympian Mansion, at 9 Conduit Road in Hong Kong's Mid Levels. The Mid Levels were aptly named, a sort of consolation zone for those who aspired to the higher splendors of the Peak but had to make do with this compromise altitude halfway up its flanks. The Peak held no allure for me. I had much earlier dismissed it in a poem entitled *Envoys from a Lost World*:

> "Down here the dawn
> of another
> South China Morning,
> with tea and Post;
> Up there, who knows?
> We haven't seen them
> for almost a week,
> those inscrutable
> Peak dwellers.
>
> Only their envoys
> cheerlessly commuting
> in their near perpendicular
> antique funicular
> to survive the noise
> and pressures of sea level,
> hurrying at five
> for a grateful ascent
> into healing vapours.

Perpetual cloud
protectively enshrouds
their Lost World
and its timeless rituals.
If it should clear
they would crowd the view
to enthuse at its beauty
and see what is new
since last year."

One of Our Aircraft is Missing

To celebrate the Queen's twenty-fifth year on the throne, it was decided that Hong Kong should stage a week-long Silver Jubilee pageant in November 1977, to be held at the Government Stadium in So Kong Po, where Pope Paul VI had celebrated his alfresco High Mass seven years earlier. I was put in charge of the arrangements.

A letter to my mother, dated November 19th 1977, records how I was nearly unseated by a military coup in the final stages of preparation:

"Last night's second full dress rehearsal was marvellous, and a cause for no minor elation on my part. It's all coming together beautifully. Very satisfying in view of the near mutiny on my hands from the military. A combined deputation of the Joint Services requested a meeting in my office yesterday morning to voice their gripes over the way the military are being relegated to the supporting cast in the pageant or 'broken down to the ranks' as one might say in military parlance. It was a forbidding assembly: Colonel David Goodman, the personal representative of the Commander in Chief, British Forces (I quite like David: he's the most nearly human of the lot of them); the band leaders of all the military bands, pipes and drums and whatever (there are so many of them I lose count) and various assorted majors, captains and lesser ranks.

"I knew what was coming, because resentment had been brewing for some weeks, so I ordered coffee, tea and beer to put them at their ease. It was very much a case of the thin red line in reverse. Their combined forces against one ex-Royal Army Pay Corps Private (National Service, retired).

"The first salvo came from the Band Leader of the R.A.F. Central Band, flown out from the UK at great expense and 'for what? To be given five minutes lost in the serried ranks of the combined bands display?' I said yes, five minutes and no more, and explained we had a very tight programme.

Awfully sorry and all that; I'm sure they play beautifully and look perfectly splendid but we're already overdoing the military stuff anyway.

"*Then I got it from all sides: the Red Devils, the Royal Naval gun teams, the Police Band, the Gurkha Pipes and Drums, the Light Infantry etc. etc. Barrage after barrage, headed by artillery spotter Major Aubrey Jackman to make sure the shells landed more or less on target.*

"*I was inflexible. I said far from giving them more time (pointing out they were practically up to 45 per cent of total programme duration already) I wanted to cut them down. I said 'Gentlemen, you have all been labouring under a false assumption. You have assumed this is a military tattoo with mufti elements. You are sadly misinformed. It is a Hong Kong community presentation with military elements, and the sooner we grasp that fact the better.' I reminded them who holds the purse strings (I do) and who has to answer to the Governor (I do, via Grahame Blundell). We had our instructions quite clear. It was a pity they didn't have theirs. I hinted we might seriously reconsider whether we should ever ask for military participation at all in any future extravaganza of this scale, since I was personally convinced that the people of Hong Kong had sufficient talent, and versatility, and professional, imperturbable temperament, to carry such a show on their own, unassisted by any military elements.*

"*That shut them up pronto. I then went on to deprive them of their entire Symphonic Salute (a sort of bastardized Dvorak with elements of Tchaikovsky) on the grounds that it was running four minutes over time. If the civilians could keep to time, surely the military could?*

"*Gillian Newson was magnificently supportive. I couldn't have done without her. She exercised a moderating influence, for I must say I've reached the stage now where I'm not impressed by multitudes of brass and rattlings of sabres. I tend to become, if anything, even more stubborn and intractable.*"

Gillian was a Godsend, the most perfect aide I could ever have wished for, and recruited by mere chance when, out of the blue, she arrived in Grahame Blundell's office to ask if there were any vacancies for candidates with organisational skills. She had them in abundance, having previously worked as assistant to Lorin Maazel, Music Director of the Cleveland Orchestra. Married to Mike Newson, a senior executive at Swire's, we thought at first she might just be another bored expatriate housewife looking for diversion, but she soon dispelled that impression by steering us through countless minefields and diplomatically defusing potentially hazardous situations. She proved to be just the girl I needed to translate my wild flights of fancy into workable realities.

Among her earliest tasks was that of repairing the damage wrought by one of these wilder flights, when I inveigled a local aero-modelers club into lending us their superbly detailed miniature aeroplanes. The club in question might—had things gone according to plan—have added another military element to the pageant, for its members were drawn from locally based military personnel. But alas things went hopelessly awry.

Gillian and I had met with them to discuss my idea of staging a wireless-controlled aero-model dog fight in the arena. Could this be done? Was it practicable? They thought it was. Deploying individually controlled planes on different frequencies it should be just a matter of rehearsing a workable choreography. Would there be any danger to spectators? They thought not, but they would need to conduct test flights in the arena to make sure.

On the day in question, they arrived to put some of the finest examples of their handiwork through their paces and it soon became clear that all was not well. The miniature aircraft were not responding to commands as promptly as they should. One model—a beautifully detailed World War Two Lancaster bomber as I recall—failed to respond at all and never returned from its mission. It sailed majestically over the rim of the stadium and into thick woods beyond, beyond hope of recovery. A deep gloom and despondency descended over all concerned.

Another of these wilder flights was my idea of staging the largest multimedia presentation Hong Kong had ever seen, using the entire width of the arena to erect a multi-panel screen that would be fed by images projected from batteries of slide and movie projectors. Given that multimedia techniques were new to Hong Kong, and had only recently been introduced by photographer/impresario Frank Fischbeck in a highly successful extravaganza staged at the World Trade Centre in Causeway Bay, could we achieve a similar result on a larger scale in an outdoor setting, afflicted by relatively high levels of nocturnal luminance produced by the stadium surroundings?

We went to television producer Robert Chua, who said he would have a shot at it. Singapore born Robert came highly recommended. Back in 1967, at the age of 21, he became the youngest producer at Hong Kong's fledgling pioneer in terrestrial television broadcasting, Television Broadcasts Ltd. One of his referees in Singapore had said of him: "His programmes have shown that he possesses not only an above average command of production techniques but also a highly developed imagination which is so necessary for the implementation of original ideas in programme production."

For his new employers Robert created a variety show entitled *Enjoy Yourself Tonight* (quickly dubbed EYT). This was TVB's first ever live presentation, staged five nights a week and immediately shooting to the top-rated slot. It was to last more than 30 years, the longest-running show in Hong Kong television history, and its multi-presenter and guest format was quickly copied by rival channels.

Gillian and I put our heads together and realised that in Robert we had found more than the answer to our multimedia show; we had the producer who could pull the whole pageant together, coaxing even the potentially rebellious military elements into submission. And so it proved. The only hitch was that on the opening night, with Acting Governor Sir Denys Roberts in attendance and a capacity crowd of more than 22,000, the multimedia show came on entirely without sound—owing to a fault we desperately and belatedly traced to a cable break.

After it was over Sir Y.K. Kan, leading Unofficial member of Hong Kong's Executive Council and chairman of our pageant steering committee, said "Come on Peter, let's celebrate." He took Gillian and me to his private supper club, from which we didn't get home until two in the morning. He recognised, as I already knew, that in Gillian we had a jewel we must strive to hold on to. Full of fun, and easy to get on with, she was also amazingly efficient and organised, quick to respond to any crisis and reveal the flash of steel under her velvet glove. When she caught one particularly nasty, bumptious little army bandmaster bullying one of our jun-

One of Our Aircraft is Missing   217

ior Chinese staff she told him "If you don't lay off my staff I'm going to lay the point of my boot in your balls with such force that you won't be able to conduct so much as a conversation for the next two months."

Since we never lost an opportunity to drive home a little community education, we arranged that one of the acts in the pageant would feature a giant wire, cane and papier-mâché effigy of Arthur Hacker's creation *Lap Sap Chung*. Mobilised on wheels, like an especially hideous carnival float, this monster was supposed to terrorise Hong Kong like King Kong run amuck in Manhattan, until squads of young CYCs descended on him with brush and pan to drive him away. CYC was the acronym for "Clean Your City", an organisation I had founded with the help of the Education Department two years earlier, to spearhead community involvement in the Clean Hong Kong campaign.

Once the pageant was over there was a distinct possibility that this initiative would fade into oblivion, so Gillian and I met with the Education Department to ascertain whether they could find the means to continue supporting it. Fortunately there was sufficient enthusiasm among participating school heads to keep the idea afloat so that, under their new name of Community Youth Clubs, the CYCs continued to grow and flourish, extending their involvement to other community issues in Hong Kong and providing an outlet for the very positive and easily-motivated energies so abundantly evident in this city.

With the pageant out of the way, we could focus more intently on promoting Hong Kong's two rival arts festivals, the international Arts Festival staged around Chinese New Year and the Asian Arts Festival mounted in late autumn. I always regarded the two as arse-about-tip, because the former was supposed to bring to Hong Kong tourists who would invariably have more convenient access to its content on their home ground, while the latter—which would have been an infinitely more effective magnet for a tourist influx—was aimed primarily at Hong Kong citizens.

Of the two, the international Arts Festival was the earlier, making its first appearance in 1973, thanks to an initiative by British Airways aimed at finding new pretexts to carry greater numbers of passengers to the Orient. However its initial offerings were so wildly extravagant, with no less

218   No Babylon

than three orchestras—the New Japan Philharmonic under Seiji Ozawa, the London Philharmonic under three conductors, Erich Leinsdorf, John Pritchard and Edo de Waart, and Sir Yehudi Menuhin conducting his Menuhin Festival Orchestra—two ballet companies, the London and the Royal Danish, the Bristol Old Vic theatre, Royal Classical Javanese Dancers and Paco Peña's Flamenco Puro, to say nothing of Elisabeth Schwarzkopf. Tom Paxton, LuLu and a surfeit of exhibitions ranging from Indian miniatures to contemporary French tapestries, that the whole extravaganza quickly ran out of money and seemed doomed to an early demise.

Enter the Dragon, Sir Run Run Shaw, to take over the reins as Chairman of the Arts Festival Committee and lend his immense weight and authority to the entire enterprise. Let the bells peal and the hosannas ascend, for the Arts Festival was saved; not forgetting its debt to Anthony Chardet and Hubert Willis, in whom we found two impresarios with their feet on the ground and the knowledge of how to engage affordable artists. Another to whom the festival owed its survival was modest, unassuming and perpetually cheerful Charles Hardy, who was one of its original promoters and who faithfully returned to Hong Kong each year to volunteer his services receiving performers at the airport and ferrying them to their hotels.

Observing this renaissance with interest, A. de O. Sales, the Chairman of the Municipal Council and therefore de facto Mayor of Hong Kong, decided there was room for more than one arts festival in his city, most of whose citizens couldn't afford ticket prices within reach of a largely expatriate minority. So in 1976 he introduced the first Festival of Asian Arts, starring the Kyoto Municipal Symphony Orchestra, the Tokyo City Ballet, Shinichi Yuize on the *Koto*, Amjad Ali Khan from India, performing on the *Sarod*, the National Classical Music Institute of Korea, the Bayanihan Dance Company from the Philippines, the Phakavali Institute of Music and Dance from Thailand and the Singapore People's Association Chinese Orchestra. Gillian and I now had two arts festivals to promote, and we had better make sure we didn't mix them up.

We also handled public relations for the fledgling Hong Kong Philharmonic orchestra and helped organise overseas tours for Hong Kong musicians, choral groups, dance troupes and other sundry artists. In 1980, when David Ford was serving the first of two spells as Hong Kong Commissioner in London, he called on us to organise a major extravaganza to be entitled Hong Kong in London 1980. I persuaded C.Y. Tung, founder of the Orient Overseas Line, last owner of the late *Queen Elizabeth* ocean liner and father of Hong Kong's first Chief Executive, to sponsor the River Thames' inaugural dragon boat races. I also persuaded his rival shipping magnate, Sir Y.K. Pao, to donate a specially built junk commemorating the voyage of a similar vessel as China's first overseas trade mission to London in the mid-nineteenth century.

There could hardly have been a greater contrast than that which separated these two maritime tycoons. C.Y. was kindly, paternalistic and benign while Sir Y.K. struck me first and foremost as wily, calculating and opportunistic. *Asiaweek* described the latter as "the first the Hong Kong businessman to achieve truly global stature" and said of him "Sir Y.K. navigated the great capitalism-communism divide as well as any Hong Kong businessman. He accepted a knighthood from Britain's Queen Elizabeth II in 1978 and frequently golfed with Denis Thatcher, husband of prime minister Margaret Thatcher. He contributed generously to the British Conservative party. But he also counted Chinese leader Deng Xiaoping as a friend. At his funeral, the then governor of Hong Kong, David Wilson, sat in the front row. Just behind him was Zhou Nan, director of the local Xinhua News Agency and China's unofficial representative in the territory."

Hong Kong in London was staged in Battersea Park, overlooking which Gillian would eventually buy an apartment when she retired from Hong Kong to run her own arts agency. Among its contributors was the young, beautiful and highly talented Cheung Man-Yee, who had been dispatched to London by Radio Television Hong Kong to study at Henley Management College. Together with Wong Wah-Kay, Wong King-Keung, Wong Lo-Tak, Yung Wai-Mi and Wong Sum, Man-Yee had directed some of the most memorable episodes of *Below the Lion Rock*, a groundbreaking television series based on a fictional family living in Wong Tai Sin resettlement estate. Its numerous episodes, spanning a quarter of a century from the seventies through to the nineties, portrayed the lives of the grassroots community at the bedrock of Hong Kong's success.

Among the many who fell under Man-Yee's charismatic spell was Lord George Howard of Henderskelfe, Chairman of the BBC from 1980 to 1983. Howard was a surprise choice as head of the world's most august broadcasting authority. Nicknamed "Gorgeous George", he frequently dressed in caftans, owned Castle Howard, the largest house in Yorkshire and chaired the County Landowners' Association. He once said he would have given up his castle to be BBC Chairman. He defended the BBC's impartiality and public service status during the Falklands war and his astonishingly wide range of interests ranged from art to engineering, valuable when programme content and new technology were crucial issues. They also included Man-Yee.

The story goes that during one of Henley's colourful regattas, Lord Howard had himself punted across the Thames with a picnic hamper, falling on one knee to serenade Man-Yee beneath her window. She accepted his invitation to visit Castle Howard, set on an elevated prominence in the North Riding of Yorkshire, where its magnificent façade was visible for miles around. It had been the home of the Howard family since the 17th century and became the setting for *Brideshead Revisited*, the highly successful television adaptation of Evelyn Waugh's novel of that name. Man-Yee was staying there as Howard's guest during filming of some of the key episodes.

A Cork in the Bottleneck

By 1976 Gerry Jackson had found a bolthole from Tokyo that allowed him to escape its stress levels and traffic noise for his weekend breaks. I fell in love with his rented, timber-framed residence at Abaratsubo, situated beside an inlet of the sea much frequented by the Japanese yachting fraternity.

"You need something like this yourself," Gerry told me. "There must be thousands of potential hideaways in the New Territories you could reach within minutes of your office."

I resolved to heed his advice. A year earlier, I had stumbled across the little island of Ma Wan, located off the north-eastern tip of Lantau like a cork in the bottleneck of the Lantau Channel. Accompanying a party of young CYCs, I had called there by boat on an operation to clean up its one and only public beach. I decided this was where we should begin our search for a second home, but since I was then immersed in preparations for the Silver Jubilee pageant I sent Mukti on the initial scouting expedition.

He returned that evening with the unexpected news that he had already found what we were looking for, and had come to a verbal agreement with the owner of the property to rent the establishment on my behalf. I should not have been surprised. Mukti was entirely capable of such initiatives.

He had stepped off the half-hourly *gaido*, the battered old wooden ferry plying the only route of access from Sham Tseng, on the southern littoral of the peninsular New Territories, and his gaze had immediately fallen upon an abandoned two-storey dwelling which constituted the sole habitation on the opposite side of the bay. "That's it," he said to himself, and then proceeded to inquire into the whereabouts of the owner, who proved to be Mr. Yuen, retired headmaster of the picturesque village school. Recovering from his surprise that anyone should actually wish to rent his erstwhile home, Mr. Yuen suggested a figure of $500 a month, and Mukti bargained him down to $400. I could hardly wait to see what he had landed us with, but when I did I was thoroughly elated with his serendipitous discovery. It was everything I could have wished for, and Gerry thought so too when he came to visit us a few months later.

Ma Wan kept a low profile. It was an island easily overlooked. Viewed from Sham Tseng it blended indistinguishably into the background bulk of Lantau. Approached by sea, via the twelve-minute ferry ride, its insularity was evident only as one rounded the light beacon and found oneself in narrow Kap Shui Mun (Fast Water Channel), one of the most dangerously turbulent straits in Hong Kong waters.

The house itself was in a serious state of neglect, but still habitable and rainproof. Although supplied with electricity, it lacked mains water, or indeed any source of potable water other than that available from the public well on the farther shore, which entailed a considerable hike with buckets and whatever other containers we could muster. Its principal delight was the first-floor balcony, overlooking the entire sweep of the bay. From there, over our next eight years of occupation, I would observe Ma Wan's comings and goings, arrivals and departures, floodlit—since the house faced due west down the Lantau Channel—by full frontal dawns or backlit by extravagant sunsets.

Over those eight years my camera would capture, in unintended and unmethodical time-lapse photography, the slow dissolve of that distilled-life landscape, the subtle tampering by time with the evidence of history. Ma Wan's closest brush with any consequence had befallen it in 1794, when Lord Macartney, stopping off in Macau on the return from his failed embassy in Beijing, commissioned Lieutenant H.W. Parrish of the Royal Artillery to conduct a survey of the island with a view to fulfilling King George III's wish for "a grant of a small tract of ground or detached island" as a depot for the hoped for exchange of Sino-British merchandise. It was not to be. Parrish reported that Ma Wan failed to meet the requirements of a satisfactory harbour for trading ships owing, among other things, to the rapidity of its offshore currents, which even today swirl past the old Ma Wan pier at six knots on the ebb-tide.

A Cork in the Bottleneck   223

Forty seven years after Parrish packed up his theodolite and departed, the tide surged in an entirely different direction when Captain Charles Elliott planted the British flag on another, larger island just nine kilometres due southwest. And sleepy old Ma Wan continued its uninterrupted slumber.

Just as enchanted by the bucolic delights of Ma Wan as I was, my friend Norman Butler asked if he could share the rent with me. Delighted to have his unfailingly harmonious company, I agreed, and we settled into an entirely satisfactory routine wherein he occupied the top bedroom and I the bottom, he would do the cooking and I the washing up.

Hailing from Kettering, in Northamptonshire, where his widowed elder brother still resided, Norman reminded me of one of my favourite movie stars, Leslie Howard, whom I had first seen in a 1942 movie entitled *The First of the Few*, based on the story of the Supermarine Spitfire which, more than any other aircraft, won the Battle of Britain. I was less than ten years old when that film, flown out to India to boost the morale of British troops fighting the Japanese on the Burma front, made its appearance at the Kanchrapara railway institute where my father was secretary, but Howard's performance as Spitfire-designer Reginald J. Mitchell effectively marked the beginning of my love affair with aviation.

Norman Butler resembled Howard not only in his slimly elegant physical appearance but in his manner; quiet, reticent, unflappable and utterly British. He was himself, in a way, the last of the few; a throwback to an earlier, more gracious age of polo sweaters, West End matinees and good, honest, unpretentious cooking. He had joined the R.A.F. during the war, so well-versed in the new science of radar that he was sent to Canada to impart his knowledge to flying cadets on the other side of the Atlantic. War's end found him in Australia, whence he hitched a ride in a Dakota to newly-reoccupied Hong Kong where, with a black-and-white wind-up 8mm movie camera, he captured footage of Japanese prisoners of war paraded through the streets and—before it was demolished—the enormous monument the Japanese had erected atop Wanchai Gap to commemorate their defeat of the British garrison in December 1941.

A gifted mechanic, Norman arranged to revive a long-neglected well closer to home to pump a supply of other than drinking water, which we continued to transport in pails from the more distant communal well. Like other Ma Wan villagers, of whom there were then some 1,800 in all, we preferred to use the communal well for our ablutions, stripping to our underwear and hauling up the chilled liquid to pour over each other by the bucketful.

On one such occasion we found ourselves surrounded by a party of excited young Girl Guides, who had probably never in their lives seen *gwailos* in such an advanced state of undress. Armed with notebooks and cameras, they added us to the collections of island specimens they had no doubt been instructed to amass, firing questions which I was happy to answer but Norman chose to ignore. When they eventually dispersed I asked Norman why he had seemed so discomfited by their interrogation.

"So who's Fauna and who's Flora?" he petulantly replied.

◆　　　◆　　　◆

By now it was abundantly apparent that Mukti and Asarah were drifting irreconcilably apart. Her preoccupation with her factory job, which gave her ample scope to cultivate her own friends and earn her own living, had left him free to act the playboy, courting the attentions of young Filipinas flooding into town to take up employment as care-givers. There was no mounting tension, no heated exchange, no pent-up hostility; just a mutual acknowledgement that the time had come to go their separate ways. She felt she had reached the stage where she wanted to settle down and start her own business back in the kampong. She had developed a finely-honed spirit of independence—rare among rural Javanese women—which made that possible.

Although obliged by Muslim law to do no more than announce "I divorce thee" three times, Mukti offered a generous settlement. He would give her half of his prime piece of land alongside the main Kuala Lumpur-Kuala Selangor highway at Batu Lapan, Kampong Ijok. Asarah accepted and they parted company in the same amicable spirit as had marked their arranged marriage some seventeen years earlier.

I felt sorriest for the boys, both of them attending Island School and embarking on their perilous teenage years of self-discovery. Mazli, then aged sixteen and born in the Year of the Ox, was the serious, dependable one who could be counted on to quietly make the best of a difficult situation and not let it show. Mazlan, aged fourteen and born in the Year of the Rabbit, was more vulnerable and also less predictable. It didn't help that they were coming home from school to find dishes of food laid at the front door, bearing messages from various inamorata competing for their father's affections. Some of these examples of Filipino cuisine, I had to concede, were quite delicious but I hoped that criteria other than culinary skills would guide Mukti's choice of a future partner.

In the end we all breathed a sigh of relief when he settled for Diosy Maglupay, who had played the sensible game of not making any effort whatever to chase after him. Hailing from a large family in Bohol, a tiny island in the Visayan region of the southern Philippines, diminutive Diosy was a delight; unfailingly cheerful, straight-from-the-shoulder forthright and unafraid of anybody. In many ways she was the perfect reflection of Mukti's own better qualities. They were married in April 1979 and later flew to Bohol to meet Diosy's parents. Her father took an immediate fancy to his newest son-in-law and, forgetting that Mukti was Muslim, roasted a pig in his honour, whose meat Mukti was the only one to decline.

En route back to Hong Kong, Mukti and Diosy stayed overnight at a hotel in Manila, where they befriended Isaac Ekuogomo, a crippled Ibo victim of the Biafran war of independence in eastern Nigeria. Isaac was at the end of his tether. A pen friend in the Philippines has assured him that the bullet lodged beneath his skull, in an area too delicate for surgical extraction, could be removed by a certain Filipino faith healer. Investing all his savings in a one-way ticket, Isaac had flown halfway across the world to consult this supposed miracle worker, who had failed to produce the desired result.

When Mukti and Diosy met up with him, Isaac was fast running out of the last of both his money and his hope of ever returning home. Mukti assured him there was a Nigerian consulate in Hong Kong who would repatriate him to his homeland, so Isaac invested what remained of his funds in a one-way ticket to Hong Kong.

When I turned up at Kai Tak airport to welcome the newlyweds home I was surprised to find them escorted by an African invalid on crutches. Mukti, who could be counted on to bring home virtually every waif and stray, naturally assumed, as he invariably did, that I would share his willingness to provide shelter to another so patently in distress. It was one of the traits that most endeared him to me.

Isaac shared the boys' bedroom and proved the most charming and amenable of guests. Speaking excellent English, he was reticent about describing how exactly he came by his near-fatal injury, though he did admit he was a serving soldier in Lieut. Col. C. O. Ojukwu's army of independence, following the latter's declaration, on May 30th 1967, of Biafra's secession from the rest of Nigeria. At first the Biafran freedom fighters did well, but by early October of that year the federal forces had captured their capital at Enugu. Despite attempts by the Organization of African Unity to end the civil war, hostilities continued until 1970, by which point the federal forces had starved the Biafran population into submission. Ojukwu fled the country on January 11th, and a delegation to Lagos formally surrendered on January 15th 1970, thus ending the existence of the Republic of Biafra.

Isaac was, at a guess, somewhere in his mid-thirties, in full possession of his faculties except that he was completely paralysed down his left side. He showed us the point where the bullet had passed through, and lodged under his skull. The doctors in Nigeria had declared his condition inoperable. Now that he had lost his last hope of a miracle, he wanted only to return home to serve as a warden in his local parish church. Mukti took him to the consulate general of Nigeria, where he was told there were no funds available to repatriate him. However they promised they would inform Lagos and report back to us whatever results this overture might produce.

As the weeks went by, our every inquiry met with the same response that they were still awaiting word from Lagos. Although he remained a model guest, Isaac became increasingly depressed at the thought that he might be facing permanent exile. Finally I could accept this situation no longer. I put through a call to the consul general. I reminded him of Isaac's condition and said that if we did not receive a positive response from Lagos within the week I would call a press conference to expose the heartless neglect to which Nigeria was subjecting one of its citizens, presumably because he had received his war injuries while serving with the rebel forces. The following day we received a call to say that Isaac's ticket home was on its way for collection at the consulate general.

For years after his repatriation, we received regular Christmas cards from Isaac, with whom we finally lost touch only because of our numerous subsequent changes of address. They never did find a cure for his disability, but he became steadily more reconciled to it and—as far as we were aware—never again looked for miracle cures, or exchanged correspondence with pen friends in the Philippines.

Skittle in a Bowling Alley

Meanwhile, back at the office there had been numerous developments. David Ford had been replaced in 1976, as Director of Information Services, by Richard Lai Ming, a tall, cultivated Mauritanian Chinese who kept a generally low public profile but did much to advance the careers of promising local officers, at a time when his directorate was still dominated by expatriate 'old timers'. On his retirement in 1978, Richard was succeeded by John Slimming.

John's only rival for the post—and there was certainly no love lost between them—was Grahame Blundell, who had just left GIS to emigrate to Alberta, where he took over the management of a ballet company. John chose me to replace Grahame as Assistant Director in charge of the Publicity Division. He made it clear that he wasn't really interested in publicity, so he would give me a free hand to do whatever I saw fit.

John had a moustache, wore a monocle and was reputed to be with MI5. As I have recounted in *Distant Archipelagos*, he had served in Burma as a British Council representative and later in Malaya as an Assistant Protector of Aborigines. During that spell he had encountered David Akers-Jones, who was District Officer at Alor Gajah in Malacca before joining the Hong Kong civil service in 1957. They became such firm friends that John and his Chinese wife Lucy, whom he had met while on a language course in Kuala Lumpur, held their wedding reception in the Akers-Jones' garden.

John and Lucy arrived in Hong Kong much later than David and Jane Akers-Jones. They did not "switch lifeboats", as I had by then begun to think of it, until the aftermath of that spillover of the cultural revolution in 1967–68. I was delegated to receive them at Kai Tak airport and install them in The Hermitage, whose spartan accommodations I had declined three years earlier.

228

John joined our GIS newsroom, applying to our press releases his talents as a writer of no mean reputation. Aside from *Temiar Jungle,* his account of a journey through the jungle with the semi-nomadic Temiar tribe under his protection, he wrote *The Pepper Garden,* an excellent novel about a Malayan rubber planter whose world is torn apart firstly by the Japanese invasion of 1941 and then by the communist terrorist insurgency. Other titles included *In Fear of Silence* and *Green Plums and a Bamboo Horse: A Picture of Formosa.* In the aftermath of the 1969 race riots in Malaysia, he persuaded then Director Nigel Watt we needed to study the causes of that communal conflict to see if there were any lessons to be drawn for Hong Kong. I personally couldn't see why since the Malaysian situation was entirely unrelated to our own, in which race had not proved a factor at all. But John got his way.

The result was a book, published by J. Murray, rather provocatively titled *Malaysia: Death of a Democracy.* A recent review of its content, by a Chinese reader who admits to having grown up in Malaysia without knowing much of the incidents described there, states "Some people may find this book pro-Chinese. I think the author tried to stay neutral, but he failed, probably due to his sympathy towards the discriminated Chinese".

It was a work typical of John, a man of passionate persuasions, liable to throw moderation aside in his total commitment to a cause. Just such a cause presented itself again when the mass exodus of Vietnamese, predicted by Queen Elizabeth back in 1975, grew from a trickle to a flood. During John's first year in office as Director, a total of 3,356 refugees were rescued at sea and a further 2,441 arrived directly aboard their own small craft, many so laden with their human cargoes that they were barely seaworthy. These numbers did not include some 3,000 aboard the Panamanian freighter *Huey Fong,* which at the end of 1978 was still anchored just outside Hong Kong waters, denied permission to enter because she had originally been bound for Taiwan and only diverted after picking up her unscheduled passengers.

John's particular talent was to anticipate the downside of almost every development. I had discovered this for myself when, on June 30th 1977—twenty years before the New Territories lease was due to expire—I chose to make that date the topic of a speech I was invited by the Hong Kong Tourist Association to deliver to a group of students about to depart for universities overseas as 'goodwill ambassadors'. When I subsequently reported to John the lively discussion that had ensued on the prospects of Hong Kong's reversion to China, he was greatly dismayed. It was not, he felt, a subject to which anyone should be drawing attention, leave alone a senior member of his own department.

For John the implications of the rising refugee influx were nothing less than disastrous. He became obsessed with this particular issue to the point where, because he was unwilling to delegate responsibility, it began to take an appalling toll of his health. At a dinner party in his flat, where he would normally be the most entertaining of hosts, regaling his guests with hilarious anecdotes or improvised scenes from Shakespeare, he called on the gathering to assemble on a circular carpet in the centre of the room. Since this was so small that they had to press close together and hold on to each other, they assumed it was some kind of party trick, perhaps to see how long they could avoid collectively falling to the ground. At the point when they were in imminent danger of doing so, John told them that this was how our latest batch of refugees had arrived, so crowded into their battered little fishing boat that they had stood in this appallingly close proximity for more than a week, sleeping on their feet.

An additional burden was his anxiety for his beloved wife Lucy, whom he somehow found time to visit every day of her prolonged treatment at Queen Mary Hospital. Yet in the end it was John who preceded Lucy's demise through his sudden death from a massive heart attack in 1979.

We first learned that something was wrong when John's driver phoned the office to say there was no sign of John, and no response to repeated ringing of the doorbell. The Slimmings were at that time residing at The Albany, a rather desirable block of government quarters situated in the Mid Levels near the junction of Albany and Robinson Roads. It has long since been demolished and replaced by one of Hong Kong's most prestigious residential properties. I drove up there to find out what was wrong, and arrived shortly after the Fire Brigade had broken down the front door.

John was lying on the floor, quite dead, in a gas-logged kitchen where we were careful not to switch on any lights as we gingerly opened all doors and windows. One of the firemen turned off the gas, which had been left burning, unlit, beneath a saucepan coated with the residue of burnt milk. It wasn't difficult to establish what had happened. John had lit the stove to heat the milk, and was headed for the door, with an unlit cigarette in his mouth, when he was felled by a massive stroke that killed him instantly.

His body lay a few paces from the kitchen door, which was of the kind fitted with a spring designed to close it automatically. The milk had boiled over and extinguished the flame, leaving the gas to fill the relatively airtight kitchen. A medical examination placed the time of death in the very early hours of the morning, but since John had made numerous calls that night, many of them preoccupied with Lucy's health and his anxieties over the refugee situation, the rumour spread that he had committed suicide. I was infuriated by this disservice to his memory. Having frequently accompanied John on his visits to hospital, to witness his devotion to his wife and his concerns for her increasingly debilitated condition, I knew there was no way he would desert her while she still needed him.

And why would a prospective suicide seek to die in a gas-filled room while reaching for a match to light the cigarette in his mouth? I testified at the post-mortem, describing the scene exactly as I had found it. But still the rumour persisted, contributing, I believe, to Lucy's own death shortly afterwards in a Singapore hospital.

Clearing out John's desk drawers when he replaced him as Acting Director, "Johnnie" Johnston found copious notes of observations on the manner in which the "boat people" had made their desperate voyages in hope of a better life, as though John had half toyed with the idea of using these for a future account of their remarkable odysseys.

There was no denying that an immense drama was unfolding in the South China Sea, where Hong Kong was increasingly becoming the primary destination because of its humane treatment of those who survived the perilous journey. We were the first skittle in the bowling alley for those headed east. And more and more did so once we began reading horrific reports of Thai fishermen plundering, raping and slaughtering aboard those boats that headed south towards Australia, while others who survived that brutal gauntlet were driven off the east coast of Malaysia at gunpoint. One will never know how many thousands perished at sea.

I visited Hong Kong's earliest refugee encampment, established in one of the few surviving warehouses along that part of the West Kowloon waterfront bordering Canton Road. When I first arrived in Hong Kong, this had been a long, unbroken stretch of wharves, godowns and dockside installations, but now much of it had been surrendered to developers erecting office blocks, hotels and shopping malls. In the full heat of summer, the corrugated sheeting that enclosed the cavernous dormitory made it seem like a giant, cacophonous incubator. Row upon row of stacked bunks, several tiers high, were crowded so close together that one moved sideways down the narrow corridors between. I was reminded of the view from my window across the alleyway, when I first arrived to stay at the Merlin Hotel. Hong Kong had been through this before.

The inmates, many in little more than their under-garments, were queuing at communal water taps, lining up for food, dining collectively in small family groups atop their allocated bunks or fast asleep with arms wrapped around their slumbering infants. The slow process of sorting out which were genuine refugees, and which were economic migrants, had already begun. Some would be subjected to repeated interrogation to establish their right to resettlement in one or other of the countries they had identified as their preferred destinations—America naturally being first on the list.

I remembered too America's paranoia over communism, and the domino theory that if one country toppled it would bring down another and another...but this wasn't the way the dominoes were supposed to fall. Our overcrowded city, composed largely of people who had all too recently been refugees themselves, wasn't equipped to deal with this invasion.

Already thoroughly familiar with the refugee issue, "Johnnie" Johnston—unlike his predecessor—took it in his stride, not letting it get in the way of everything else. Though he organised special documentary films, booklets and information kits designed to highlight the burden posed for an already overcrowded territory that was not receiving the co-operation it needed from countries far better equipped to share the load, and often personally organised briefings and conducted tours of improvised refugee centres, he also busied himself with other departmental priorities, including the importance he attached to recreational events organised by the staff club. For relaxation he embarked on weekend excursions to the New Territories and outlying islands with his wife Gwyneth, a noted authority on butterflies who succeeded in rearing lesser-known species in a special room assigned for the purpose in their government quarters in Mount Austin Road. Together they collaborated on a book ISD commissioned on Hong Kong butterflies.

More intimately involved with refugee matters were David Roads, a veteran AP correspondent who had been based in Hong Kong almost throughout the post-war years, and Matthew Cheung, who was later to leave ISD and make his mark in the ranks of the administrative grade. These two formed the nucleus of the Overseas Public Relations Section established in 1977 under the Public Relations Division. The most famous holder of the post, however, would later be Mark Pinkstone, whose unfailing good humour, accessibility and helpfulness prompted his "clients" to award him a rare life membership of the Foreign Correspondents' Club, to which David Roads had belonged since it first moved to Hong Kong from Shanghai in 1949.

During the coming years, following my appointment as a Justice of the Peace, I would visit refugee centres and learn for myself something of the variegated human dramas that had brought these tides to our shores. As the selection process became more refined, in the aftermath of ugly incidents provoked by those already admitted into their host countries, the mood of the ones remaining shifted from perseverance to despair. There seemed no end in sight to their effective imprisonment. Yet even when Vietnam agreed to accept those who wished to return, there were few volunteers, and many scheduled for repatriation—because they had failed the litmus test of genuine refugee status and were accounted economic migrants instead—had to be carried screaming and kicking to the waiting aircraft.

234   No Babylon

Hong Kong was to carry the cross of its refugee centres for many years to come, constantly defending its policies and raising the issue in the world arena to focus attention on the unfairness of its struggle to cope, largely unassisted and with little sympathy for the dilemma it faced. Not until June 1997, on the eve of Hong Kong's reversion to Chinese sovereignty, did the numbers of Vietnamese migrants in detention centres decline to the point where the government could afford to close the largest—and most contentious—at Whitehead. Inmates at this Sha Tin facility had frequently staged violent protests against efforts to repatriate them. Less than a year later, the last of the detention centres was closed bringing to a humane conclusion a saga that had dogged Hong Kong's development for more than two decades.

The Crochet Club

On January 15th 1980 police inspector John MacLennan was found dead in his flat, with five bullet wounds in his chest. The Special Investigations Unit officers who discovered his body had arrived to arrest MacLennan on charges of homosexuality. To gain entry they had to break through a door locked from within. Despite the purported existence of a suicide note, and the fact that there appeared to be no other means of access to the apartment, few people readily accepted the official finding that MacLennan had died by his own hand. Was it conceivable that he would shoot himself in the chest five times before eventually expiring?

I had maintained links with Hong Kong's gay community since my arrival in 1965. I had known some of my fellow members since my previous sojourn in Malaya, and found many parallels in the restraint, caution and conservatism that governed our social conduct. Numbering a wide spectrum of often highly placed individuals, both in commerce and in government, we were compelled to exercise the very height of discretion. We met only at small social gatherings, to let our hair down and relax among kindred spirits. Where I had thought of the Malayan equivalent as the knitting circle, I regarded the Hong Kong group as the crochet club, almost surgical in the precision with which we wielded our hooks and gathered our stitches.

As had been the case in Malaya, most members had formed lasting and monogamous attachments. Others had outlived their partners, considering themselves too old to seek new ones or, like me, had found substitute relationships that were more emotionally fulfilling. There were only two known gay haunts in the city and most of us avoided them like the plague. I never set foot in either of them myself. They were for the young, the reckless and the tourists. We were homebodies, with our books, our music collections, our gourmet meals and our television.

The Hong Kong government had first attempted to "legalise" homosexual acts, between consenting adult males in private, back in 1968. The issue found favour among liberal British expatriate legislators but was strongly opposed in the local community, who maintained this was yet another case of the decadent west attempting to pollute innocent Chinese.

By 1980 it had become apparent that the government was embarked on what smacked of a witch hunt, and none of us knew how far this would reach, who its targets were and where it would end. MacLennan's inadequately explained death caused our crochet club to come thoroughly unstitched. No one and nothing seemed safe any more. We were like a spy circle threatened with exposure if just one of us cracked. We dug even deeper underground.

A general public outcry over the nature of MacLennan's death, and the jury's return of an open verdict—despite instruction by the coroner that almost all the evidence pointed to suicide—compelled Governor Sir Murray MacLehose, on July 9th 1980, to order a commission of inquiry headed by Mr. Justice Yang. When its report was eventually published, the main conclusion came as no surprise—and yet has done little since to dispel the still lingering suspicions. It found that John MacLennan had committed suicide.

The still colonial government again attempted to introduce homosexual law reform, and was again fiercely resisted by sectors within the Chinese community, which insisted that homosexuality was a western vice, unknown in Chinese tradition. As Mark McLelland has pointed out, in his *Interview with Samshasha, Hong Kong's First Gay Rights Activist and Author*, "The fact that the law against homosexuality was itself a colonial imposition, which had no parallel in the legal codes of either the People's Republic or Republican China, went unmentioned. Instead, conservative Chinese groups organized and conducted a media battle against the proposed changes, asserting that 'Church leaders, educators and social workers [are] unanimous in attacking legalised homosexual activities as 'deviant behaviour'.'"

Years later there came a perceptible shift in the prevailing public attitude when the government launched one of the first AIDS awareness campaigns in Asia. Although still insecurely encased within my metaphorical closet, I personally took charge of the publicity drive, aided by the eminently knowledgeable and highly motivated Dr. E.K. Yeoh, who would later become Hong Kong's Secretary for Health, Welfare and Food.

E.K. and his colleagues arranged for me to interview a delegation of young Chinese gays, to obtain their advice on the tactics we should adopt in addressing our principal target audience. There was no need for me to pretend ignorance of the prevailing trends in Hong Kong's gay underground of that time, for by now I really was totally unenlightened in that regard.

I found these youngsters refreshingly forthright and candid. I asked them what would be the most effective approach to drive the message home through our main medium of television. They told me to put two young men in bed and show one of them reaching for a condom. So we did. Ours became the first publicity campaign in Asia to employ such a direct approach. And it worked. We never had a single complaint from an outraged viewer. All those hypocritical claimants who had so vociferously contended that this sort of thing didn't happen in China suddenly fell unaccountably silent.

But it was not until 1991 that homosexuality was finally decriminalised. As Mark McClelland has pointed out, this followed "two years after the Tiananmen Square massacre, when growing concern over human rights issues as Hong Kong approached the handover to China in 1997, as well as the need to monitor the spread of HIV infection, created an environment among the Chinese community in Hong Kong in which the colonial administration could finally bring the laws relating to homosexuality in line with those in Britain".

◆   ◆   ◆

On September 9th, 1980, Diosy delivered her son, Mazmois Melchor, at Tsan Yuk Maternity Hospital in Sai Ying Pun, while I was away on another of my peregrinations through India, Europe, America and Japan. It had not proved the most successful of vacations. I found San Francisco greatly changed since my last visit some eight years earlier. I sat in Union Square at eight o'clock on my first morning and witnessed a sequence of events so bizarre that it set all my remembered impressions askew.

A young Hispanic male had climbed atop a piece of public statuary to deliver an oration, apparently with me as his only audience. Since he chose to do this in what sounded like Mexican it made no sense to me, but from his wild gestures and somewhat furious tone of voice it was clearly incendiary and filled with expletives. Seemingly oblivious to this spectacle, a rotund blonde in a rumpled dress was seated on the grass in the middle distance, accompanied by a trio of black males and giggling almost uncontrollably while they plied her with alcohol from bottles in brown paper bags. I didn't want to think where that would end.

Then an elderly and emaciated Asiatic man, who struck me as Japanese, made an appearance in a dirty raincoat from stage right, furtively creeping through the bushes until he came upon a group of peaceable pigeons scavenging on the gravel pathway. Approaching these as close as he could without revealing himself, he hurled a large and extremely stale loaf of French bread at the grazing birds, which promptly took off in alarm. Breaking cover, he rushed out to retrieve the loaf before returning to his hideaway to await the return of the wheeling flock. This process was repeated three or four times before the pigeons decided to migrate elsewhere, at which point he tucked the loaf under his arm and made his exit.

From stage left appeared another Hispanic, attired entirely in mauve, from his dyed hair, sunglasses, battledress and suede shoes to his mauve poodle on a mauve lead. He minced across my range of vision until he disappeared through the park gates.

I next saw a grim-looking middle-aged Chinese woman take up a position on a park bench on the opposite side of the square, glaring around her until she rose to confront a young Caucasian couple, who appeared to be the only relatively normal looking people I had seen so far. Haranguing them in Cantonese, she switched to English to shriek "You not welcome here. You go back where you belong." Startled, they hastened their pace and gave her a wide berth. At which point her eyes fastened upon me and she started heading in my direction.

I didn't wait a moment longer to heed her advice. I decided to go back where I belonged on the next available flight.

When I returned to Hong Kong, Mazmois, or Mel as we all called him, was about six weeks old. We got off to an awkward start. Cradling him as he lay contentedly asleep in my arms, I surrendered to an irrepressible sneeze which made him open his eyes, scowl at me with a look of extreme disapproval and then doze off again.

He profoundly changed my life. I stopped smoking to avoid any risk to his health, and invested in my first video camera to spend virtually every moment of my spare time recording his progress. He was the most engaging and rewarding child I had ever known. He almost never cried or complained, was incessantly curious about everything and knew, from the start, exactly how to manipulate the camera lens, surmounting an otherwise recognisably human physique, that followed him everywhere and became his first perception of me.

I would hoist him astride my neck and take him for long walks on the hills behind Olympian Mansion or in the Botanical Gardens below, where we would be gazed at askance by Filipina domestics tending their employers' largely Caucasian progeny. Exiting the house for one of our longer excursions, I bent down to press the button for the lift, forgetting that, at his higher elevation on my shoulders, his head would come into fairly abrupt contact with the lift door. The bump caused me some concern but failed to elicit any protest from him so that I assumed all was well. Halfway through our expedition, along a remote water catchment path overlooking Kennedy Town, I was suddenly aware that he was failing to respond to my running commentary on the ships anchored in the harbour. I hauled him down and found him as limp as a rag doll, not roused in the least to my efforts to awaken him.

Convinced he was suffering a delayed reaction from that blow to his head, I panicked, ran down the hill, laid him in the back seat of my car and took off like a lunatic for Queen Mary Hospital in Pok Fu Lam. In the worst possible display of colonial arrogance, I ignored the reception counter at the outpatients' clinic, rushed into the waiting room and shouted for immediate attention, declaring that the child in my arms was suffering severe concussion. This produced the desired effect of a doctor and two nurses rushing to attend to him and laying him out on an examination bench.

Knowing that his parents would be made anxious by our delayed return, I sought out a telephone to put through a call to the house. Diosy answered and listened patiently to my explanation.

"There's nothing wrong," she assured me. "He's just asleep."

"But I shook him repeatedly and there was no response."

"He always sleeps like that."

I recognised an outraged yell from across the room. "Excuse me," I said, "I'll find out what's happening."

Mel had awoken from his slumber, indignant to find himself surrounded by masked strangers probing his vital organs. I had no alternative but to explain to these medical personnel that there had been a mistake. I apologised.

It wasn't that easy. I had reported a case of concussion, which required that the patient be kept overnight for observation. Mel could only be discharged with parental consent. There was no way that either Mukti or Diosy could get there to sign the discharge sheet. They were preparing dinner for our guests that evening; a function for which I was already running way behind time.

I led Mel to a bench in a quiet corner of the reception room and explained that we were going to play a game called "Running away from Hospital". He entered into the spirit of this exercise with enthusiasm and together we tiptoed out through the entrance and made a dash for the car. For weeks afterwards I worried that the police would arrive at our doorstep with a warrant for my arrest on a charge of child abduction.

Consorting with the Enemy

With Diosy taking charge of our domestic arrangements, her husband was free to look for a job. The Argentine consul, Julio Ferrari, whose consulate adjoined our first-floor apartment at Olympian Mansion, engaged him as a chauffeur. Ferrari was a quiet, kindly bachelor, much liked and respected. Mukti, who was always particular about choosing employers, developed a great fondness for him.

In the early spring of 1982 I took a fortnight's vacation and headed for Kanazawa, on the western coast of Japan's main island of Honshu. This was the relatively less industrialized littoral bordering the Sea of Japan, with long, near pristine beaches interrupted—like frets through the silken strings of a *koto*—by romantic, pine-covered headlands. It was remote, arcadian, largely unspoilt and precisely the kind of repository of tradition that most attracted me to Japan. But because of all these things, it was also out of touch with the English speaking outside world.

I had learned by now that the best way to get around Japan was to profess not to speak any Japanese at all. Discovering a helpless *gaijin* wandering like a lost soul in their midst, the indigenous populace felt morally obliged to take me under their wing. I had only to ask directions at any street corner, with an appropriately bewildered expression on my face, and a little knot of people would converge to debate what was to be done with me. Kindly escorts would conduct me to the nearest *ryokan*, ensuring that I removed my shoes before entering. I loved *ryokans* with their paper-thin walls, sliding *shoji* screens, beautifully timbered floors and *tetami* mats. They were infinitely preferable to the cheap but stereotyped business hotels with their western-style beds and miniscule, prefabricated bathrooms.

Buried in rusticity, without English newspapers, radio bulletins or television coverage, I was oblivious of the rapidly deteriorating relations between Britain and Argentina, unaware that both countries were plunging headlong into war over an insignificant archipelago in mid-Atlantic. I found a public telephone and put through a call to Hong Kong to ask Mukti how things were faring on the home front.

Everything was fine, I was assured, but Mr. Ferrari was about to be posted back to Buenos Aires, and would be leaving just three days after my anticipated date of return. Could we invite him to dinner on his last night in Hong Kong?

Of course we must, I naturally replied. He was a family friend and we would all miss him.

Thinking nothing more of it, I rounded off my vacation and headed by train for Tokyo, where I was due to spend a couple of days with my old friend and colleague Gerry Jackson. Gerry met me at the door with a copy of that day's *Japan Times* in his hand. Unfurling the headlines, he held up the front page for me to read. "What do you think of this?" he asked.

I assumed at first it was some kind of excessively elaborate April Fool hoax. A British naval task force setting sail for the Falklands? Flag-waving mobs at the quayside shouting jingoistic phrases like "Bash the Argies"? It was too absurdly picaresque to take in; no more plausible than a Gilbert and Sullivan operetta. Was it a joke?

No joke, said Gerry, pointing to a boxed paragraph at the bottom right-hand corner of page one. The Hong Kong Government had instructed Argentine consul Julio Ferrari to pack his bags. He was to be deported on the Wednesday following my return.

"But I've invited him to dinner on the eve of his departure," I protested.

"What?" thundered Gerry. "Get on the phone immediately and call it off."

"I can't. He's a friend of the family."

"You're mad. A senior government official consorting with the enemy? Not only consorting but offering him succour! You'll be accused of treason."

"It won't come to that. He's a diplomat. He'll find a diplomatic way to decline."

I flew back to Hong Kong, where Mukti was waiting for me in the teeming Kai Tak arrival hall.

"Did you invite Ferrari to dinner?" I asked.

Mukti nodded.

"He declined of course?"

"No, he accepted."

"Mukti, what have you landed me in? Why didn't you tell me he's being deported?"

"What difference does it make? He's our friend."

I thought about it. What difference indeed? Does a disagreement between heads of state suddenly turn a neighbour into an enemy?

Back home again, I leafed through back issues of the *South China Morning Post* that had piled up in my absence. On the front page of one of the most recent of these was a full-spread photograph of a mob of journalists besieging the doors of the Argentine consulate. Barring them entry was the "consular official" who informed them that Mr. Ferrari wasn't available for comment. The "official" was Mukti, who must have bewildered them by wearing his habitually congenial grin.

I refrained from ringing Ferrari. If the media hounds trailing him everywhere should follow him to our front door, I would arrange for Mukti to greet him there, while I remained in hiding in the kitchen. In the event he rang me in my office on the Tuesday afternoon, some four hours before he was due to arrive for dinner. He apologised for the fact that pressure of work would prevent him making an appearance. I tried to keep the tone of relief from my voice, picturing him bent over a wastebasket in his near empty office, burning the last of his top-secret documents.

However he had something he wanted to give me. Could I meet him in the forecourt of Olympian Mansion at six o'clock? The forecourt, I thought to myself, in full public view, just below the Argentine flag hanging outside the consular office. I swallowed hard and said yes.

It turned out that what he wanted to give me was his consular limousine, a Toyota Carina with automatic transmission and consular plates. I said no, I couldn't possibly accept. He protested that he didn't have time to sell it and had no other way of disposing of it. I said I would buy it, but

HK$ 4000 was all I had at the time in the way of spare funds. He said it was a done deal. I wished him luck, we shook hands and that was the last I saw of him.

The following morning Mukti drove him in the Carina to the airport, where the media were assembled in wait for him. Lawrence Pottinger, the Gurkha officer I had befriended at Sek Kong in 1967, had by now left the army and taken up a government appointment as Hong Kong's Assistant Protocol Officer. It fell to him to see Ferrari safely aboard the first leg of his flight to Buenos Aires, and he told me afterwards that Ferrari, doyen of the consular corps, was a consummate gentleman to the last, who would be much missed by his peers.

The Carina gave us long and faithful service until I retired from government eleven years later and surrendered it to a secondhand dealer. Mel, who was by then thirteen years old, had become so attached to it that he demonstrated the fact by strapping himself into the back passenger seat. It took our collective powers of persuasion to coax him into accepting the inevitable.

Boadecia Redux

Fresh from her conquests in the Falklands, and almost palpably clad in the armour of Boadecia Redux, heir apparent to the Celtic queen who had fought so bravely to save Britain from the Romans, British Prime Minister Margaret Thatcher made her way to Beijing in September 1982 for discussions with the Chinese leaders over the future of Hong Kong.

The timing of her visit could hardly have been less propitious, for myself personally as much as for Hong Kong at large. I had just returned from another trip to Canada, to coincide with my mother's arrival from the opposite direction so that the two of us could converge on the home of my brother Paul and his family in Metchosin. There I had so far surrendered to the attractions of the Canadian lifestyle that I placed a down payment on a property barely a mile from my brother's house, embracing some two acres of rocky terrain in the vicinity of beautiful Lake Matheson, named after the offshoot of a family that had contributed one of Hong Kong's best known founding fathers.

We could hardly deny the necessity for Mrs. Thatcher's visit. Some three years earlier our anxieties over the future had been partially allayed, and our confidence slightly boosted, by an invitation from the Chinese Minister of Foreign Trade, as a result of which Sir Murray MacLehose made the first-ever official visit to China by a Hong Kong governor. Our hopes were further raised when Sir Murray returned from Beijing with an assurance from Deng Xiaoping that Hong Kong people could "set their hearts at ease". But "Big Mac" had given us only an abbreviated version of this exchange. What Deng in fact told him was:

> "We have always maintained that the sovereignty of Hong Kong belongs to the People's Republic of China. As Hong Kong has its unique position, we shall discuss the settlement of the Hong Kong

question in the future on the premise that Hong Kong is part of China. But we will take Hong Kong as a special region. Hong Kong may practice its capitalism over a considerable length of time while we shall pursue our socialism."

We weren't given the full version at the time, for if we had known, something approaching panic would have set in. After all, there weren't too many lines to read between. Deng knew this, so he advised Sir Murray to "set their hearts at ease".

Sir Murray had not gone to Beijing empty-handed. He took with him a proposal put forward by Britain's then Foreign Secretary, David Owen, calling for an 'exchange of sovereignty for ruling right.' The youngest politician to hold that post for more then forty years, Owen was subsequently to break away from the Labour Party as one of the so-called 'Gang of Four' who founded the Social Democratic Party.

In his history *The Return of Hong Kong*, Wang Yincheng writes:

> "Owen planned to unveil the programme to the Chinese Government during his visit to China in April and asked Hong Kong Governor Murray MacLehose, who would visit China one month earlier, to sound out China's stand.
>
> "In line with the instruction of the British Foreign Office, Murray MacLehose told Deng that Britain hoped China could permit the British Hong Kong Government to extend the land lease concerning the New Territories beyond June 30th 1997 and change the lease's deadline to 'be effective during the British Queen's reign of the territory.' This was aimed at obscuring the deadline of June 30th 1997. Deng saw through the British Government's intention and told Murray MacLehose no matter what wording was included (in the document trying to extend the land lease), it was a must to avoid touching upon the issue of 'British reign.' In other words, Deng turned down the British side's proposal."

While self-determination had seldom been viewed as a realistic option for Hong Kong—since it was felt China would not countenance such a development—some, at an earlier point in time, had publicly disagreed with this assessment. Under the governorship of Sir Alexander Grantham, prominent legislator Man Kam Lo had put forward a motion advocating partial elections to the Legislative Council, staggered over a number of years. The motion was approved by councillors and by Grantham, but retracted at the last moment because unofficial legislators were anxious as to how China might react.

On June 4th 1969, exactly twenty years before the Chinese government moved to stamp out the pro-democracy movement in Tiananmen Square, eighteen Urban Councillors, including Elsie Elliot, Henry H.L. Hu, Denny Huang and M. H. Huang, jointly sent a letter to British newspapers in the UK. They requested a change in Hong Kong's political system to a "wholly local, internal, self-governing administration", rationalizing that China would

> "surely tolerate a more sophisticated, egalitarian and enlightened ordering of that society devoted to the interests of the overwhelming Chinese majority of their own compatriots".

The letter achieved some publicity but negligible result. Nevertheless, by 1981 it was believed that a limited franchise could be safely extended to apolitical areas of the administration that affected public services and amenities. In January of that year the government approved a district administration scheme whose aim was to give the people of Hong Kong more say in those government services and policies that affected the districts in which they lived, and to make it easier for the needs of each district to be identified and provided for.

It was announced that a new system based on electoral constituencies would be introduced for both the Urban Council and district board elections. The first district board elections would be held in the New Territories in March 1982, followed by the urban areas in September 1982. The first elections to the Urban Council on a constituency basis would take place in March 1983.

Against a background of continuing economic prosperity, and a cautious experiment with limited forms of representative government, tempered with concern for renewal of the New Territories lease and a settlement of the growing crisis of illegal immigration, Hong Kong held its bated breath when Margaret Thatcher announced her intention of calling on Beijing to discuss the Hong Kong question with Chinese leaders. Those old communist warhorses were known to dislike dealing with uppity women, and especially members of the female sex mounted on warhorses.

One hundred and eighty nine years had elapsed since Lord Macartney headed in the same direction, only to receive his humiliating comeuppance. But that was long before Hong Kong came into existence, and even longer before it became rich and famous.

Our bated breath was collectively exhaled in a dismayed sigh when the reassurance that Maggie hoped to receive failed to materialize, when it became unmistakably clear that, once the lease of the New Territories expired in 1997, China intended to recover the indivisible whole, including Hong Kong and Kowloon. According to Wang Yincheng, Mrs. Thatcher

> "grudged giving up the pearl on the crown and decided to bargain with China with her remaining influence as the victor in the case of the Falkland Islands. The card she played was the three unequal treaties China's Qing Government signed with Britain in the 19th century. According to the treaties, Hong Kong and southern Kowloon were land ceded to Britain in perpetuity and only the New Territories was the leased territory. China's announcement that the three treaties were unequal could not bind Britain because the international law understood by Britain proved the three treaties effective, said Mrs. Thatcher."

Wu Jiping, who was present during the subsequent Sino-British negotiations in the role of interpreter and translator for the Chinese team, says in his book *The Hong Kong Deal*:

> "The British still had the illusion that they could continue to rule Hong Kong after 1997 by signing a new treaty with China. Alternatively, the British might propose recognition of China's sovereignty over Hong Kong in exchange for China's recognition of its continued administration. One such analysis, drafted by my colleague Zhou Con-

gwu. stated that 'inspired by Britain's victory in the Falkland Islands war, Mrs. Thatcher would make full play of her reputation as the "Iron Lady" and take a hard-line stance in her coming visit'. But the British, strong in appearance but feeble in reality, were in a weak position on the Hong Kong issue. Mrs. Thatcher herself was aware Hong Kong was not the Falkland Islands and China was not Argentina."

Wang Yincheng says that Deng Xiaoping told Mrs. Thatcher:

"No latitude is allowed in the issue of sovereignty. Frankly speaking, sovereignty is not negotiable. Now the time is ripe. It should be made clear that China will take back Hong Kong in 1997. In other words, China will not only take back the New Territories but also the Island of Hong Kong and Kowloon. China and Britain (should) conduct negotiations under this precondition to find the way to settle the Hong Kong issue. We've waited for thirty-three years. It will be forty-eight years in fifteen years. Our long wait has been based on the people's full confidence. If we couldn't take back (Hong Kong) in fifteen years, the people would have no reason to trust us again and any Chinese Government would be forced to relinquish power and step down from the stage of politics of its own accord. There can be no other choice.

Deng also told Mrs. Thatcher:

"We have a clear-cut position regarding the Hong Kong issue, which involves three things. First, it involves the issue of sovereignty. The second question is about what method China will adopt to govern Hong Kong to maintain its prosperity after 1997. The third question is that both the Chinese and British governments should carefully discuss how to ensure that no major fluctuations will occur in Hong Kong from 1982 to 1997."

Deng added:

"We hope to co-operate with Britain to maintain Hong Kong's prosperity. But this doesn't mean that Hong Kong's continuous prosperity must be achieved only under British rule. Fundamentally speaking, the territory's ability to maintain its prosperity depends upon the adoption of policies suited to Hong Kong's circumstances upon China's resuming the exercise of sovereignty over, and administration of, Hong Kong. Hong Kong's existing political and economic systems, even most of its laws, can be maintained. Of course, some reform measures should be introduced. Hong Kong will still practice capitalism and many systems fit for it should be maintained.

"We should exchange views with people from different walks of life in Hong Kong to formulate our principle and policies in and after the next fifteen years. These principle and policies should be accepted by both Hong Kong people and other investors in Hong Kong. First, they should be accepted by the British, for they'll benefit them too."

As her own account of this meeting has testified, Deng's inflexible stand came as something of a shock to the British Prime Minister. Wang Yincheng describes how she reacted:

"Mrs. Thatcher thought that China's administration of Hong Kong would have a disastrous effect. Deng replied: 'It's thought that fluctuations will take place once China announces it will take back Hong Kong in 1997. To me, small fluctuations will be unavoidable. (But) if China and Britain solve the problem with the attitude of co-operation, major fluctuations can be avoided. We've also considered one question we are unwilling to consider. What should we do if major fluctuations took place in the fifteen-year transitional period? If that happened, the Chinese Government would have to reconsider the time and method of taking back Hong Kong. What I worry about is how the fifteen-year transition could be smooth and is that major disorder would emerge in the transitional period. The disorder would be man-made. It would be created by both foreigners and Chinese. But it would be created mainly by the British. It's easy to create disorder."

Whatever Mrs. Thatcher conveyed of this conversation on her return from Beijing—and she was certainly guarded in what she said—the fluctuations were not long forthcoming. The Hong Kong dollar fell on foreign exchange markets and the stock market dropped to its lowest ebb since the global economic crisis of 1973. Business activity declined markedly and foreign consulates and commissions—particularly those of the United

States, Canada and Australia—were swamped with applications from would-be emigrants.

It did not make for smoother Sino-British relations that in her references to Hong Kong, Mrs. Thatcher continued to use the word 'colony', which had been virtually taboo in Hong Kong Government parlance throughout the previous decade. Says Wu Jiping:

> "The term 'colony' may be a neutral word in the vocabulary of the West in reference to an entity, but in the Chinese language it has a strong sense of degradation. It is highly irritating to the average Chinese ear."

To employ another term later popularized by Hong Kong's last governor, Chris Patten, I was 'gobsmacked' by this unexpected downturn of events. Landed with a hefty Canadian mortgage at suddenly vastly unattractive exchange rates, I was tempted to pin Maggie's portrait to my darts board and practice improving my aim.

A Touch of Positive Interventionism

Sir Philip Haddon-Cave, who had been Financial Secretary from 1971 to 1981, had famously coined the phrase "positive non-interventionism" to describe the principal governing his economic policies. But now that he was Chief Secretary, faced with a distinct crisis of confidence in the aftermath of Mrs. Thatcher's visit to Beijing, he decided to positively intervene in the conduct of our information policy. To clear the decks for action in response to suddenly altered times, he appointed Peter Tsao Kwang-yung as Director of Information Services. It was a decision equivalent to commanding a storm to take control of a teacup. We really weren't big enough to contain Peter's energies, so he turned us into a cooking pan forever on the stove.

Overnight I was transformed from the youngest member of his directorate into its oldest. "Johnnie" Johnston was leaving us on retirement, Joseph Cheng was moved up to an information post in the Secretariat and I was suddenly the sole survivor of the "Old Guard". Peter himself was only two years older than me. Born in Shanghai in 1933, he emigrated to Hong Kong at the age of seventeen and enrolled in St. John's College. He made a positive boast of the fact that he had never been to university, and I believe developed something of a soft spot for me because he knew I hadn't either.

Because of his multiple talents, his career was both chequered and accelerated. He served as a computing officer in the Royal Observatory, played guitar in his spare time with a local hotel band, as its only non-Filipino member, negotiated intricate trade deals that spared Hong Kong the worst impact of the numerous trade embargoes erected against us, and—after a spell on attachment to Radio Television Hong Kong—was appointed Director of Trade, Industry and Customs in 1979.

I fondly recall an evening in his home when Peter provided the guitar accompaniment to the late Denis Bray as the latter sang the old Yorkshire folksong "On Ilkley Moor Bar Tat" in Cantonese. I also remember his habit of alerting his directorate, at his regular morning briefings, that he was feeling "particularly robust this morning" and therefore, by implication, would expect an even greater contribution of brilliant ideas and suggestions.

In my earlier years as Secretariat press officer I had occasionally experienced the sensation of being surrounded by ideas flying faster than the speed of thought. In Peter Tsao's case the speed was supersonic, and the ideas ricochetted around the inside of his think tank like bullets rebounding off steel plate. I wanted to duck for cover.

Sir Philip Haddon-Cave had indulged Peter in his choice of the best people he could find for this think tank, and he chose well—Cheung Man-yee from Radio Television Hong Kong, Kerry McGlynn, who had headed various departmental press units, and Irene Yau, who brought with her to the GIS news room the team that had supported her in the Police Public Relations Bureau. I was left to continue running the Publicity Division because Peter admitted he didn't know or care enough about it to interfere.

Sir Edward Youde succeeded Sir Murray MacLehose in May 1982 as Hong Kong's 26th governor. He joined the British delegation, headed by Sir Percy Cradock, at the bilateral talks on the future of the territory, nobly bearing up to the scrutiny of television cameras and the interrogations of the media in his frequent commuting between Hong Kong, Beijing and London. Comments Wu Jiping:

> "Sir Edward was very good at dealing with reporters, always appearing very polite. Nevertheless, they hardly got anything out of him. The British really kept their lips sealed as far as the negotiations were concerned. This was said to be a good tradition of the British Foreign Office. But on China's part, there was always somebody revealing internal policies. Some were authorised to do so deliberately, others

simply slipped up. One example was the former Defence Minister, Geng Biao, who said China would not station troops in Hong Kong. He leaked something that was being considered at the time, so an irritated Deng decided to send troops."

Despite the oft-repeated statement that the talks were "useful and constructive"—the term carefully agreed between both parties as their concerted response in all dealings with the media—the impression grew that they were running into serious difficulties, that both sides were negotiating from irreconcilable standpoints.

The situation turned critical when it became apparent, in the late summer of 1983, that Britain and China were quarreling over the British claim that the territory should remain under British administration. At this point the adjectives "useful and constructive" disappeared from the communiqués and the Hong Kong dollar fell still further. China viewed the financial crisis with considerable distrust. As Wang Yincheng comments in *The Return of Hong Kong,* the Chinese felt

"the British Government had intended to play the 'economic card' through Hong Kong's economic fluctuations to shake the Chinese Government's stand of resuming the exercise of sovereignty over Hong Kong and arouse Hong Kong citizens' dissatisfaction with the Chinese Government. But the Chinese Government was not affected. While meeting with Hong Kong guests on September 27th, Ji Pengfei, director of the Hong Kong and Macao Affairs Office of China's State Council, announced that the Chinese Government would never permit Hong Kong to be independent, and that it must take back Hong Kong on July 1st 1997."

Wang attributes the impasse to the British stand of "separating sovereignty from the ruling right".

Wu Jiping, in *The Hong Kong Deal,* describes an exchange between members of the Chinese team in the aftermath of a prolonged position statement delivered by Sir Percy Cradock in July 1983, at another of their series of meetings:

"Taking the lead Luo (Luo Jiahuan, head of the first division of the Department of Western Europe in the Foreign Ministry) said 'It seems that the British are going to have a seesaw battle with us'. Lu Ping (Secretary-General of the Hong Kong and Macao Affairs Office) said 'So the British really believe that we are going to allow them to stay on in Hong Kong after 1997. How naive they are'. Ke (Ke Zaishuo, Director of the Foreign Ministry's Hong Kong Negotiations Office) added 'I think the British are prepared for the worst and working hard for the best. They know sovereignty is out of the question, so they talk about administration. They have said a lot to convey only one message: We cannot prevent you from taking back sovereignty, but you're so poor in administration we should be in charge'. Yao (Yao Guang, Executive Foreign Vice Minister) added 'This old gentleman is just blowing his own trumpet. Is it really because of you, the British people, that Hong Kong has achieved so much today? What nonsense! Anyway, let them continue talking and see if they have anything more to say'."

Deng Xiaoping told former British Prime Minister Edward Heath on September 10th, in the course of a visit by the latter, that Britain's proposal of exchanging sovereignty for ruling right was not acceptable, and that China would have to announce its own principle and policy on the settlement of the Hong Kong issue in September 1984 if an agreement could not be reached by that time. But Mrs. Thatcher, according to Wang, "still wanted to have a bet".

The resulting financial crisis forced a review of British tactics and the British delegation suggested that the two sides should examine whether it would be possible to build a tolerable future for Hong Kong on the basis of the so-called Chinese twelve points. In the end this proved the way out of the minefield. The British side, says Wang Yincheng, had to return to the negotiation table when they found the 'economic card' didn't work.

On October 7th 1983, at a meeting called by Mrs. Thatcher at 10 Downing Street, Sir Percy Cradock submitted a letter suggesting that confrontation be avoided and negotiations be pushed forward. Mrs. Thatcher finally accepted his suggestion and gave up her confrontational stance. On October 14th, she wrote to Chinese Premier Zhao Ziyang, saying that both sides could discuss Hong Kong's permanent arrangements on the basis of

256   No Babylon

China's suggestions. At the fifth and sixth rounds of talks, in late October and mid-November, the British side abandoned their stance of exchanging sovereignty for the right to rule. Some progress was being made at last. Britain was no longer seeking any form of joint administration of Hong Kong by both countries.

The *Pearl of the Orient* had once been memorably portrayed, in tourist posters, as delicately suspended by a pair of chopsticks. The opposing implements were now Chinese and British. In the course of transferring the pearl from one platter to another, the fear was that somebody would fumble that precious orb and let it slip.

Of the two sides, it was demonstrably apparent that the Chinese had all along been the better prepared, and the more determined to stick to their guns. They had in their favour the fruits of various carefully laid initiatives, going back over many years, for the reclamation of their sovereign rights in regard to Hong Kong. They had laid the foundations for their negotiating position with great care, and were well armed against any proposals to internationalize the issue. Despite what Roosevelt had said at the Yalta Conference in February 1945, in his celebrated aside to Stalin, the Chinese had no intention of even considering Hong Kong as some kind of international free port, under the jurisdiction of a world body such as the United Nations.

Back in 1972 China had taken pains to specifically preclude such a possibility. By adopting the resolution of its Special Committee on Decolonization, the 27th UN General Assembly had recognized China's demand concerning its sovereignty over Hong Kong, in line with the principle of international law. It had also effectively ruled out the possibility of other countries (including the United Nations) participating in the settlement of the Hong Kong issue (for example through any so-called 'joint international administration').

Wang Yincheng records that when meeting British guest Louise Helen in October 1972, Premier Zhou Enlai said:

> "The future of Hong Kong must be determined. When the term of the lease (of the New Territories) expires, the Chinese and the British must enter into negotiations. Both countries now have normal diplomatic

relations. It is a matter of course for Britain to participate in the negotiation in due time. The land taken away from China must be returned...China's policy is that it won't take action in haste in terms of these things."

Yet to all intents and purposes Hong Kong had indeed become a focus of global concern. Just about every nation's interests were represented in, if not closely and intricately bound up with, its huge and complex net of banking and financial services, its manufacturing industries and commercial organisations. And everybody stood to lose if the pearl of Hong Kong were to fall between the platters; America and Japan more than most.

Given the distance to be covered in bringing both parties to any kind of reconciliation, and the fact that they were racing against the clock to meet the deadline of September 1984, as stipulated by Deng Xiaoping, the final product of the protracted talks surpassed expectations. British Foreign Secretary Sir Geoffrey Howe, returning from a meeting with Deng, held a press conference in Hong Kong on August 1st 1984 at which he presented the broad outlines of the agreement about to be initialed in Beijing.

Sir Geoffrey said the purpose of his visit to Beijing had been to "review progress of the negotiations, to make real headway on remaining issues and to strive for the best possible result for the people of Hong Kong." The two sides, he announced, had agreed to the framework and key clauses of a legally-binding accord which would preserve Hong Kong's unique economic system and way of life. Furthermore, he added, there would be satisfactory provisions for liaison and consultation after the conclusion of the agreement.

Reaction was bullish. The stock market climbed as the Hong Kong public eagerly awaited proof of Sir Geoffrey's assurances in the Sino-British Joint Declaration. By now Sir Percy Cradock had vacated his chair as head of the British negotiating team and returned to London, to oversee negotiations as foreign affairs adviser to Mrs. Thatcher. Wu Jiping was one of those who went to the airport to see him off. He says, in *The Hong Kong Deal*:

"The first time we met Sir Percy, we thought he was a serious and con-scientious old man who sometimes showed extreme impatience and mild rudeness that was just typical of an old-fashioned British diplo-mat. It was not until after regular contacts that I knew Sir Percy had a keen interest in China and its culture. He was, genuinely, a pleasant person. Given authority by Mrs. Thatcher Sir Percy had adopted a firm approach in the first round of talks in which he fought primarily for British interests. After the resolution of Hong Kong's sovereignty Sir Percy displayed sincere concern for Hong Kong and worked hard to lobby Chinese leaders. Contrary to his previous agenda, he never spoke a word about British interests."

Lord Wilson, who joined the British team in the final stages of the negotiations—and well before his eventual replacement of Sir Edward Youde as governor of Hong Kong—recalls (in *Hong Kong Remembers*) that the last lap was intense and absolutely exhausting.

"Matters were complicated by the fact that the Chinese text of the agreement was as important as the English, and would be read by more people in Hong Kong. We didn't want a separate negotiation on the Chinese version of the text after an English one, however, so the two were negotiated together. We were aided by the use of modern tech-nology with a computer in the Embassy which could transmit in cipher the Chinese text of what was being agreed. The Chinese side either had to use a typewriter or revert to pens. I believe the use of this sort of information technology for diplomatic negotiations was probably unique at the time."

Peter Tsao made me responsible for overseeing publication of the draft agreement on September 26th 1984, in the form of a white paper. I worked closely with the Government Printer, in conditions of utmost secrecy, to produce this on time. Its appearance on the counters of government publi-cations outlets and in the various district offices led to queues that wound through the streets of Central and other areas, as thousands filed their patient way to receive their free copies. They had heard that the seemingly impossible could be made achievable; that it really was feasible to have one country with two systems. They wanted, in their own hands, tangible evidence to support this miracle, to justify claims of life after 1997.

Tempting Providence

To recover from the stress and tension of those climactic years, I badly needed another holiday, and chose Egypt as my destination, reluctantly accepting the fact that, in order to cruise down the Nile, I would need to join a tour group. I met up with them in January 1985 at a hotel in Cairo, whence we were flown to the massively relocated temple of Ramesses II, above the waters of Lake Nasser on Egypt's border with Sudan. Our next destination was Aswan, where I sought to escape from my fellow travellers by plunging into Nubian back streets and bazaars, only to keep running across a fellow escapee by the name of Joyce Williams.

Recently widowed, and still grieving for the all too premature loss of someone she had loved very dearly, Joyce proved as independently-minded as I was, and equally loath to become embroiled in any more than the merest acquaintanceship with the married couples who made up the majority of the group. We weren't particularly anxious to team up with each other either, except that it seemed churlish to keep ignoring each other when chance brought us so constantly and consistently together.

We got into conversation, and in the end adjourned to the terrace of the legendary Old Cataract Hotel, overlooking Elephantine Island and the gull-white sails of slow-moving feluccas negotiating the waters below. So popular had this haunt of the rich and famous proved, from its inception in 1899, that within two years of its opening the management were forced to erect tents in the grounds to accommodate the overspill.

Joyce was from Rotherham, born in the same year as me, shared my Chinese zodiac sign of the pig, spoke with a charming hint of a Yorkshire accent, and had inherited from her recently deceased husband the national chair of her professional body, the parent organisation of the worldwide and far-scattered physiotherapist community. In her appetite for travel,

260

and her insatiable curiosity for everything she encountered, I recognised a kindred spirit.

But where I was content to survey the general panorama of the scene before us, she would devour the details, quarrying the minutiae of the landscape, querying the particulars, how the fields were irrigated, how they ground the corn, what they fed the camels. She was not in the least bit like any tourist I had ever met. She conducted her travels with the thoroughness of an anthropologist, botanist and economist combined. She could not pass a food stall on the street, no matter how fly-infested, without inquiring into the ingredients of its mysteriously inedible looking offerings and wanting to sample them herself. She claimed that her tough, working-class, street-smart upbringing had made her impervious to germs.

To my surprise, never before having been especially attracted to any member of the opposite sex, I found I was beginning to like her enormously, which I decided was not only an unfamiliar but also an extremely hazardous state of affairs. I was tempting providence, and felt impelled to caution her that I was not what she might take me for.

To my initial dismay, she replied that she wasn't in the least deterred from continuing the relationship because, if anything, she felt safer knowing that I was not just one more predatory male whose overtures she would end up having to politely but firmly discourage. Another emotional entanglement was the last thing she wanted. We could both rest assured that neither of us posed the slightest danger to the other.

For me the effect was both astonishing and unprecedented. I could pursue a friendship with a member of the opposite sex without placing myself at risk. With her and through her, I could grasp something of hitherto uncharted feminine psychology while simultaneously permitting her to satisfy her curiosity as to my own. I felt downright comfortable sitting beside her, discussing the trials of contending with the vicissitudes, frequent unreliability and generally unromantic nature of the male sex.

On completion of our four-day cruise down the Nile to Luxor, we entrained for the overnight journey back to Luxor—only to discover that the booking clerk had assigned us the same two-berth compartment. This added a further dimension to our relationship, to which I surprised myself—and I suspect her too—by adjusting without demur. It deepened rather than jeopardised our curious liaison, and provided the foundation for something more intimate, yet still unthreatening.

Hotel-bound by an unseasonable sandstorm in Cairo, we happily kept each other company in our respective bedrooms and confirmed the suspicions of our fellow travellers without ever acknowledging the full nature of our "affair", which remained our best kept secret.

Meeting Joyce was one of the great landmarks of my life; the commencement of a relationship that has sustained me over the past twenty years. And it could not have come at a more opportune time for either of us. We were both in our fiftieth year, with the bulk of our lives behind us and uncertain prospects looming before us. I was on the cusp of male menopause, poised in a brief interlude between delayed adolescence and premature senility. And I was feeling very much "yesterday's man", an ungainly relic of an earlier, less uncertain age; an anachronism in the new order at GIS, where I was making so little contribution to the latest agenda of putting a positive spin on negative circumstance. As much as I consoled Joyce in her widowhood, so she persuaded me to accept that I may not necessarily be as defunct as I felt myself to be.

◆   ◆   ◆

True to the form we displayed whenever our backs were to the wall, Hong Kong collectively decided we must shrug off any appearance of anxiety over the fact that we were now in "countdown" for the great return of the prodigal son to China in 1997. We would take part in only the second world Expo in which we had ever ventured to appear, and since Grahame Blundell was by now busy taking charge of the Alberta pavilion, the task of coordinating our own pavilion fell to me.

Once again I set about wheedling and cajoling, one of the consequences of which was that the first-ever dragon boat races would be staged in False Creek, Vancouver, an event that I understand has since become a fixture on the Vancouver calendar. I was also inspired to propose that thousands of blank postcards should be printed and distributed to schools, inviting their students of all ages to draw or paint on these, or append whatever messages they wished, as contributions to be handed out to pavilion visitors. Even Jan Morris, author of my all-time favourite work on the rise and fall of the British Empire, the *Pax Britannica* trilogy, contributed elegant sketches of junks sailing through Hong Kong harbour, which some unwitting recipients might have acquired without ever grasping their value.

Jan was at that time in town to research material for her book *Hong Kong*, which remains the classic of its genre. I was fortunate enough to be assigned by Peter Tsao to offer whatever assistance she might require, and we established an immediate and lasting friendship.

The planning committee for Expo 86 comprised key players of "Hong Kong Inc." that unofficial conglomerate of banks, commercial and public institutions that collectively responded to any such opportunity to demonstrate the city's strength through unity. Together we launched an international competition for the design of our pavilion, which happily was won by our own Hong Kong architect and conceptualist, Tao Ho. A man of all seasons, catholic tastes and positively Renaissance versatility, Tao Ho came up with the idea of a pavilion encased in bamboo scaffolding, symbolising the ever-changing nature of Hong Kong and its refusal to be straitjacketed into any fixed and static notion of itself.

The idea was for the scaffolding to remain in a constant state of incompletion, either in the process of being erected or dismantled for reinstallation in new configurations. Visitors would be able to observe actual Hong Kong scaffolding workers in action, demonstrating their highly trained, surefooted talents. But of course we had reckoned without the density and obtuseness of Canadian paper-pushers, who had apparently never heard of such skills and were not about to entertain them now.

I equated their stupidity with the same stupefying obstinacy that Grahame Blundell had encountered in Osaka sixteen years earlier. No amount of reassurance, that the workers would at all times wear safety helmets and harnesses, could satisfy minds as thick as several planks lashed together. We had to do without the workers, substituting their life-sized, plaster-cast facsimiles instead. At one stroke of a bureaucratic pen, the whole concept of the pavilion was destroyed. We became the static fixture that we had sought to demonstrate Hong Kong was not.

Despite this setback, Tao Ho did he best to provide us with a pavilion of which we could be proud, the principal feature being a nine-minute multimedia show, depicting twenty-four hours in the life of Hong Kong and designed for us by Frank Fischbeck, who had pioneered this art form in Hong Kong several years earlier. The remaining exhibits took as their theme the contrast between "Silk and Silicon" to show the transition from Hong Kong's historic role as a coastal trader to its status as the industrial, financial and communications mecca of Asia.

I flew to Vancouver for the opening and met up there with Joyce, travelling from the opposite direction. Together we watched with the crowds lining False Creek on May 2nd 1986, as Prince Charles and Princess Diana arrived to declare the Expo open, marking the highlight of Vancouver's hundredth anniversary. We dined with Grahame, exchanging reminiscences of our many happy years together, and then Joyce and I crossed to Vancouver Island for the trip down to my brother's home at Metchosin.

We borrowed a motor home from Paul's father-in-law, Leo Cornford, and—since it was still somewhat early in the season—discovered we had most of the up-island provincial parks and campsites to ourselves. There we barbecued our sausages in empty moonlit landscapes to the call of the loon and found ourselves, on one occasion, dive-bombed by minute and almost invisible humming birds because we had strayed too near their nest.

We partly retraced the route I had followed three years earlier, when I took Mukti, Diosy and Mel for their first visit to Canada, renting a slightly larger motor home to traverse virtually the entire length of Vancouver Island from Victoria to Port Hardy. It had proved a glorious holiday, which commenced and ended with brief stays at the home I had bought the previous year, then occupied by my niece Kate and her husband Simon. In fact it was so enjoyable that, forgetting the old adage that one should never attempt to live in a place where one has enjoyed one's holidays, we started contemplating the possibility of eventually living in Canada, if anything should prevent us staying on in Hong Kong, where at that time the future seemed so dark and uncertain.

◆　　◆　　◆

Back in Hong Kong, having moved but two years earlier from Conduit Road into a flat at Trinity Court in Harbour City, Tsim Sha Tsui, I learned that those premises were about to be pulled down and was offered something equally transitory in the former Victoria Barracks, across the road from St. John's Cathedral. This was a curious but delightful relic of bygone times, a lost world in the heart of busy downtown Hong Kong, consisting of former military married quarters housed in three-storey brick and tile-roofed blocks that cascaded in serried ranks down a hillside run riot with neglected vegetation. We loved it there, islanded amid trees raucous with cockatoos, and we wanted to stay forever, but the ceaselessly moving finger of the civil service quartering office was already writing; nor all our piety, nor wit, could lure it back to cancel half a line.

Eventually this sanctuary would become the green oasis of Hong Kong Park, but only years after we had moved elsewhere—initially to a ground floor bachelor flat at Mount Nicholson, which offered a walled garden to make up for a lack of interior space that compelled us to convert the dining room into a bedroom for the family. Our last government quarter was situated on the topmost floor of the front block of this delightful retreat, where our balcony commanded a spectacular view of the harbour and the aircraft still making their perilous descents into the old Kai Tak Airport.

◆　　◆　　◆

Sir John Bremridge had succeeded Sir Philip Haddon-Cave as Financial Secretary, and in October 1983, to stave off concerns over a free-floating Hong Kong dollar during those darkest hours of pre-agreement jitters, had announced the decision to link the Hong Kong and US dollars at a fixed exchange rate of 7.8 to one. He had also declared that he was shelving the plan for a new airport to replace overburdened Kai Tak.

I was relieved. There had already been extensive exploratory excavations on Ma Wan with a view to building a bridge to this proposed new airport, which was to be constructed by completely obliterating the natural environment on the unpopulated islet of Chek Lap Kok, off the north shore of Lantau, and turning this into a vast podium that would house the new runways and all their ancillary services. Ma Wan itself would have been entirely defaced and transformed, losing all the charm that had attracted me to it in the first place.

Rumours of the new airport had led to a brief flurry of speculation in the late seventies and early eighties, but now the commotion had died down, and Ma Wan was going back to sleep again. It seemed the perfect time to buy, secure in the knowledge that our insulated kingdom would remain undisturbed. I decided we would look around for something to purchase rather than continue renting the increasingly dilapidated two-storey structure we had occupied for the past decade. Norman Butler had moved back to his home in Kettering where, some years later, he would be discovered dead in his drawing room, having tripped and smashed his skull against the corner of a table; a sad and lonely end for such a dignified and charming man.

In our quest for suitable accommodation we received invaluable help from Jonathan and Irene To. Jonathan To Siu-kwong had long been embraced into our extended family as one of our dearest friends. When we first moved to Ma Wan in 1976 he was the delivery boy who would willingly arrive at any hour of the day or night to supply our groceries from one of the few village stores we could call upon for this purpose. I admired his determination to fight against all the odds to make something of himself.

Born in 1959, he was a mere infant when his mother had brought him and his elder sister into Hong Kong in 1962, successfully smuggling them across the border amidst the great surge of illegal immigrants that had poured across the Shum Chun River that year, when authorities on the other side had relaxed their customary controls and Hong Kong's own security forces had proved inadequate to the magnitude of the task of rounding them all up and sending them back again. It was precisely the fear of a repetition of this hopelessly unmanageable influx that had governed so much of the PolMil discussion during my own stint on the border in 1967.

Jonathan's mother was penniless, jobless and desperate. She arrived on Ma Wan to seek out distant relatives who had left China themselves during a much earlier purge of landowners, and who know managed a chicken farm and a small grocery store. She explained to these tenuously remote kinfolk that she was incapable of looking after her children, left them in their care and disappeared from their lives. The chicken farmers fed and raised Jonathan and his sister and—without treating them unkindly—employed them as unpaid labour to manage both the farm and the store.

Jonathan was eighteen when he first came into our lives. He had chosen to name himself Jonathan because in 1973 he had seen the movie *Jonathan Livingstone Seagull*, whose plot is summarized in the Internet Movie Database as follows:

> "Jonathan is sick and tired of the boring life in his seagull clan. He experiments with new, always more daring flying techniques. Since he doesn't fit in, the elders expel him from the clan. So he sets out to discover the world beyond the horizon in quest of wisdom."

The name suited Jonathan to a To. I could see that his willingness to place himself at our beck and call stemmed from his hope that we might somehow offer him a means to escape his island prison. The flat we occupied at the time, in Olympian Mansion, Conduit Road, had a small servant's quarter at the back. We placed this at Jonathan's disposal, rent-free, together with a seat at our table. Isaac Ekuogomo, the crippled Ibo war victim, had by then been repatriated to Nigeria.

Jonathan proved the personification of that "try anything" Hong Kong spirit that had so inspired our love for this city. He set out to learn all of it at once, French, German, quantity surveying, concrete mixing, any and everything that would allow him to improve his life. We urged him to focus and he eventually did, getting a job first at a Gammon construction site and then applying for, and being accepted as, a trainee fire services officer. He met and married Irene, equally ambitious, who taught herself classical calligraphy, Chinese painting, western painting and photography and who would eventually acquire a degree in humanities through an open university course. They made a delightful pair and produced an equally delightful son, whom they named Anthony.

Although by 1986 Jonathan had long left Ma Wan, he still retained his sentimental ties with the village and would keep us informed of properties for sale. One of these proved particularly appealing, a three-storey house located at the end of Sports Road, facing south and flanked by a hillside amidst just about perfect *feng shui* surroundings. The moment Mukti, Diosy and I set eyes on this, we resolved we would make it our own.

The immediate portents were not especially propitious. Disembarking from the battered old *gaido* that took us back to Sham Tseng, I slipped on the seaweed-covered stairs of the unprotected jetty and lost my balance. Desperate to save my video camera, I held this up at the fullest extension of both arms as I slipped headfirst on my back, step by step, into the sea. Mel, who was six years old at the time, remarked to his mother that I looked exactly like a dead cockroach.

A flurry of arms reached for me as I struggled in the water, the camera by now hopelessly unsalvageable. It struck me at the time that nobody laughed at the stupid old *gwailo* who had got himself into such a fix. Even though most of my would-be rescuers hardly knew me, they were all too busy saving me and ensuring I was all right. Another of those heartening little reminders of why I felt so at home amidst these people. They wouldn't necessarily give any evidence of even being aware of your existence unless you were in trouble, and then they would collectively rush to your aid.

Although I had escaped relatively unscathed, but for the loss of my camera, I felt it my duty to report this circumstance to the Tsuen Wan district office, within whose jurisdiction Ma Wan fell. The next victim, perhaps older than me, might not be so lucky.

Within a few weeks I received a courteous reply. Measures had been put in hand to remedy the situation. The pier had been renovated and a new roof placed down the entire length of it to provide shelter from the sun and rain. Adequate lighting had been affixed to this to ensure the safety of

Tempting Providence 269

gaido passengers, fishermen and boat owners, night and day. The steps had been replaced and thoroughly cleaned. The accident I had suffered was regrettably due to the fact that moss was deposited on these steps.

I replied to this with a single sentence. "Correction. Moss was deposited in the sea."

My reminder was pinned to the Tsuen Wan district office staff notice board, where I understand it remained on display for some time.

Changing Horses in Midstream

The untimely demise of Sir Edward Youde, on December 5th 1986, deprived Hong Kong of one of its most beloved governors and forced it to change horses in midstream. Sir Edward, who died, aged sixty-two, at the British Embassy in Beijing, in the course of one of his frequent China visits, had hoped to see Hong Kong through the most difficult stages of the transition period, and would have been well qualified to do so. His role in the Sino-British negotiations had played no small part in securing the Joint Declaration. One of his last public appearances had been as escort to the Queen and the Duke of Edinburgh during their second—and last—visit to Hong Kong.

Small and clerkish in appearance, with a disarmingly shy smile, Sir Edward possessed an astute intellect and a thorough understanding of the Chinese. The despair of his public relations team, because he declined our image-building proposals to make him seem more visibly gubernatorial, he was nevertheless esteemed by the public as a tireless champion who literally risked his life in Hong Kong's cause.

Knowing how well he understood them, the Chinese had regarded his presence on the British negotiating team with suspicion, and had insisted he take part simply as a member of the British delegation and not in his capacity as Governor of Hong Kong. Says Wu Jiping, in *The Hong Kong Deal*:

> "Despite this the people of Hong Kong could only express their will and request through the Hong Kong Governor. Sir Edward did not disappoint—he had indeed spared no efforts to fight for the interests of the British and Hong Kong people till he died in office. Although he did not want to speak Chinese at formal occasions, all of us knew he

spoke it very fluently, so we were always alert and careful when discussing issues before him."

Elsewhere in his book, Wu Jiping says Sir Edward:

"played all sorts of tricks. That's why Luo (Luo Jiahuan) had said: 'Youde is as slippery as an eel'. Sir Edward demonstrated his cunning over and over again in later negotiations, so much so that the saying 'as crafty as Youde' is still part of the vocabulary of the Foreign Ministry, especially in the Department of Western Europe."

I was utterly taken with him myself, mostly for his kindliness, humanity and concern for those with whom he worked. When Lawrence Pottinger was due to retire as Assistant Protocol Officer, Sir Edward gave a small farewell luncheon for him at Government House. I was among the dozen or so diners at the table, thoroughly disarmed when Sir Edward rose to deliver a brief but beautifully phrased farewell address, in which he admirably encapsulated all of Lawrence's best qualities; not least his humility and unfailing cheerfulness, no matter what consular carryings-on or diplomatic fracas he might be called upon to referee.

It was the sort of thoughtful personal touch, away from the public eye, so typical of Sir Edward. I regarded both him and Lady Pamela as a breath of fresh air after their dour Scottish predecessors in Government House.

When his body was returned from Beijing, thousands of mourners streamed past his coffin in the hallway of Government House to pay their last respects prior to his funeral cortege. He was succeeded, after a brief interval when Sir David Akers-Jones held office as acting-governor, by Sir David Wilson, also from the Foreign Office, steeped in Chinese affairs and returning to Hong Kong after having served as political adviser to Sir Murray MacLehose. Like Sir Murray, Sir David cut a patrician figure in his formal attire, complete with plumed helmet. It was a reversal to old form.

In his *History of Hong Kong*, Frank Welsh says

272   No Babylon

"In selecting MacLehose, his successor Sir Edward Youde, and later Sir David Wilson, all from the Foreign Service, successive British governments were indicating that the most important task facing governors was not that of looking after Hong Kong, but of dealing with Beijing. Anyone who might 'go native' and manifest undue enthusiasm for Hong Kong interests would be dangerous."

Youde had come close to courting that danger, but there seemed no risk of Wilson doing the same. However committed in his intentions to govern Hong Kong, leaving to others the task of continued negotiations with China, it was inevitable that Wilson would be heavily involved with the delicacies of paving the way to an agreeable and satisfactory convergence—and the Chinese had got his measure through the last stages of the talks leading to the Joint Declaration.

◆   ◆   ◆

The Easter break of 1989 found me alone in my "music room" on the top floor of our house in Ma Wan. The family had gone off to the *kampong* at Batu Lapan Ijok, in Selangor. I had acquired my first electronic word processor and I had long wanted to put this through its paces. I got to work on the novel that had been hovering in the back of my mind, the story of a disillusioned member of the former Nazi Youth movement, who was once described as the youngest station master in Germany, and who fled to Brazil at the end of the war, consumed with guilt at the role he played in directing the traffic to the Nazi death camps. He believes himself to be the last surviving Nazi war criminal, and is relieved when his long awaited Nemesis arrives in the form of a young Jewish butterfly hunter. To complicate matters, despite their age difference, he falls in love with her.

I had never been to Brazil. I had never been anywhere near South America. But I had acquired a huge number of bound volumes of *National Geographic*, together with an index. I set to work trying to find out what it would be like to be a "station master" in some remote corner of the Amazon basin, managing a rubber estate in Indian territory. Mel, who was then nine years old, had become so central to my life that I had to put him into the book, as the young Indian boy Eduardo. I wrote, with minimal sleep and nourishment, for ten days, almost never stopping. It was like taking dictation, as if Kristian Hardy were at my shoulder, reliving his memories. At the end of that Easter break I packed up my word processor and returned to the office with a completed first draft of approximately forty-eight thousand words scattered on various floppy disks.

I had an appointment the following week with Chris Holmes, son of one of Hong Kong's most distinguished civil servants, the late Sir Ronald Holmes. Chris and his American wife Stephanie had recently returned from London to establish Hong Kong's first literary agency. I had been sufficiently emboldened by this development to offer them a huge tome of a historical saga entitled *Possession Point*, recounting the fictional memoirs of a reclusive expatriate, retired to London and looking back over his years in the colony and all the characters he met there. Mercifully none of that manuscript of some two hundred and fifty thousand words has survived. I laboured over it for many months before the advent of my word processor.

Chris had suggested we meet at the new *Spices* restaurant in Pacific Place. He had my voluminous manuscript with him, and was clearly steeling himself to break the news that it was not worth submitting. I saved him the trouble by suggesting a swop; the return of *Possession Point* in exchange for my new novella, tentatively entitled *The Music Room*. With that out of the way we went on to enjoy a very good lunch. A few weeks later Stephanie arrived at my office in Beaconsfield House, asking me to sign a contract that would allow the agency to market my novella.

A few months after that she passed on to me a letter from Liz Calder, publishing director of relatively newly founded *Bloomsbury Plc.* and discoverer of such authors as Salman Rushdie, Anita Brookner and Julian Barnes. She wanted to publish my book.

The following year, on a spell of home leave, I met Liz, who took me to lunch at the *Groucho Club*, so called because the late Groucho Marx had declared he would never join any club that would have him as a member. *Bloomsbury* was then still making its mark, and had not acquired quite the reputation it enjoys today, with numerous Booker, Pulitzer, Whitbread and Nobel prizewinners to its credit and no less than the *Harry Potter* books making them a fortune.

Liz asked me how long I had been in Brazil. It was a country she had lived in for many years and was still in love with. I felt compelled to admit I had never seen it, hastily adding that I had always wanted to. After a slightly worrying silence she said she had only asked because I wrote about it so convincingly. Thank God, I thought, for all those volumes of *National Geographic*.

In the end we had to change the title. Somebody else had come out with a book called *The Music Room*. We settled for *The Singing Tree*.

◆   ◆   ◆

One of the landmarks of Sir David Wilson's gubernatorial tenure was his announcement, in the course of his policy address to the Legislative Council on October 11th 1989, that the immensely costly new airport project at Chek Lap Kok, publicly abandoned by Financial Secretary Sir John Bremridge on February 25th 1983, was back on again. Hong Kong needed a shot in the arm after the massive loss of morale it suffered because of what had taken place in Beijing's Tiananmen Square on June 4th 1989.

The Tiananmen incident was one of those pivotal points by which you could calibrate the epochs of Hong Kong's history. The colony's citizens had watched with considerable admiration and sympathy the progress of the pro-democracy student movement enacted in that arena. Thanks to a massive presence of international print and electronic media, who had virtually camped out at Tiananmen since the state visit of Russian President Mikhail Gorbachev, the world was given a ringside seat as the students rallied under a large plaster-cast figure suggestive of the State of Liberty.

I had personally entertained the direst misgivings as to how long this state of affairs would be allowed to continue. Would any other country have countenanced the prolonged occupation of its capital heartland by a potentially riotous multitude for so great a duration without seeking to put an end to it? Surely I wasn't alone in believing that—all other efforts to defuse the situation having failed—this could only culminate in a bloodbath? Even some of the original instigators of the demonstration were having second thoughts and trying to apply the brakes. But the heady exhilaration of the mood they had inspired, and the apparent inability of the authorities to effectively deal with the situation, were proving devastatingly infectious. Thousands of youngsters were pouring into Beijing from elsewhere in China to join the brouhaha. Why was the western world virtually exhorting them to further manifestation of their demands in the face of the all-too-apparent dangers?

China was an extremely large and potentially volatile country that could all too easily slip into anarchy. In my own lifetime it had disintegrated into independent fiefdoms incompetently governed by disputatious warlords. The present rulers in Beijing had only to look to developments in Gorbachev's own nation, following *Glasnost, Perestroika* and the collapse of the Berlin Wall, to witness the outcome of relaxing the reins and permitting too much too soon.

Yet Hong Kong had seemed carried away by the general euphoria, staging its own rallies in support of the Beijing students. Two marches were held on the consecutive Sundays of May 21st and 28th, running like broad rivers several kilometres in length from Statue Square in Central to Victoria Park in Causeway Bay. I had been with the Tilbrooks on a visit to Macau during one of those weekends, observing much the same massive demonstration of empathy staged in the forecourt of the ruined cathedral. It was very contagious, that mood that China might actually be on the threshold of some momentous, incoherently articulated change. One could so easily overlook the sheer impossible scale of the dream envisaged, and so readily ignore the potential risk of expecting that impossibility to arrive overnight.

When the storm inevitably and finally broke, I was aboard the government's elegant old flagship the *Lady Maurine*, named after the wife of former Governor Sir Alexander Grantham, and heading for the drug addiction treatment centre of Hei Ling Chau with my fellow members of the Action Committee Against Narcotics. The only one aboard with a radio was our chairman, Dr. Gerald Choa. His was a tiny pocket-sized device, to whose broadcasts he listened with headphones. It was therefore incumbent on him to deliver the chilling blow-by-blow account in the same solemn tones he employed to summarise the main points in the minutes of the last meeting.

The tidings he conveyed, of troops of the People's Liberation Army sent in to crush the demonstration, sent shock waves round the world, and shook Hong Kong to the carefully-laid foundations of its entire future prospects. It was as if nobody had anticipated such an outcome, or even stopped to consider where all that elation might lead. Was I the only one who had seen it coming?

The prevailing mood was so fraught with disbelief, anger and dismay that it would have been tactless and insensitive of me to murmur "I told you so". My own private anger was directed at our collective failure to discourage that euphoria from producing the Greek tragedy enacted on that fateful but horribly predictable day. Having been born on June 4th 1935, Mukti chose forever after to celebrate his birthday elsewhere on the calendar. His anniversary became a movable feast.

The colony sank into deep, sorrowful depression. Thousands wore black armbands or black patches, taxis and private cars flew black ribbons from their radio antennae, and the marchers rallied again en masse for candlelight vigils to grieve for those who had died in defence of their democratic ideals.

These were not Hong Kong's first expressions of public indignation. The French bombardment of Foochow in August 1884, during the Franco-China war, had killed some three thousand civilians and provoked wide-scale anti-French demonstrations which included a refusal by Hong Kong port workers to service French vessels. A second example was local reaction to the shooting of Chinese demonstrators by British troops in Shanghai in May 1925. A third had been the concerted and crippling community boycott of mainland department stores in 1967, when it was discovered that some of them housed perpetrators of terrorist acts inspired by the violent excesses of the Cultural Revolution.

Once roused to action, the Hong Kong public could unite in a way that forcefully and unmistakably signified its disapproval. Even so, reaction to

Changing Horses in Midstream   277

Tiananmen was by far the largest expression of public outrage Hong Kong had ever witnessed. Jan Morris, in her own, regularly updated book on Hong Kong, says:

> "Hong Kong had never exhibited itself like this before, allowed its pent-up fears and resentments to show so frankly, or declared itself so politically aware."

Driven to review the provisions of its Nationality Act, the British government announced, on December 20th 1989, a selection scheme to award full British passports for fifty thousand households. Applicants would be processed on a points system. They demurred at granting any broader concession because of domestic constraints—neither of the two main political parties would tolerate large-scale immigration from Hong Kong.

In the urgent search for counter-measures to restore confidence and stem a dramatically increased brain drain, it was felt that news of a massive and far-sighted injection of funds into a bold new airport project would be greeted with enthusiasm. In most quarters it was, but China, refraining from any immediate condemnation, slowly dug in its heels and brought the underground railway of joint consultation to a virtual standstill.

As if to punish me for having so prematurely presumed that Ma Wan would remain pristine and uncontaminated by any further schemes for a replacement airport, I was put in charge of the campaign to milk the propaganda potential for all it was worth.

An Imminently Virtual Reality

Our task was to portray a project that didn't exist, except as an idea in the mind of Principal Government Town Planner Dr. Ted Pryor, who had headed the team exploring all possible options as to where it should be located. Since no plans had been commissioned for the airport terminal, runway layout or any other key feature, he suggested we use our imaginations—something he was very good at doing himself, but with the added bonus of all his engineering experience behind him.

Because we knew computer graphics would have to play a key role in this presentation, to "conceptualise" the as yet non-existent airport, its approach roads, bridges etc., and we also knew that computer graphics—then still in their infancy—were astronomically expensive things to produce, we asked for and were given a budget of approximately three million Hong Kong dollars.

I decided to depart from the customary procedure by which we invited tenders for government contracts, and instead call a meeting of all interested parties, adding in anyone else we could think of who might conceivably be interested in this kind of work. I explained the scale of what we wanted and put it to them that we had a total of three million dollars to play with. The tender that offered the best results at the cheapest price would win the contract.

But what was the airport going to look like? they all wanted to know.

We had no idea. It was quite simply anybody's guess, which was why I had laid emphasis on the "best results"—by which I meant the most convincing and persuasive.

We gave them all the preparatory studies and all the background material we could lay our hands on and sent them away to think about it. Some five weeks later we did the rounds, visiting them all to see what they had come up with. They had some great ideas and striking examples of computer graphics to present to us, but on balance we decided the job should go to Salon Films, which by now had established an impressive track record of producing government documentaries and televised public messages. They had done their homework and come up with the best package.

In the event the film they produced for us garnered at least two international awards and was shown around the world, either *in toto* or in the form of news-clip excerpts. I still feel it has stood the test of time and could serve, even now, as an acceptable introduction to how the airport came about. It was quite a story. The problems faced were enormous and, in many cases, unprecedented.

Just to lay the platform for this enterprise, it was necessary to wrest nearly nine and a half square kilometres of land from the sea, in some places to a depth of ninety metres, in only two and a half years. Where did one get the material? And how would it be placed on site so that, at minimum cost for removal and transport, one obtained maximum stability where one needed it: where planes would land and major structures rise? The original granite island of Chek Lap Kok was only three hundred and two acres in extent. The upper strata of the seabed around it were geotechnically too unstable to provide the foundations for an airport. Up to thirteen giant dredgers, equipped with suction and gripper arms, were deployed to retrieve the masses of submerged sludge, marine deposit, and chalk. Only when the dredgers had finished, could the specialists at last start preparing the groundwork for the airport by dumping rock into the sea, together with sand obtained from a host of other locations.

Our film, of course, had to anticipate all of this by presenting an airport already in existence, together with a terminal not yet designed, an arterial road system still on the drawing board and a massive suspension bridge whose model configurations were yet to be subjected to wind tunnel and other tests to see if it would resist typhoons. Working with Salon Films, we designed the whole lot, together with the control tower and the massive new reclamation along the yet to be created West Kowloon corridor to carry the express train all the way into Central, well before the first contracts were let.

Author Simon Winchester, who had yet to publish some of his best known works, such as *The Surgeon of Crowthorne* and *Krakatoa*, generally looked me up when he was in town, and happened to be living in Hong Kong at the time to launch a company with his wife Catherine. The company was called InterOptica Publishing, and it had embarked on the design and production of a relatively new communications medium, the CD-ROM.

Relatively new to the notion of personal computers myself, and yet to acquire my own, I had never heard of a CD-ROM, so Simon took me to his Mid Levels apartment to show me what it could do. I was bowled over by the notion that you could cram so much instantly accessible information into something the same size as a compact disk. GIS ended up commissioning InterOptica to produce a CD-ROM of the airport. It was perhaps a step just a little ahead of its time, for unhappily not enough of the people to whom we distributed it were able to play it. They probably used it as a rather nicely designed place mat.

But the airport film continued to do well. What we did not count on was that the exposure it received would be considerably magnified as a result of China's opposition to the scheme, which kept the story in the headlines for months to come. China questioned the need for so huge an investment at this late juncture in Britain's tenure. Based on 1989 prices, the Chek Lap Kok venture was estimated at HK $127,000 million, without allowing for cost-overruns. How could Britain defend this enormous depletion of financial reserves? China's suspicions were that the elaborate scheme was a convenient device for clawing back Hong Kong's hard earned capital savings in the form of pay-outs to British consortia queuing up for a piece of this farewell cake.

Wang Yincheng summarizes their position:

> "For half a year, the British Government had not notified the Chinese side of any facts about the new airport.... Not until spring was changing into summer in 1990 did the British Government turn round and ask for support from the Chinese side. The airport project could not start as the Hong Kong government dealt with unexpected difficulties when raising funds. Investors in and outside Hong Kong hesitated to

inject money into the new airport project as it was not approved by the Chinese Government. The reality was that the Chinese Government found no way to approve it."

Whatever the arguments for and against, it was clear no headway could be made without some serious reconsideration. Hong Kong's planners and financial advisers went back to their drawing boards and their calculators to see where cost-trimming might be applied. Perhaps creative accounting could overcome some of the major objections. One result of this review was a division of all airport-related projects into separate component packages.

The Chinese government demanded the right to scrutinize all documents, all calculations and all papers connected with the whole enterprise. The British were reluctant to oblige, pointing out that the intention was to complete just about everything during the remaining years of their administration, before the 1997 deadline and within the projected costing. There is some justification for supposing that at least some of these expectations might have been met, but once the wrangling set in, the window of opportunity began to close rapidly.

Former Financial Secretary Sir Piers Jacobs comments (in *Hong Kong Remembers*):

> "The Chinese seemed to think that we had produced a snow job. So it was decided that we should resolve the matter through so called 'expert talks', but, by that time of course, the Chinese realised that they had a very valuable political lever in their hands and, ultimately, in order to reach an agreement for the project to go ahead, they managed to secure John Major's visit to Beijing to sign the Memorandum of Understanding."

When the so called 'expert talks' failed to allay Chinese anxieties, they were followed by two rounds of official talks with a team headed by Andrew Burns, the Assistant Under-Secretary from the Foreign Office representing Britain and Hong Kong. These also failed to overcome Chinese objections. Douglas Hurd, the Foreign Secretary, tried his hand in April, again without success. Eventually Sir Percy Cradock, the Prime Minister's

Foreign Policy Adviser, flew to Beijing in June. He negotiated and initialled the airport agreement, which was greeted with relief and thanksgiving in Hong Kong.

A feature of the negotiation, and a useful lever on the British side, was the Chinese wish that John Major should come out to Beijing to sign the agreement, thereby helping in China's rehabilitation after Tiananmen. It was widely believed in Hong Kong that John Major was deeply embarrassed and unhappy at having to go to Beijing in this way, that he blamed Sir David Wilson for helping to bring about a humiliating situation and that Sir David lost his post in consequence. But Sir Percy Cradock has reminded me that there is no solid evidence for this, and that furthermore the decision to replace Sir David with a politician had been taken in principle long before Major's trip. It only remained to find a suitable name.

Within months of his return to London, and days of the re-election of his government on April 10th 1992, the Prime Minister declared that Chris Patten would govern Hong Kong through its remaining years of transition. The game of guessing the identity of the next governor had absorbed Hong Kong through the closing phase of every incumbent's tenure, but few would have put their money on the chairman of the Conservative Party.

Comments Wang Yincheng:

> "Candidates for the governorship would not come from the Ministry of Foreign Affairs as before, because China experts were not fit for the changing China any longer. The next governor must be substituted by an iron-handed politician."

Patten had been accorded much of the credit for steering the Tories back to power, and had earned considerable sympathy for the fact that his preoccupation with the broader objective had cost him his own seat in the constituency of Bath. However the award of the governorship of Hong Kong was viewed by many as a somewhat unlikely consolation prize. He took one weekend to make up his mind before announcing his acceptance.

From the outset the Chinese were suspicious of his intentions. They remained obstructive on the airport until they could see the colour of his money. When they saw their suspicions confirmed, the airport became enmeshed in the Sino-British political quarrel and its completion was further delayed in consequence.

Martin Lee remembers that he first saw Patten's face when viewing live televised results of the election at the Hong Kong Club:

> "He was the party chairman, and yet he had lost his seat, while everybody else had won. I thought then that this was an interesting politician. Most people in those circumstances would have put on a brave face and at least pretended to be happy. But apparently this guy couldn't do it. So my first impression of Mr. Patten was that he was an honest man. I think he has viewed me as both an ally and a thorn in his side."

In his book *The Soong Dynasty*, Sterling Seagrave describes Sir Halliday Macartney, a descendant of the same Lord Macartney whose abortive mission to China served as the prelude to Hong Kong. Sir Halliday was hired by the Chinese Government to handle its diplomatic affairs with the Court of St. James, and was one of those who, in 1896, endeavoured to conceal from the British authorities the imprisonment in the Chinese legation of the eventual Chinese Nationalist leader Dr. Sun Yat Sen, due to be returned to China to face trial as a revolutionary. According to Seagrave, Sir Halliday was "another of those fastidious British mandarins whose oriental natures were more inscrutable than the Chinese themselves".

The tradition had survived through nearly a hundred years, but Patten's appointment signalled a distinct departure. He leapt on stage as vigorously as Mark Antony, come to bury all dead caesars and definitely not to praise them. He looked every inch the man who should have been in charge a great deal earlier, bent on demonstrating that even now it was not too late. He had about him a slightly cheeky quality of boyish ebullience, set to roll up his sleeves and get things done. I saw him as a knight in shining armour, riding in at the eleventh hour to slay the dragon. I felt there was a distinct danger of him accidentally killing the damsel in distress.

Robert Cottrell, in *The End of Hong Kong*, says

"The new governor brought with him to Hong Kong a populism
which was a world away from Wilson's fastidious discretion. Patten
declined the customary knighthood, discarded the white ceremonial
uniform and drew crowds so large that the police could barely secure
his route."

Steeped in the thrust and parry of parliamentary debate, Patten
eschewed the convolutions and obfuscations of diplomatic language. Probably his greatest service to Hong Kong was to demystify the inscrutable, to
force a laying of all cards on the table. On the debit side, he left little margin for the paramount observance of 'face', held so dear by the Chinese, so
that they descended to vituperation and outright vilification in responding
to him. Indeed they so lost their self-control that they were driven to curs-
ing him and his issue for a thousand generations.

Dan Waters, in *Faces of Hong Kong*, comments

"With changes in British policy Governor Patten brought a western
approach and an occidental mind to a Chinese situation. These differ-
ing postures, with Hong Kong having to live with the consequences,
took on proportions not always appreciated in London. Making the
opposition lose face is not the way to succeed."

Patten always admitted that, as a democratic politician who lost his parliamentary seat in the polls, face was a difficult concept for him to grasp.
What he deemed more important was honour. Whether face or honour, it
sounded to hapless observers like an unwinnable round of that popular
Chinese fingers game of scissors-hammer-paper—honour covers face while
dignity outranks honour and face expresses dignity.

The leadership in Beijing had never dealt with his like before, and
clearly did not like what they now had to deal with. They were used to
Foreign Office sinologists who thought of themselves as steeped in the
mysteries of the Great Within. They expected discussions to take place
behind the scenes, from which stiff upper-lipped British negotiators would
emerge to utter—no matter how much they may have been compelled to
concede backstage—bland, reassuring sentiments that revealed nothing of

An Imminently Virtual Reality   285

consequence. Patten wasn't going to play that game. He wanted the drama enacted in full, stage front, under the spotlight.

When they grew tired of insulting him, and it became evident that no amount of protest would force a restoration of the old colonial style—because both the Conservative and Labour parties, in a rare display of unity, made it clear that Patten was their man—the Chinese did their best to ignore him, as if he simply didn't exist. Which wasn't easy, given his immense popularity among the masses in Hong Kong. Big business may have loathed him for imperiling, at the last moment, the whole carefully negotiated nod-and-a-wink of a deal, but to the common man he was a hero.

Wang Yincheng supplies some insight into the Chinese stance:

> "Chris Patten on October 7 unveiled his maiden policy speech of a blueprint for Hong Kong's last five years before 1997, in which he proposed the 'democratic reform' that would safeguard Hong Kong's future prosperity after its return to China. The speech, recognized by *The Times* as the most important address in Chris Patten's political life, was aimed at overhauling Hong Kong's electoral system and it caused immense dispute in the crucial time of Hong Kong's transitional period.

> "Chris Patten failed to conduct any consultative discussion with the Chinese side before his proposals were delivered. Moreover, he showed no sincerity in his talks with the Chinese side after the latter lodged a protest.

> "After learning the content, Lu Ping, in his reply to Patten, expressed his wish not to publicize the report before thorough talks between the two sides, so as to ensure the smooth handover of Hong Kong and reduce unnecessary political disputes. But it did not prevent Patten from promulgating it without modifying even one word."

Being a highly controversial figure, Patten inevitably attracted—as well as strong support—considerable criticism, not only from the Chinese but also from Hong Kong businessmen and from professional British diplomats. The main charge against him was that, for all his claims to advance democracy in Hong Kong, by antagonising the Chinese and disregarding their repeated warnings against unilateral action, he was leaving Hong Kong with less democracy rather than more. He was also accused of ensuring that, as a result of the bitter political quarrel with China, Britain would get worse terms in the handover negotiations and Hong Kong would be left with less, not more protection against China after 1997.

He claimed to be doing the honourable thing in defence of civic rights and liberties, and he certainly acquired a considerable reputation in Western countries for his stand. But his critics contended he was making a short-term gesture which—he had been warned—would only provoke a damaging Chinese backlash after he left for home. These same critics questioned which was the more honourable course: to engage in such posturing, or to cooperate with China in securing the highest possible level of democracy and liberal values after 1997.

Certainly his impact was divisive. In response to his changes, China set up a so-called *second kitchen*, in effect a parallel administration for Hong Kong. During his last six months of tenure there would be two legislatures, one in Hong Kong and one appointed by the Chinese, operating in Shenzhen, just over the border. Hong Kong society was polarized, compelled to choose between present and future masters, the one dilemma they had wished to avoid.

Offerings to the Gods

Meanwhile the on-off-on-off airport was on again, and making great strides. Our little home on Ma Wan became a gathering point for those wishing to view some of its major works at close quarters. These included the three separate structures that made up the Lantau Fixed Crossing, the costliest and most time-consuming link of the entire new highway stretching from Central, via an equally new cross-harbour tunnel, to the airport itself. Like a triptych on a highly avant-garde altar to the gods of engineering, this crossing comprised two double-decked suspension bridges and an intervening viaduct connecting Tsing Yi Island to Lantau Island via Ma Wan. All three had to cater for both road and rail traffic, the railway occupying the lower deck in an almost entirely enclosed tunnel.

The longest and most spectacular of the three was the 1,377 metre main span Tsing Ma Suspension Bridge (the world's second longest), which would end up being 2,032 metres overall. At the other end of the viaduct, crossing the narrow channel which had prompted surveyor Parrish to advise Lord Macartney against a British settlement on Ma Wan, the Kap Shui Mun Bridge would have a main span of 441 metres and measure 691 metres long overall.

Over the entire length of the three-component crossing, the forty metre-wide bridge deck would comprise two carriageways on the upper level, each of three lanes, for road traffic, and the lower level would accommodate two rail tracks and two protected emergency lanes for road traffic, should wind strengths associated with tropical storms exceed certain limits of safety.

My fellow villagers looked to the island's only incumbent *gwailo* for advice. What could they do about this situation? There was no indication that we would be allowed any access to that crossing poised so high above our heads, yet we were expected to live in its shadow, suffer its noise and—most distressingly of all—endure the unfavourable consequences to our environmental *feng shui*. In ordinary circumstances government paid compensation to those whose lives and livelihood were disrupted by public works on any scale. Here was an example of public works on an unprecedented scale, yet no offer of compensation, no redeeming benefits of any kind.

A group of villagers decided to present a case to the Tsuen Wan district office, through the Ma Wan rural committee, stating that the goddess Tin Hau, secluded in her tiny but elegant little jewel of a temple on the waterfront, was being sorely distracted by the revolutions of a radar scanner set up on a prominence above the opposite shore of Lantau. Its gyrations were making her dizzy. I sighed. If that was the best we could come up with, ours really was a lost cause.

My old friend and colleague David Ford had now replaced both Sir Philip Haddon-Cave and his successor, Sir David Akers-Jones, as Chief Secretary. With that elevation had come a knighthood. He was now Sir David Ford. To celebrate the fact that I had sold *The Singing Tree* to *Bloomsbury*, I invited a gathering of my closest and dearest friends, including his name on the list. He accepted, and in due course arrived by helicopter, landing on the nearby football field and attracting considerable attention.

After lunch I took him for a stroll around the island. As was his style, he asked a great many questions and you sensed he was making a careful mental note of all the information these elicited. Not long afterwards, the chairman of our rural committee came to me with an offer to buy my house. I was aware that he had been making similar offers to other villagers and knew what he was up to. He was using privileged information to swell his own pockets. I reported his conduct to a contact in the district office, but unfortunately by then some of my unsuspecting neighbours had fallen for the con, selling their properties at prices far below what they could have earned had they held out.

Shortly afterwards the official offer became general knowledge and was circulated throughout the village. We were invited to sign agreements with a subsidiary of an unnamed company, whom I knew to be Sun Hung Kai, one of Hong Kong's largest property developers. The agreement stipulated that in exchange for our existing three-storey dwellings we would each be provided with a new dwelling of the same size, together with an additional flat in another building. I accepted with alacrity, and hoped that my fellow villagers would do so too. Not all of them did. Some demurred because they genuinely did not want to move from homes they had grown to love; others were downright greedy, believing they could extort far more by employing delaying tactics.

Sun Hung Kai presented their proposals to the government. They sought to build a residential development of low-rise buildings that would transform Ma Wan into one of Hong Kong's most desirable resorts. We would have fast jetfoil ferries to Central and Tsuen Wan, beautiful gardens, even a theme park. They further requested permission to construct, at their own expense, slip roads from the fixed crossing down to the island, to provide vehicular access. The government replied that the latter wasn't feasible, because there was no room for such slip roads. Sun Hung Kai responded with engineers' plans and drawings that demonstrated there was, that it could be done and that it wouldn't cost government a penny.

◆　　◆　　◆

I was by now in my final months of government service. Instead of seeking to switch to the permanent and pensionable establishment, which would have entailed repaying all the gratuities I had earned at the end of previous tours of service, I had always chosen to remain on contract terms. Never endowed with the slightest shred of financial acumen or even practical foresight, I had treated my gratuities as pocket money, and had continued to blow most of them on my protracted holidays—Spain, Norway, Ireland, Wales, India, Thailand and Malaysia with Joyce, South Africa, Australia, New Zealand, Papua New Guinea, Vanuatu, Fiji, Tahiti and the Solomon Islands on my own. It was my nature to recklessly indulge myself, and my dependants, in the lifestyle to which I felt we were accustomed. "Live for the moment" had been my motto, and the moments had been many and memorable.

But there had been moments, too, of rational choice and reasonably sensible decision-making. I had bought a home for my parents in Sussex, one for Mukti and Diosy at Batu Lapan Ijok in Selangor, where they possessed the only two-storey dwelling in the kampong, right opposite the mosque and right next door to Mukti's ex-wife Asarah, and I had even invested in a house in Canada, not to mention the house we were now being asked to exchange for a better one on Ma Wan. My Guardian Angel must have been on the lookout, even if I wasn't.

My mother was about to celebrate her eightieth birthday. Her anniversary would fall on July 10th 1992. Paul wrote to suggest that we should once again stage a reunion in Canada, bringing our younger brother Bob over with her to celebrate in style. I heartily agreed and we duly converged on his delightful pastoral home in Metchosin, organised family group photographs, a dinner cruise of Victoria harbour and countless other diversions too many to recall.

All went well until Paul's eldest son, Nick, suggested an afternoon drive for just the two of us. He took me up Mount Matheson, at the foot of which lay the lake near the property I had bought ten years earlier. There was a "For Sale" sign at the entrance to a large empty lot he wanted to show me. It was an eight-acre plot the family had been in love with it for years. They had frequently come up here to mull over the possibility that they might one day get enough capital together to own it. We left the car by the road and walked down a forestry trail to a promontory overlooking the view.

I was simultaneously flabbergasted, gobsmacked and hopelessly undone. Not since I was a child, making the scenic circuit of the pony trails in Darjeeling, where my family retreated during the hot Indian summers, had I seen such a vision. Below us, the site's eight acres of forest fell away to a plateau of mist that spread across the entire Juan de Fuca Strait to the snow-capped peaks of the Olympic Mountains in Washington State, USA. It was my boyhood memory of Kanchenjunga recalled, the "Five Treasures of the Snow", glowing radiant across the deep-shadowed chasms of the Himalayan ranges that lay between. If my Guardian Angel

Offerings to the Gods   291

was screaming caution in my ear, I never heard her. I **had** to have this land. I could not live through the rest of my life without it.

I rang the estate agent that same evening, made an offer and awaited the outcome. The owners made a counter offer. They were going to raise the price unless I accepted the first figure. I accepted, and from that moment on, I lived to be in Canada, yearned to be on that promontory, overlooking that view. Whatever threadbare filaments of reason and common sense might have survived, in the jumbled fabric of my mind, slipped away silently that night, like the proverbial rats deserting a sinking ship. Did I but know it, I was already lost.

The following year I brought Mukti, Diosy and Mel with me for another motor home holiday, this time in a rented, thirty-two foot, air-conditioned behemoth which we parked in the embryonic, grass-covered driveway overlooking that spectacular panorama. With us was Diosy's nephew Clement, aged fifteen, whom we planned to take with us on our visit to his mother Cleofe, in Calgary, Alberta. Vultures wheeled high above, gathering for their migration south across the Juan de Fuca Strait to Washington and beyond, a bald eagle flapped its wings to settle in a pine tree below, we glimpsed deer at the edge of the escarpment, a family of raccoons came down from the trees in the evening to forage in the vicinity of our camp fire. It was like living in a *National Geographic* wild life special, not least because the cul de sac which ended in our property was called Wilderness Place. It seemed almost too much to believe that it was all ours.

After four days of blissful retreat from worldly care, exploring our forest, picnicking on rocks suspended above sheer drops, watching fishing boats from Sooke Inlet and Pedder and Becher Bays playing the channel for salmon, we drove our motor home down to where we could tank up with fuel and fresh water, discharge its waste and do all the things that are required for the maintenance of such recreational vehicles.

We camped overnight at French Beach, on the road to Port Renfrew, and returned the following, remarkably hot day, slogging up Mount Matheson Road at a speed I felt to be surprisingly sluggish, even given the prevailing temperature. Mukti took the wheel to reverse us on to the site, a laborious process interrupted when Mel, then aged thirteen and still in his pajamas, rushed round to the driver's cab to inform us that the motor home was on fire.

Idiotically, I assumed the fire had started in the engine, so I reached for the catch below the steering wheel to open the hood. Unfortunately I tugged at the wrong handle, releasing the hand brake instead. Mukti and I had already vacated the cab, only to watch helplessly as the by now flaming motor home started to roll gently downhill. I ran alongside it, intending to leap aboard again and arrest its progress. The motor home bounced off a boulder and started to roll over on top of me. Fortunately, before it succeeded in doing so, it crashed into the trunk of an arbutus, which rolled it back upright again.

The rest of the family came rushing up to see if I was all right. Mel was carrying Hugo the Hippo, a stuffed woollen toy I had bought him when he was two years old, and which had accompanied him everywhere ever since. His first priority had been to save Hugo, but mine was to save our motor home. I grabbed Hugo from him and used its stuffing to protect my hand as I endeavoured to unscrew the radiator cap. Why it would have occurred to me to do so I cannot now recall. Abandoning the effort to get at the radiator, I saw that Diosy had retrieved a fire extinguisher from inside the cabin. I took this from her and—before anyone could remind me that this wasn't the source of the fire—emptied its contents through the radiator grille. Behind us, the cabin was by now beginning to glow, layered from the ceiling downward in dense black smoke.

I rushed to my bunk, groping blindly for my video camera and my wallet, from which I had removed the two thousand Canadian dollars I had cashed at the bank that morning. I found the camera and the wallet but not the money. Being a great deal more organised, Diosy had already retrieved all our passports and air tickets, which she had taken the precaution of safeguarding in a bedside drawer. With the fumes choking my lungs, I at last surrendered to the shouted appeals from outside to vacate the patently unsalvageable vehicle. I could only join them and watch from a safe distance as the blaze evolved into a devouring inferno. One or two mature firs in the immediate vicinity candled into spectacular Christmas trees, tongues of flame racing through their upper branches. Oh Christ, I thought, the whole forest is going to go.

Our neighbours were few and far between, their houses mostly invisible in the trees. Somebody, I decided, ought to be told about this. I raced off in search of a telephone. About three hundred yards down the road, a family in a U-Drive removal van was in the process of shifting household effects into a weatherboard vacation rental. "Can I use your phone?" I panted. "I'm afraid the forest is on fire."

The wife, caught in the act of hauling a large suitcase, turned to her husband and yelled "Honey, put it all back again!"

I found the phone and dialled 911, but by now a helicopter was circling overhead. I returned to the scene of the crime. The butane gas tanks were screaming and wailing like creatures in the last tortured throes of distress. There was really nothing one could do about it until the fire brigade arrived. But no, wait a minute…I still had my video camera. I started recording the scene, just as two enormous ribbons of flame leapt from the butane tanks into nearby shrubbery.

Panic-stricken residents started to emerge from the trees down the road. I turned round to introduce myself, my video camera still running to record their incredulous expressions. "Hello," I said apologetically. "I'm your new neighbour. I'm sorry about all this."

The East Sooke Fire Brigade arrived to take control of the situation. I remembered that I was supposed to meet John Chan at the BC Ferries Swartz Bay terminal. John had taken over as Director of Information Services when Cheung Man-yee left that post to return to Radio Television Hong Kong as Director of Broadcasting. Small, chubby, affable and bright as a beacon, he was at that time Secretary for Education and Manpower. Holidaying with friends in Vancouver, he had expressed sufficient interest in my neck of the woods to ask if he could come across by ferry through the Gulf Islands and see it for himself. I had to go and explain to him that, by that time, it might not actually exist any more.

In addition to the motor home, I had rented a Ford Lincoln as a "run-about". Still covered in soot, as visible proof that I wasn't just making excuses, I used this to race up the Saanich Peninsula to Swartz Bay and explain the situation to John. He was most understanding, deciding to investigate the Butchart Gardens instead. Good choice, I said.

I returned to Wilderness Place to find the blaze had been extinguished. Firemen were still combing the underbrush, snuffing out the last smouldering vestiges. It was a good thing, they told me, there hadn't been a breath of wind that day, or the whole mountain might have gone up in flames.

Very lucky, I murmured, surveying the crumpled, molten metallic ruin of our thirty-two foot, air-conditioned, rented motor home.

Mukti, Diosy, Mel and Clement had been taken in by our immediate next door neighbours, seventy-seven-year old Vernon and Lesley Footner. In terms of providing us with post-traumatic succour, fate could not have been more providential. Where others had been concerned only to save themselves, Vernon and Lesley had thought first and foremost of rescuing us, complete strangers though we were.

We all fell immediately in love with them and their house, which Vernon, a retired building contractor, had designed and constructed entirely on his own. It was shaped like a squat but massive pagoda, with the bedrooms sensibly in the basement (since one never needs to look out of the window at night) and the top floor given over entirely to one spacious and inviting living area, its huge windows offering views on all sides. I was so taken with his architectural as well as building skills that I immediately asked him to design the house I planned to build next door.

Vernon declined, pleading old age and the fact that he hadn't built anything in years. But a week later, when we all returned from our peregrinations through the Rockies in the Ford Lincoln, in the course of which we revisited Grahame and Lisbet Blundell in the outskirts of Edmonton and returned Clement to his mother in the heart of Calgary, I was delighted to learn that Vernon had changed his mind. His grandson Robin wanted to follow him into the construction business himself and saw this as an ideal opportunity to make a start.

Vernon introduced me to Robin and the three of us paced out the plot while I described the basic configuration I had in mind. I wanted to take maximum advantage of the land by aligning the structure along the lip of

Offerings to the Gods   295

the rock ledge. I thought that a spacious living room should act as the pivot, with two wings on either side containing four en suite bedrooms, an office, dining room and kitchen. The basement floor would consist of an even larger living area and a rumpus room which could also serve as a viewing theatre for a built-in cinema. Combined with a two-car garage, we calculated that the whole floor area would run to approximately six thousand square feet.

By this time the molten remains of the motor home had been towed away for scrap. The owner had recovered the full value with his insurance policy, which did not allow any coverage for those hiring it. But Mukti, Diosy, Mel and I were undeterred. We felt we had made our offering to the gods of Wilderness Place. And what did possessions matter so long as we ourselves had escaped unscathed?

A Gross Miscalculation

The lack of a pension, on my retirement from the civil service at the age of fifty-eight, meant that I would have to continue working in order to keep some money flowing in. I accepted an offer from Ogilvie & Mather, which had bought out the highly successful public relations company founded by the late Michael Stevenson when he left Government Information Services more than two decades earlier. When Mike died in office, at an indecently early age, Bill Fish, another old friend and colleague from my younger days, had taken over, only to meet the same end through a stroke at roughly the same age. By one of those curious twists of fate, Mike and Bill had recruited their former boss, Nigel Watt, who in turn was followed by Drew Rennie—all of them ex-GIS. I was effectively the fifth in an unbroken line of "god speakers".

But I didn't much care for this other side of the fence. I found it phoney, full of manufactured self-importance, grandiloquent mission statements, motivational pep talks and very little substance. The only aspect I enjoyed was organising crisis management exercises, for which I borrowed freely from the absurdities of our old departmental exercise days, when we sought to provoke widespread nervous breakdowns and massive coronaries by bringing public bureaucracy to its knees.

For one such exercise, to train the staff of the Island Shangri-La Hotel, I engineered a scenario in which, during the course of the day, a helicopter crashed into the swimming pool and guests were incited to near-mutiny by a breakdown of the water supply and air-conditioning plants. For minor diversions I arranged for the principal wife in the travelling harem of a Middle Eastern potentate to set fire to the drapes, by endeavouring to cook sheep's eyes on a kerosene stove, and for a strippergram girl to deliver Yom Kippur greetings at the bedroom door of a highly Orthodox Jewish rabbi.

A particular quandary affected my work for two rival organisations which, by sheer chance, both happened to have fallen within my portfolio. The Hong Kong Hotels Association, consisting of the general managers of most of the leading hotels in town, lived high off the hog by organising splendid meetings in palatial locales, usually preceded by an excellent buffet lunch and generous quantities of wine. On the other hand the Hong Kong Hotel Owners Association, whose members actually owned the very same hotels, conducted their meetings abstemiously over sandwiches and tea in unobjectionably modest surroundings, with the excesses of the rival organisation frequently tabled for discussion.

I would be called in by Michael Li, Executive Director of the Hotel Owners, to compose a mildly critical letter addressed to the Hotels Association, suggesting the courtesy of extending an invitation to the Hotel Owners to contribute their views before making representations to the relevant government department on matters affecting the future of the industry.

Taking exception to the tone of this communication, Manuel Woo, Executive Director of the Hotels Association, would summon me to discuss a suitable reply, conveying just a touch of reproof at the way in which the Hotel Owners had couched their suggestion.

Michael Li, reading more into this response than I had intended, would ask me back to compose a slightly sterner riposte. Hardly had this reached his desk when Manuel Woo, incensed by the latest communiqué, would be on the phone to me requesting my urgent assistance in composing the next salvo.

Both knew, of course, for I frequently reminded them of this blatant conflict of interest, that I was involved in the preparation all of these missives, but neither was willing to dispense with my services. And so it continued, like playing both courts in a solo badminton match.

◆　　　◆　　　◆

With my departure from government came the loss of my quarter at Mount Nicholson, if not the largest at least the most delightful we had ever occupied, with easily the most panoramic view. So bucolic were our surroundings there that we had frequently to stop the car to allow a family of porcupines to cross our path on the long access road. From now on we would be living full-time on Ma Wan, commuting by the hourly *gaido* service, at the wheel of which was a veteran with half his face grievously scarred and both arms amputated at the elbow, thanks to a youthful misadventure with an illegal fish bomb that exploded in his hands before he could drop it into the water.

During our absence the house on Sports Road had been ably looked after by two Sri Lankans, Ravi and Babu, who contributed Singhalese and Tamil dishes to our weekend feasts, while authentic Thai input came from Boon Som, whose muscular torso was so badly burned in a factory fire that he had covered it with tattoos to conceal the scars. We never lacked for friends, among them Filipino musicians like Boyet Samonte and Baby Apostol, Filipino engineer Rino Cantillano and cost controller Felix Barraca. In fact we did more entertaining there than at any time in our lives, with weekend barbecue parties of thirty or more spilling through the house and up the adjoining hillside.

Most of our "regulars" were domestic workers drawn from the great soft underbelly of Hong Kong's Filipino community, who were making it possible for the city's middle and upper classes to enjoy increasingly affluent lives. Many of these care givers had married partners from other ethnic groups in similar employment. Some were serving in Hong Kong's finest homes, to many of which I would be invited through the back door when their owners allowed the staff to entertain. It gave me a whole new perspective on Hong Kong. I felt I was not, like so many others, limited to the shallow surface waters but could swim at virtually any depth and mingle with far wider and often more interesting spectra of fellow denizens of the deep.

Among our dearest friends—aside from aforementioned Jonathan and Irene To—were Komar and Medi, he from Bandung in Java, she from Luzon in the Philippines, and Benjamin Cario, a hot-blooded islander from the pirate-ridden Riau archipelago who had served in Soekarno's red berets and had dropped by parachute over Johore during the dark days of the Indonesian-Malaysian confrontation, married to quietly self-effacing Shamshir, who shared my birthday. Then there was Sarto, a Sundanese married to Lettie from La Union, and Diosy's many brothers and sisters working in Hong Kong, including Lolong, Linda, Mario, Junior and Tita, the latest to arrive from an extended family whose roots were firmly anchored on the island of Bohol in the Visayas. Another from the Philippines was Berlina, married to Tony, from Bali, who back in 1976 had accompanied Mukti on the house hunting quest that produced our first Ma Wan residence.

It was a particular joy for me to observe the progress achieved by the progeny of these assorted marriages, beautiful, talented children growing up together in one large extended family amidst our richly metropolitan environment, schooled sometimes in Cantonese but mostly in English, often attaining high scholastic honours. Another example even closer to home was the marriage of Mukti's eldest son Mazli to Jennifer Chu, daughter of a Shanghainese father and Cantonese mother. Moving to Malaysia, where Jennifer went by her Muslim name of Rohani, they had produced two similarly beautiful and talented children in Anna Liza and Ross Ariz, both of them educated in English, Malay and Mandarin. This, I thought, was the way the world should be, without boundaries imposed by religion, race and culture, confirming my view of Hong Kong as the perfect melting pot, embracing all-comers and receptive to all influences.

On Ma Wan I felt entirely at home, a villager—a non-Cantonese speaking *gwailo* perhaps but nonetheless very much *persona grata* with the indigenes, who would arrive at our front door every Chinese New Year's Day, drums thumping, gongs clanging and crackers exploding, to perform the traditional lion dance. This colourful if raucous performance would end with the lion grasping, in its large, grinning array of teeth, the cabbage suspended from our balcony attached to *ang pau* (a red packet of lucky money). And every year I would contribute to the community fund-raising for the annual Chinese opera, staged in its temporary bamboo and corrugated iron shed on the clearing before the Tin Hau temple normally reserved for the noxious preparation of Ma Wan's only domestic product, its pungent but popular shrimp paste.

One Saturday morning Tao Ho arrived for lunch, compact and buoyant as ever, bearing a sheet of paper on which he had sketched the outline for the future flag of the Hong Kong Special Administrative Region. The ink was barely dry on the paper. He had come straight from a meeting of the panel of judges appointed to choose the winning result from an international competition. The judges couldn't agree on any of the designs so they sat down to individually and anonymously submit their own, dropping their unsigned efforts into a box from which they collectively selected the best entry. Tao's had won the most votes.

I didn't know quite what to say. It looked like the sort of decorative design we had employed years ago to adorn street lamps for the long-defunct Festival of Hong Kong. It was supposed to represent the floral emblem of Hong Kong, the *Bauhinia blakeana* or Hong Kong orchid-tree, but to me it looked like a spinning catherine wheel, desperately trying to run away from an imminent appointment with history. Was this insubstantial, inelegant thing intended to express all I had known and loved of Hong Kong?

I couldn't hurt Tao's feelings. I saw him, in Longfellow's words, as "a youth, who bore, 'mid snow and ice, a banner with the strange device". "Excelsior!" I murmured to myself, for the dye had already been cast. For Tao's benefit I nodded. "Very nice."

And I inwardly mused that the day would eventually come when it might be declared a crime to burn that device. I felt an almost irrepressible urge to burn it there and then.

◆　　　◆　　　◆

Another dye was already cast. I had my heart set on the plot of land I had accidentally chanced upon at the southernmost tip of Vancouver Island. I was still besotted by that view.

I exchanged almost daily faxes with Vernon Footner and his grandson Robin, who sent me plans so impressive that I seldom had cause to suggest changes. It was all turning out exactly as I had hoped. To enable actual construction to commence, I arranged a bank loan repayable at a hefty fifteen per cent. Accompanied by Mukti, Diosy and Mel, I presented myself at the Canadian consulate to apply for admission to Canada as a landed immigrant. I was told the family would be regarded as my dependants. We were all duly interviewed and our applications put forward with a recommendation to that effect.

Then things went horribly wrong. I was accepted but they were not. When I tried to find out why, the consulate responded with a series of brief form letters stating, in effect, that the decision was final.

I had already burnt my bridges behind me. I had to press on. When one leaps before one looks, there has to be a quick reconnoitering in midair to choose the least uncomfortable landing. I decided I would go ahead, taking Mel with me on a student visa, to pursue channels at the Canadian end. Surely the Canadian immigration authorities were not so inhuman and implacable that they would not be prepared to lend a sympathetic ear? What a gross miscalculation that proved to be.

They were.

◆　　　◆　　　◆

Mel and I took possession of our new home in September 1995. The house was gorgeous. Vernon and Robin had done a fantastic job in making the most of the view, the sheer sweep of which—from every window along the front—took one's breath away.

Crossing the Rockies from Edmonton, Grahame and Lisbet Blundell came to visit, timing their stay to coincide with Brian and Moyreen Tilbrook from Hong Kong. Cheung Man-yee called while they were there, and Joyce Williams arrived on the first of several visits shortly thereafter. Other arrivals included Man-yee's predecessor as head of broadcasting, Stuart Wilkinson; Maggie, daughter of Kevin and Evelyn Voltz, whom I had last met in Brunei; Swee Ngor and Cyril Pereira, originally hailing from Malaysia; Jonathan, Irene and Anthony To; my former secretary Linda Lee from Toronto; Betty Shum and Nita Wan, two more old colleagues from GIS; Gillian Newson from London; Manuel Woo and his wife Anna; Chris and Stephanie Holmes, who had by then moved to Bainbridge Island, near Seattle; Nigel and Daphne Watt and Keith and Lindsay McGregor, who had run the *Banyan Tree*, Hong Kong's most elegant interior furnishing store, where Mukti had spent his last years of employment.

I should have been happy. Despite nearly demolishing their environment with that blazing motor home, I had made many delightful friends among fellow denizens of Mount Matheson. My walls were lined with books, I had the three thousand five hundred or so CDs I had been busy collecting over the years and there was that fabulous view, of whose existence my brother Paul would keep ringing up to remind me. "Have you taken a look at it yet?" he would ask, "or are you still crouched over your computer?" "Hang on," I'd reply, leaving my desk to cross the room and draw the curtains. "Yes, it's still there."

Something didn't fit, and I boiled it down to the fact that it was almost certainly me. I would listen to the sound of chainsaws buzzing all around, from neighbouring properties, whose owners were out there, sleeves rolled up, to immerse themselves in chopping down trees, discarding deadwood, improving their surroundings. I had nothing against those surroundings. They were pretty, and as far as I was concerned they could go on being pretty and looking after themselves, as they had done for millions of years before I ever moved there. All I needed to do was cross the floor, draw the curtains and take an occasional peek at them to indulge myself in a fleeting fit of self-congratulation.

Often there would be a small herd of deer nibbling at the outcrops of grass on the moss-covered rocks below, tiny humming birds hovering at the flowers in the trees, blue jays arriving for crumbs, raccoons sauntering out of the woods, their delicate little hands fastidiously picking at food from the dishes laid out for our four cats. Once I spotted a trio of killer whales sporting in Becher Bay, clearly visible through my telescope. And always there was that bald eagle settled in the crest of a tree halfway down the slope.

One by one the cats began to disappear, and my neighbours suggested this could be due to the fact that the house lay alongside a cougar trail. Although I never saw a cougar myself, Mukti did. On one of his annual visits, in the days when we still held on to the ever-diminishing hope that the immigration authorities would relent in response to my repeated appeals, he was driving alone up Mount Matheson Road when he came upon a cougar by the roadside. It sat erect and unalarmed, observing him for a moment before it turned and made its majestic withdrawal back into the timberline.

Then one night a freak storm brought down a number of old forest giants. In the crown of the tallest was an eagle's nest, containing eighteen cat collars.

Farewell the Trumpets

Sally Chow rang from Hong Kong to ask if I would be interested in returning to write a book on the handover for the *South China Morning Post*. Would I? Yes please, I replied, just say when.

I had first met Sally when she arrived in my office at GIS many years earlier, to persuade me not to withdraw the government's recruitment advertising from the *Post* because, not only was it more visible and widely circulated there, but she could offer me a better deal. She accomplished her mission and established an immediate and lasting friendship.

Sally and her husband James were both Calcutta Chinese, and spoke better Hindustani than I did. Though he was there many years after me, James was a fellow graduate of Calcutta's St. Xavier's College. We shared many happy memories and a taste for Indian curry, which led to our establishment of an informal "Calcutta Club" to explore the many and various Indian restaurants of Hong Kong in search of the ideal cuisine. No mean cook herself, Sally would frequently entertain us in their Mid Levels apartment, where fellow guests would often include Lindley 'Lin' Holloway and his Singapore wife Anne, who at one time had been a racing driver in the Macau Grand Prix.

I had known Lin since 1961, when I was working in Kuala Lumpur for the *Straits Times Press Limited*, which he joined that year. He used to come to lunch with Gerry Jackson and me in the flat we shared at 6, Chiu Yoke Road. He held the position of Chief Executive of *Singapore Press Holdings Limited* for twelve years and left in 1986 to join The *News Corporation* in London. He was first associated with the *South China Morning Post Group* in 1987 and became its Chief Executive and Director in 1990.

From our long-distance telephone conversation that early spring day in 1997 I learned that Sally and Lin had discussed producing a souvenir pub-

lication with which the *SCMP* would mark the handover, and had decided
that I was the best person to write it.

I was suffering withdrawal symptoms of the kind experienced by drug
addicts endeavouring to go "cold turkey". I would wake up in the middle
of the night in cold sweats thinking "What the hell have I got myself
into?" I was rapidly getting deeper into debt. The promised new house on
Ma Wan had not materialised, so there was no chance of selling it to
achieve that hoped-for windfall that would see me through the rest of my
life.

The pay-off from my insurance policy had run dry, and there was no
money coming in other than that supplied by kindly Asian friends like
Rino Cantillano, who had by then been appointed Building Services
Coordinator working on some of the terminal facilities scheduled for the
new international airport taking shape at Chek Lap Kok. With typical
generosity, Rino and his wife Daisy were sending me a substantial part of
the income he was earning every month.

In like manner, Jonathan and Irene To sent me what they insisted was
an outright gift of thirty thousand Canadian dollars to "see me through"
what they hoped were my temporary trials and tribulations. And "Manny"
Woo, newly retired from the Hong Kong Hotels Association, also contributed most generously to the rescue operation. With friends like these, why
had I ever been so mad as to leave Hong Kong? Without them I was in the
throes of sensory deprivation, lacking all the stimulus and excitement that
Hong Kong had afforded me; the very stuff of life that had kept me alive.

Retirement in my case had proved a dangerously terminal condition,
inducing stagnation and despair of the kind that would see me into an
early grave. The danger had been exacerbated by my retreat, of my own
volition, not only off stage but into the wilderness. Albeit a very beautiful
wilderness, and possibly one of the most beautiful in the world, it was not
my wilderness. I had found I could not live on scenery alone. I needed
action, the kind of *bravura* virtuosity and non-stop three-ring circus of
which only Hong Kong was capable.

According to the international press, the majority of the newspapers
and magazines that came my way, it was all going to end at midnight on

June 30th 1997, when Hong Kong was returned to China at the close of the ninety-nine-year lease of the New Territories. Rubbish, I thought. The day will come when all those doomsday Cassandras, those glib "Chinese takeaway" scribes, will be forced to swallow their own stale fortune cookies.

I returned to Hong Kong to find the city humming, all those scribes still assembling in their multitudes, the Government Information Services busy organising sophisticated press facilities to pander to their every need.

Preparing to steal a three-year lead on the Millennium, by celebrating its infinitely more momentous reversion to Chinese sovereignty, Hong Kong had chosen, as the setting for this occasion, the new Convention and Exhibition Centre on the Hong Kong Island waterfront. Like some marvellous crystal deposited in the bowl of that crucible where the alchemy first began, this edifice too seemed the product of a restless urge to reassemble and reconfigure. And emblematic of the city which it served as showcase, its undulating roof billowed like sails catching the winds of a freshly stirring history.

Approximately two miles east of here, at fifteen minutes past eight in the morning of January 25th 1841, Hong Kong Island had been formally occupied by a party of marines, who raised the British flag at Possession Point, encountering no resistance from the few and somewhat bemused Chinese inhabitants assembled to observe this curious circumstance. Now, one hundred and fifty six years later, we ourselves would be witnessing the surrender of our beloved island in this new, purpose-built landmark, which I would forever come to think of as our "Dispossession Point".

It was here that the press would be afforded a ringside seat. Thomas Chan, who had taken over from Irene Yau as Director of Information Services, accompanied me there to see how things were progressing. Our visit coincided with a tour of inspection by Anson Chan, who had replaced Sir David Ford as Chief Secretary. Spotting me, she came over to say hello and welcome me back.

Thomas arranged for me to attend the official farewell ceremony to be staged at HMS Tamar on the eve of the handover. Through him I also managed to secure seats for both Jan Morris and Simon Winchester who, years earlier, had collaborated on a book entitled *Stones of Empire* and who were now, albeit separately, back in Hong Kong to witness the removal of this last pillar of its essential fabric. What had once seemed no more than a pebble in the greater imperial structure had assumed the proportions of the final monument to its faded glories.

Jonathan and Irene To arranged to take Rino and me on a trip through the New Territories, that massive Achilles heel of an appendage whose expiring shelf life had led to this moment. On its western seaboard, south of the fishing settlement of Lau Fau Shan, where many an illegal immigrant, swimming at night across Deep Bay, had come to grief on the offshore oyster beds, we found a farming community that had impatiently precipitated its own return to the motherland. From every farmhouse, shop and lamp post fluttered the red banner of the People's Republic. The smiling inhabitants who greeted us had jumped the clock by several days, and were proud to pose for our cameras with their flags as backdrop.

I was by now well into the history that the *SCMP* had commissioned me to write, using their excellent library, and whatever other resources were available to me through the Internet, to compile some fifty-six thousand words in the space of four weeks. Sally liked it, Lin liked it, Deputy Chief Executive Owen Jonathan said he liked it but suggested we should also show it to Sir Percy Cradock, who was then on the Board of the *Post* as one of its non-executive directors.

Sir Percy compiled a closely-typed six-sheet memorandum itemising alterations and additions he required me to incorporate into the text. I accommodated all of these with varying degrees of difficulty, but the sticking point came when he insisted I alter the reference to John Major's humiliating experience in Beijing, where he had been required to stand shoulder-to-shoulder with Beijing leaders in Tiananmen Square. Sir Percy specifically wanted me to say that, on the return flight to London, John Major had declared how pleased he was with the visit.

I replied that while he might have said this to Sir Percy, he hadn't done so to me or, as far as I was aware, to anyone else. Therefore I must attribute this statement to Sir Percy. No, he responded, I must say this myself, leaving his name out of it.

308   No Babylon

I protested that nobody would believe me, for it flew in the face of popular perception of the whole episode.

As I was given to understand, the impasse was next submitted to Robert Kuok, the Malaysian tycoon who owned the *SCMP*. The decision came down that the *Post* would not be publishing my history. It would find some other way of marking the handover. But to be fair to Sally, Lin and Owen, I was paid handsomely for my labours and granted permission to use my submitted manuscript in any other way I might see fit.

The evening of the handover looked meteorologically better suited to a funeral cortege. Lowering clouds draped a black proscenium across the harbour, their curtains of rain partly obscuring the brilliance of Kowloon on the other side. We were all given umbrellas, under which we huddled on the already sodden planks of the tiered seating arranged around the open-air arena. Being taller than most, mine was trapped at a higher elevation, hemmed in by immediately adjoining umbrellas surrounding me on all sides, which were depositing their catchments directly on to my unprotected clothing. I was wringing wet and soaked through, but thoroughly elated. I wouldn't have missed it for the world. I had lost touch with Jan Morris, who was seated somewhere nearer the VIP podium, where Chris Patten was sandwiched between Prince Charles and the new British Prime Minister Tony Blair. It was Jan's book *Farewell the Trumpets: An Imperial Retreat* which had concluded her trilogy of Empire, and to which tonight's ceremony would provide an evocative postscript.

Waiting for the show to begin, my mind went back to Captain Elliot, reviled for planting that flag without prior authorisation on what Foreign Secretary Lord Palmerston described as "a barren island with hardly a house upon it". "Your proclamation," Palmerston told him, "was entirely premature." Well maybe it had seemed so to someone who had probably never been further east than Greenwich, but in the end—after many more thousands of Chinese died in the resumed hostilities of the iniquitous "Opium War"—the Treaty of Nanking, concluded on August 29th 1842, ceded that very same island to Britain in a "perpetuity" that was about to end.

The real drama was too great for this small, rain-sodden arena to contain. Even the pomp and circumstance to be enacted almost immediately afterwards, in the nearby Convention and Exhibition Centre, as the clock struck its midnight chime, could not encompass it.

This prodigious prodigal, after straying so far from its origins, was on the eve of returning to its homeland, laden with self-made fame and fortune. A long-standing historical anomaly would be finally reconciled. Almost precisely half a century after it yielded the first of its overseas dominions, Britain was surrendering the last substantial relic—and ironically the greatest jewel—of its long-defunct empire. China was regaining its most successful offspring.

My own life had straddled that half-century, had seen the beginning of the end in India and would now witness the end—and hopefully a new beginning—here in Hong Kong. For me, born of that empire and inextricably linked with its aftermath, the moment held a very particular poignancy.

Like a child sent out for schooling in a wider world, Hong Kong had carved its own career. Its achievement has astonished all beholders, and inspired many imitators. Any prediction of what this phenomenon would next accomplish must daunt even the most daring seer. But the temptation to read the tea leaves remained so compelling that few could resist. Only one opinion could be ventured with assurance. The saga had taken on a new form, but it was far from over.

Epilogue

And did we all live happily ever after? Although in real life there is no "ever after", the story so far—at least from my perspective—has fulfilled most, if not all, of my admittedly quite typically optimistic expectations.

What followed the handover is already enough to fill another book, perhaps borrowing from the title of Paul Scott's *Staying On*, which provided the postscript to his *Raj Quartet*. For I have long since rejoined the happy band of the many who *are* staying on and who, like me, feel privileged to do so.

The immediate aftermath was a rough and bumpy ride, for Hong Kong collectively and for me personally. China's newly inaugurated Special Administrative Region took several punishing body blows, from a grievous economic depression that sent the property market reeling and rendered thousands bankrupt, from successive alarms over avian influenza, better known as bird flu, and from an outbreak of severe acute respiratory syndrome (SARS) that brought our brave new international airport almost to a standstill and saw our streets filled with masked commuters.

While still resident in Canada, I lost my brother Paul to a rare but ferocious disease called Wegner's Granulomatosis, a systemic vasculitis of unknown aetiology. Diosy lost her sister Tita to a drunken driver who mowed her down at a pedestrian crossing in Vancouver. In a fit of road rage, a hit-and-run maniac in a four-wheel drive sped up behind Mel, as he headed home in my Honda Civic through Victoria's suburbs in the early hours of the morning, and battered him off the road at a nasty bend. Mel was lucky to crawl out of the crumpled wreck unscathed. Also in the early hours of another morning, a reporter for Paul's old newspaper, the *Times Colonist*, rang my Hong Kong hotel room, where I was working on a book for *FormAsia Publications* entitled *Skylines Hong Kong*, to inform me that my land on Mount Matheson had caught fire again. "The good news," he said, "is that your house is safe. The bad news is that you have lost about a third of your estate."

Robbed of my sleep in the pre-dawn darkness, more than ten thousand kilometres from the scene of the conflagration, I rather wished it had all been bad news, at least in his terms, which could only be good news in mine. For it would have brought a resolution to an increasingly burdensome impasse by compelling me to sever my ties with a country where I did not belong and where I had never really felt at home. Knowing how deeply rooted were my links with Hong Kong, Paul had cautioned me against moving to Canada, and I had blindly and foolishly ignored his advice. Despite the many wonderful and enduring friendships I had forged with my neighbours on Mount Matheson, I believe they were as conscious as I was that I remained a square peg in their round hole.

A year later I was invited by Rino and Daisy Cantillano to spend a holiday with them at their home in Banlic Cabuyao, not far from the birthplace, at Calamba, Laguna, of the famous Filipino author and martyr to the cause of freedom, Jose Rizal. During the countdown to midnight on December 31st 2000, the whole *barrio* exploded in a non-stop barrage of pyrotechnics, crackers exploding, rockets streaming to the stars and dogs alternately barking and whimpering in terror. I could hardly have chosen a more exotic locale in which to celebrate the advent of the third millennium.

The following day we observed the time-honoured Filipino custom of seeking out a fortune teller to predict our respective futures. Rino and Daisy knew a Vietnamese soothsayer patronised by some of Manila's leading celebrities. She lived down a narrow lane, festooned with pennants, above the mountainous hot spring spas of Los Baños, and she used Tarot cards for her readings, a method of prognostication to which I had not previously resorted.

Her explanation for the curiously illustrated cards I was called upon to select, and her interpretation of what they foretold, struck me as remarkably convincing, given that she knew nothing about me, which made the import of her final analysis all the more compelling. The last upturned card produced a shake of her head and an audible *tut-tutting* that had me gripping the arms of my chair. I lived, she said, in a large house in a foreign land that was fast becoming a black hole, draining my wealth and my health and giving nothing in return. It was a millstone round my neck and I must take immediate steps to extricate myself from its burden.

If I did so, where would I live?

In a place whose name was eight letters long, in two words evenly balanced.

"Hong Kong?" I murmured.

She looked up from the cards and nodded. I should never have left it.

◆   ◆   ◆

I rang Mukti in Malaysia to tell him I would book us on the first available flight to Victoria, where we would retrieve Mel from the Edward Milne Secondary School in Sooke, empty our house, freight as much as we could of its contents, try and sell whatever was left and give away what remained. We had two weeks in which to do this, because—thanks to my old colleague Charles Wang—I was by now employed by Salon Films and caught up in the work of designing the exhibits for Hong Kong's new museum of history.

Those two weeks were a nightmare. Like the survivor of an air disaster, I got through them in a daze, just putting one foot before the other to walk away from the scene of the crash as fast as I possibly could. I had arrived in Canada five years earlier with a forty-foot container of my possessions, accumulated over my long sojourn in the east. I now watched four vans drive away, loaded with my books, while others arrived to relieve me of much else. But I would have been content just to depart with a suitcase, closing behind me not only the front door but that whole chapter of my life. The one compensation was the relief I felt at freeing myself of my aptly named impedimenta which, over the years, had come to possess me.

Most painful of all was my leave-taking of family and friends, many of whom I would never be seeing again. In Mel's case the parting was more severe, because he had by now become well ensconced in the local lifestyle and thoroughly Canadian in his outlook. He was profoundly disconcerted at the prospect of returning with his father to Malaysia, a country he hardly knew.

Back in Hong Kong, I was sharing an apartment with Rino Cantillano and—whenever his children could take a break from their schooling in Laguna—with Daisy, Joyce Anne and Brian. We were living in an enormous residential estate called Sun Tuen Mun Centre, directly above the depot of the Light Rail Transit network that ran all the way up the western littoral of the New Territories as far as Yuen Long. Although this was, effectively, the "other side of the tracks" when compared with the rather pampered life I had enjoyed for years as a civil servant, I was thoroughly at peace in that setting, where once again I seemed the only token *gwailo* in a cast of untold thousands.

Especially pleasing to me was the thought that many of my neighbours in those forty-four-storey towers, whose sheer height and density made Sun Tuen Mun Centre by far the most populous in the entire district, were descendants of the resettled squatters housed in those primitive H-blocks of Hong Kong's original resettlement programme.

I would sit on a bench in the gardens of the estate podium, stacked above shops, restaurants and transportation hub, observing my fellow residents, looking increasingly affluent, no longer *nouveau-riche* but well established in their contented lower middle-class *modus Vivendi*. And I would think to myself how richly they deserved this, for they were the ones who had made it happen, the real power behind Hong Kong and everything it had accomplished in the forty years since I had first arrived here.

We were—all of us—once inhabitants of a tiny, temporary territory of transients, and it brought tears to my eyes to see what they had made of it; what Jan Morris has called (in the *Guardian* of October 24th 2005) "a marvellous anomaly, a historical epitome, a boast, a marvel and a show, whirling away night and day in the South China Sea".

I had watched Chris Patten's performance as our last governor with a mixture of admiration and apprehension; admiration of his style, his élan, his charisma, apprehension engendered by the bravado with which he had cocked a snoot at the last remnants of the Long March still entrenched in Beijing, daring them—if they must do so—to bully him in the full public gaze of the world arena. Like an errant knitting needle belatedly forced into the pattern, he had undone much of what had gone before. But he had also left us with a significant, even vital legacy. He had taught us the importance of speaking our minds, of refusing to be silenced.

And I saw then, as I still see, evidence of that legacy every day, in the freedom which—despite all claims regarding its steady erosion—is still enjoyed by our media, our public forums, our "sound-bite" politicians ever in search of a microphone. I may not actually join those marches for democracy, which turn the main thoroughfares of Hong Kong Island into rivers of assertive but unfailingly orderly humanity, nor may I always agree with what they say, but I am profoundly grateful for the right Chris Patten instilled in us to speak up and be counted.

It is tempting to draw this epilogue to its conclusion in those tranquil surroundings, comforted by the fact that, on that elevated podium, high above the green parks and gardens of Tuen Mun, I was in the company of Hong Kong's most important people, those who would always remain outspoken and willing to be counted.

But so much has happened in this past year that I am compelled to outline its particulars in these final paragraphs. Sun Hung Kai has at last fulfilled its fifteen-year-old promise of providing me with a new home on Ma Wan, in exchange for the one that had become too dilapidated, and redolent with might-have-been memories, to restore.

Together with Mukti, Diosy, Rino and whoever else may occasionally chance by, I now occupy a newly-built, delightful, three-storey, semi-detached villa at the foot of the island's northern slopes, bordering the curiously named Rural Committee Road (though the Post Office insist on calling us Ma Wan Main Street, Village North). Once again we can entertain our many friends from so many layers of Hong Kong's rich and closely-interwoven fabric. In the six months since we moved here, our visitors have been many, including Hong Kong's last two expatriate Chief Secretaries and, once again, Jan Morris, who in her *Guardian* article had this to say of the prospect from our rooftop:

"I think of Ma Wan (now known as Park Island) as Hong Kong in miniature. History is absorbing it into Hong Kong just as history is fusing Hong Kong with China. Behind my friend's house there is still a little grassy hillock, to remind me that only a few years ago this was just a rural islet of the South China Sea, but to the south the huge bridge rushes its traffic to the airport, cars on the upper deck, trains in a tube below. The island has become quite pleasantly suburban, and from its balconies gleeful children can watch the firework displays of Disneyland."

It sounds very halcyon, and indeed it is. Yet there is always more to come, some of it bad while much of it, I confidently feel, will be good. There are still things to do. No longer a manufacturing centre, Hong Kong has yet to crystallise its new identity, properly find its bearings and chart its new course. Most of all, we must integrate more closely with emerging power engines of the neighbouring Pearl River Delta, shaped on the map like a cornucopia pouring the contents of its horn of plenty, for worldwide distribution, through our bustling port and airport.

We are nearing the ninth anniversary of our return to China, and yet so few of those jaundiced prophecies, that were once made to seem so dark and dire, have materialised. On balance, China has been commendably, even remarkably, circumspect in abstaining from interfering in our affairs to anything like the extent that was once feared. But at the same time so little of our positive achievement has been recognised. In many respects we are better off now than we were a decade ago. We are friendlier, more caring, more conscious of ourselves as an integrated community. We are installing better infrastructure, improving our already excellent transportation systems, designing better shopping malls, better gardens, better recreational facilities and lifestyles.

But as if disinclined to tempt providence, we are reluctant to admit it, more prone to point out the flaws than to take credit for the benefits. And we have only ourselves to blame if, like yesterday's news, we have been swept off the dining table along with the bread crumbs.

Thank God, I remind myself, Hong Kong remains the proverbial never-ending story, so that I am more than ever inclined to murmur "Just

Epilogue 317

wait. And watch this space". We may not ever have been Babylon, even though fabulous enough to warrant comparison. Instead we are more, we are better, something real, tangible and enduring.

978-0-595-38087-9
0-595-38087-5

Printed in the United Kingdom
by Lightning Source UK Ltd.
111314UKS00001B/124-141